HMH SCIENCE DIMENSIONS™

Grade 3

This Write-In Book belongs to

_____

Teacher/Room

_____

Houghton Mifflin Harcourt™

Consulting Authors

Michael A. DiSpezio
Global Educator
North Falmouth, Massachusetts

Marjorie Frank
Science Writer and Content-Area
  Reading Specialist
Brooklyn, New York

Michael R. Heithaus, PhD
Dean, College of Arts, Sciences &
  Education
Professor, Department of Biological
  Sciences
Florida International University
Miami, Florida

Cary Sneider, PhD
Associate Research Professor
Portland State University
Portland, Oregon

Printed in the U.S.A.

ISBN 978-0-544-71326-0

13 0868 25 24 23 22 21

4500825250   C D E F G

Program Advisors

Paul D. Asimow, PhD
Eleanor and John R. McMillan Professor of Geology and Geochemistry
California Institute of Technology
Pasadena, California

Eileen Cashman, PhD
Professor
Humboldt State University
Arcata, California

Mark B. Moldwin, PhD
Professor of Space Sciences and Engineering
University of Michigan
Ann Arbor, Michigan

Kelly Y. Neiles, PhD
Assistant Professor of Chemistry
St. Mary's College of Maryland
St. Mary's City, Maryland

Sten Odenwald, PhD
Astronomer
NASA Goddard Spaceflight Center
Greenbelt, Maryland

Bruce W. Schafer
Director of K–12 STEM Collaborations, retired
Oregon University System
Portland, Oregon

Barry A. Van Deman
President and CEO
Museum of Life and Science
Durham, North Carolina

Kim Withers, PhD
Assistant Professor
Texas A&M University-Corpus Christi
Corpus Christi, Texas

Adam D. Woods, PhD
Professor
California State University, Fullerton
Fullerton, California

Classroom Reviewers

Michelle Barnett
Lichen K–8 School
Citrus Heights, California

Brandi Bazarnik
Skycrest Elementary
Citrus Heights, California

Kristin Wojes-Broetzmann
Saint Anthony Parish School
Menomonee Falls, Wisconsin

Andrea Brown
District Science and STEAM Curriculum TOSA
Hacienda La Puente Unified School District
Hacienda Heights, California

Denice Gayner
Earl LeGette Elementary
Fair Oaks, California

Emily Giles
Elementary Curriculum Consultant
Kenton County School District
Ft. Wright, Kentucky

Crystal Hintzman
Director of Curriculum, Instruction and Assessment
School District of Superior
Superior, Wisconsin

Roya Hosseini
Junction Avenue K–8 School
Livermore, California

Cynthia Alexander Kirk
Classroom Teacher, Learning Specialist
West Creek Academy
Valencia, California

Marie LaCross
Fair Oaks Ranch Community School
Santa Clarita, California

Emily Miller
Science Specialist
Madison Metropolitan School District
Madison, Wisconsin

Monica Murray, EdD
Principal
Bassett Unified School District
La Puente, California

Wendy Savaske
Director of Instructional Services
School District of Holmen
Holmen, Wisconsin

Tina Topoleski
District Science Supervisor
Jackson School District
Jackson, New Jersey

You are a scientist!

You are naturally curious.

Have you wondered . . .

- **is ice still water?**
- **if you could float in midair?**
- **how you can talk to your friend on a cell phone?**
- **if plants can grow without soil?**

how does a ac work in a house

Write in some other things you wonder about.

HMH SCIENCE DIMENSIONS™

will **SPARK** your curiosity

AND prepare you for

✓ tomorrow
✓ next year
✓ college or career
✓ life

Where do you see yourself in 20 years?

Write in or draw another career you'd like.

Be a scientist.
Work like real scientists work.

Plan

Investigate

Have Fun

Be an engineer.

Solve problems like engineers do.

Design

Solve Problems

Share Solutions

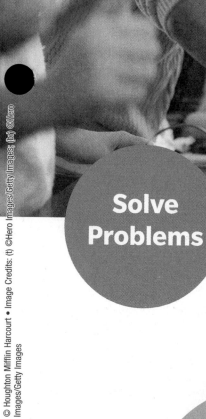

Explain your world.

Start by asking questions.

Think Critically

Make a Claim

Gather Evidence

There's more than one way to the answer. What's YOURS?

Work in Teams

Develop Explanations

Support Your Conclusions

UNIT 1 Engineering and Technology

Engineering Processes 1

ENGINEER IT **Lesson 1**
How Do We Define a Problem? 4
 Hands-On Activity: What's in the Way? 11
Careers in Science & Engineering: Interview an Engineer 18

ENGINEER IT **Lesson 2**
How Can We Design a Solution? 22
Hands-On Activity: Modeling Irrigation 29

ENGINEER IT **Lesson 3**
How Do We Test and Improve a Solution? 42
Hands-On Activity: Looking It Over 47
People in Science & Engineering: Olivia Lum 55

UNIT 1 PERFORMANCE TASK 60
UNIT 1 REVIEW 62

UNIT 2 Physical Science

Forces 65

Lesson 1
What Are Forces? 68
 Hands-On Activity: Demonstrating How Forces
Affect Motion 77

Lesson 2
What Are Some Types of Forces? 88
Hands-On Activity: Exploring Forces 100
People in Science & Engineering: Christine Darden,
The Wright brothers 103

ENGINEER IT **Lesson 3**
What Forces Act from a Distance? 108
Hands-On Activity: Build an Electromagnet 121
Careers in Science & Engineering: Electrician 125

UNIT 2 PERFORMANCE TASK 130
UNIT 2 REVIEW 132

xi

UNIT 3

Motion 135

Lesson 1
What Is Motion? 138
 Hands-On Activity: Slow Walk, Fast Walk 150
People in Science & Engineering: Mark Fuller,
     Megan Leftwich 153

Lesson 2
What Are Some Patterns in Motion? 158
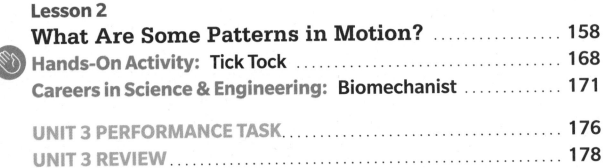 **Hands-On Activity:** Tick Tock 168
Careers in Science & Engineering: Biomechanist 171

UNIT 3 PERFORMANCE TASK 176
UNIT 3 REVIEW 178

© Houghton Mifflin Harcourt • Image Credits: ©arnaudbertrande/Getty Images

Life Cycles and Inherited Traits

Life Cycles and Inherited Traits **181**

Lesson 1
What Are Some Plant Life Cycles? **184**
 Hands-On Activity: How Do Plants Grow? **191**
ENGINEER IT X-treme Plant Engineer Group **203**

Lesson 2
What Are Some Animal Life Cycles? **208**
Hands-On Activity: Observing Mealworm Metamorphosis ... **222**
People in Science & Engineering: Steve Irwin **229**

Lesson 3
What Are Inherited Plant and Animal Traits? **234**
Hands-On Activity: Monster Traits **246**
Careers in Science & Engineering: Genetics Specialist **249**

UNIT 4 PERFORMANCE TASK **254**
UNIT 4 REVIEW **256**

UNIT 5

Organisms and Their Environments 259

Lesson 1

How Does the Environment Affect Traits? 262

Hands-On Activity: How Much Water Do Plants Need? 268

People in Science & Engineering: Charles Henry Turner,
May Berenbaum 276

Lesson 2

What Are Adaptations? 282

Hands-On Activity: Just Pecking? 294

ENGINEER IT Robotic Adaptions 297

Lesson 3

How Can Organisms Succeed in Their Environments? 302

Hands-On Activity: Battle of the Beans! 308

Careers in Science & Engineering: Wildlife Expert 315

ENGINEER IT **Lesson 4**

What Happens when Environments Change? 320

Hands-On Activity: How Can It Cross the Road? 332

Engineer It: Solving a Salmon Problem 335

UNIT 5 PERFORMANCE TASK 340

UNIT 5 REVIEW 342

© Houghton Mifflin Harcourt • Image Credits: ©AlexandraPhotos/Getty Images

Fossils 345

Lesson 1

What Is a Fossil? 348

 **Hands-On Activity:** Walk This Way! 358

Careers in Science & Engineering: What Is a
  Paleontologist? 365

Lesson 2

What Do Fossils Tell Us about the Past? 370

Hands-On Activity: What Can You Learn from Studying
  a Fossil? 380

People in Science & Engineering: Karen Chin, Mary Anning,
  Mary Gordon Calder 389

UNIT 6 PERFORMANCE TASK 394

UNIT 6 REVIEW 396

UNIT 7
Weather and Patterns................399

Lesson 1
How Is Weather Measured? 402
Hands-On Activity: Analyzing Weather Data.................. 410

Lesson 2
How Can We Predict Weather? 422
Hands-On Activity: Weather Here and There 432
People in Science & Engineering: Pam Heinselman,
    Lidia Cucurull 439

ENGINEER IT **Lesson 3**
What Are Some Severe Weather Impacts? 444
Hands-On Activity: Smashing Floods 454
Careers in Science & Engineering: Hurricane Hunters 461

Lesson 4
What Are Some Types of Climates? 466
Hands-On Activity: Looking for a New Home 476

UNIT 7 PERFORMANCE TASK.................................. 488
UNIT 7 REVIEW 490

Glossary R1
Index R17

© Houghton Mifflin Harcourt

Safety in the Lab

Doing science is a lot of fun. But, a science lab can be a dangerous place. Falls, cuts, and burns can happen easily. **Know the safety rules and listen to your teacher.**

☐ **Think ahead.** Study the investigation steps so you know what to expect. If you have any questions, ask your teacher. Be sure you understand all caution statements and safety reminders.

☐ **Be neat and clean.** Keep your work area clean. If you have long hair, pull it back so it doesn't get in the way. Roll or push up long sleeves to keep them away from your activity.

☐ **Oops!** If you spill or break something, or get cut, tell your teacher right away.

☐ **Watch your eyes.** Wear safety goggles anytime you are directed to do so. If you get anything in your eyes, tell your teacher right away.

☐ **Yuck!** Never eat or drink anything during a science activity.

☐ **Don't get shocked.** Be careful if an electric appliance is used. Be sure that electric cords are in a safe place where you can't trip over them. Never use the cord to pull a plug from an outlet.

☐ **Keep it clean.** Always clean up when you have finished. Put everything away and wipe your work area. Wash your hands.

☐ **Play it safe.** Always know where to find safety equipment, such as fire extinguishers. Know how to use the safety equipment around you.

Safety in the Field

Lots of science research happens outdoors. It's fun to explore the wild! But, you need to be careful. The weather, the land, and the living things can surprise you.

- ☐ **Think ahead.** Study the investigation steps so you know what to expect. If you have any questions, ask your teacher. Be sure you understand all caution statements and safety reminders.

- ☐ **Dress right.** Wear appropriate clothes and shoes for the outdoors. Cover up and wear sunscreen and sunglasses for sun safety.

- ☐ **Clean up the area.** Follow your teacher's instructions for when and how to throw away waste.

- ☐ **Oops!** Tell your teacher right away if you break something or get hurt.

- ☐ **Watch your eyes.** Wear safety goggles when directed to do so. If you get anything in your eyes, tell your teacher right away.

- ☐ **Yuck!** Never taste anything outdoors.

- ☐ **Stay with your group.** Work in the area as directed by your teacher. Stay on marked trails.

- ☐ **"Wilderness" doesn't mean go wild.** Never engage in horseplay, games, or pranks.

- ☐ **Always walk.** No running!

- ☐ **Play it safe.** Know where safety equipment can be found and how to use it. Know how to get help.

- ☐ **Clean up.** Wash your hands with soap and water when you come back indoors.

Safety Symbols

To highlight important safety concerns, the following symbols are used in a Hands-On Activity. Remember that no matter what safety symbols you see, all safety rules should be followed at all times.

Dress Code

- Wear safety goggles as directed.
- If anything gets into your eye, tell your teacher immediately
- Do not wear contact lenses in the lab.
- Wear appropriate protective gloves as directed.
- Tie back long hair, secure loose clothing, and remove loose jewelry.

Glassware and Sharp Object Safety

- Do not use chipped or cracked glassware.
- Notify your teacher immediately if a piece of glass breaks.
- Use extreme care when handling all sharp and pointed instruments.
- Do not cut an object while holding the object in your hands.
- Cut objects on a suitable surface, always in a direction away from your body.

Electrical Safety

- Do not use equipment with frayed electrical cords or loose plugs.
- Do not use electrical equipment near water or when clothing or hands are wet.
- Hold the plug when you plug in or unplug equipment.

Chemical Safety

- If a chemical gets on your skin, on your clothing, or in your eyes, rinse it immediately, and tell your teacher.
- Do not clean up spilled chemicals unless your teacher directs you to do so.
- Keep your hands away from your face while you are working on any activity.

Heating and Fire Safety

- Know your school's evacuation-fire routes.
- Never leave a hot plate unattended while it is turned on or while it is cooling.
- Allow equipment to cool before storing it.

Plant and Animal Safety

- Do not eat any part of a plant.
- Do not pick any wild plant unless your teacher instructs you to do so.
- Treat animals carefully and respectfully.
- Wash your hands throughly after handling any plant or animal.

Cleanup

- Clean all work surfaces and protective equipment as directed by your teacher.
- Wash your hands throughly before you leave the lab or after any activity.

Safety Quiz

Circle the letter of the BEST answer.

1. Before starting an activity, you should
   a. try an experiment of your own.
   b. open all containers and packages.
   c. read all directions and make sure you understand them.
   d. handle all the equipment to become familiar with it.

2. At the end of any activity, you should
   a. wash your hands thoroughly before leaving the lab.
   b. cover your face with your hands.
   c. put on your safety goggles.
   d. leave the materials where they are.

3. If you get hurt or injured in any way, you should
   a. tell your teacher immediately.
   b. find bandages or a first aid kit.
   c. go to your principal's office.
   d. get help after you finish the activity.

4. If you have unused liquids after finishing an activity, you should
   a. pour them down a sink or drain.
   b. mix them all together in a bucket.
   c. put them back into their original containers.
   d. dispose of them as directed by your teacher.

5. When working with materials that might fly into the air and hurt someone's eye, you should wear
   a. goggles.　**b.** an apron.
   c. gloves.　**d.** a hat.

6. If you get something in your eye, you should
   a. wash your hands immediately.
   b. put the lid back on the container.
   c. wait to see if your eye becomes irritated.
   d. tell your teacher right away.

Engineering Processes

Explore
Online

Unit Project: Building a Better Backpack

How can a backpack keep contents dry in the rain? Your team will design and test a model. Ask your teacher for details.

Powered leg supports allow this paralyzed person to walk.

At a Glance

LESSON 1

How Do We Define a Problem?..... 4

LESSON 2

How Do We Design a Solution? ... 22

LESSON 3

How Do We Test and Improve a Solution?........................ 42

Unit Review 60

Vocabulary Game: Guess the Word

Materials
• Kitchen timer or online computer timer
• Cards with vocabulary and science words

Directions

1. To take a turn, choose a word card. Do not tell the word to the other players. Set the timer for 1 minute.

2. Give a one-word clue about your word to another player. That player has one chance to guess your word.

3. Repeat step 2 until time runs out or the player guesses the word. Use a different one-word clue each time.

6. The first player to guess the word gets 1 point and 1 point if they use the word in a sentence. That player chooses the next word. The first player to 4 points wins.

Criteria

The desired features of a solution

Technology

Engineered products and processes that meet a want or need.

Unit Vocabulary

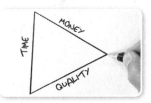 **constraint:** A real-world limit on the resources of a solution such as available time, money, or materials.

 **criteria:** The desired features of a solution.

 **engineer:** A person who uses science and math to design structures, machines, and systems to solve problems.

 **technology:** Engineered products and processes that meet a want or need.

How Do We Define a Problem?

Many classes keep an indoor garden. The potted plants need lots of care and attention.

By the end of this lesson . . .
you'll be able to define a problem.

Can You Solve It?

▷ Explore Online

A two-week holiday break is coming. School will be closed when the break begins. No one can water the plants, so students are worried. They want to design a way to water the plants with materials they have.

1. What problem does the class need to solve? Give details to tell what the problem is or what the solution should do.

_____

_____

_____

_____

_____

_____

 EVIDENCE NOTEBOOK Look for this icon to help you gather evidence to answer the question above.

Defining Engineering Problems

Where Do Solutions Come From?

When faced with problems, such as how to water plants in a closed building, **engineers** can help. Engineers design solutions to meet a want or need.

You use **technology** many times a day! But do you know what technology is? Simply put, technology is human-made devices or systems that meet a want or need.

Technology Everywhere

2. Look at the different types of technology. Then tell how each meets a want or need.

 Explore Online

This is a tablet. It can store many books or magazines in one device. Instead of carrying books or magazines, a person can bring the tablet and read on the go.

Not all technology is electric. This lightweight pop-up tent keeps you dry when you sleep outside.

Zippers are technology, too. They temporarily hold fabric together.

This ball is technology too! It can be rolled, kicked, or thrown. Is that a need or a want?

_____

_____

_____

_____

_____

_____

_____

🖐 **HANDS-ON Apply What You Know**

Meet the Need

3. With a partner, find three human-made products in your classroom. Decide which needs they meet. Write your answers in your Evidence Notebook.

How Do You Define a Problem?

The first step in a design process is to find a problem. Engineers begin by clearly defining the problem. You solve problems every day without planning or thinking about them. Cleaning up spilled milk with a towel, packing a backpack, and using a sharpener to sharpen a pencil are a few examples.

However, a lot of problems are more complex. When solving them, you need to be more careful and thoughtful. Before you can work on solving a problem, you should clearly know what you need or want. Then when you're finished, you'll need to know whether your solution worked.

When you design a solution, you need to test it to be sure it works. For complex problems, you should have specific **criteria,** or desirable features of the solution.

Bad Day Blues

4. Look at each image and problem. Give at least two criteria of a solution. The first one has been done for you.

▷ Explore Online

a bicycle with a flat tire

Problem: The tire is flat and I can't ride my bike.

Criteria
1. The tire is full of air and I can ride the bike.

2. The leak is fixed.

I'll know that the solution works when I see or measure . . . that the tire is filled with air and stays that way for a week.

getting items to the recycling bin

Problem: Sometimes recycling bins are too heavy for us to carry.

Criteria

1. _____

2. _____

I'll know that the solution works when I see or measure .

_____

_____

_____

a heavy, over-packed backpack

Problem: My backpack is too small to carry all I need for class.

Criteria

1. _____

2. _____

I'll know that the solution works when I see or measure . . .

_____

_____

_____

_____

_____

Problem

a crosswalk on a busy street

Problem: It is not safe to cross the road because sometimes we have no crossing guard.

Criteria

1. _____

2. _____

I'll know that the solution works when I see or measure . . .

_____

_____

EVIDENCE NOTEBOOK Tell how you might use a checklist to evaluate an engineering solution.

Putting It Together

5. Think about an engineering problem you know. It can be in the past or happening now.

What is the problem?

_____

_____

What are two criteria for a solution to the problem?

A. _____

B. _____

What is a solution that fufills both criteria?

_____

_____

© Houghton Mifflin Harcourt • Image Credits: © Blend Images/Getty Images

HANDS-ON ACTIVITY
What's in the Way?

Objective

Collaborate on planning a backpacking trip. Before you go, you must decide what gear you need. You'll need cooking tools as well as items for staying safe, keeping warm and dry, and sleeping comfortably. But for safety, a backpack can't be too heavy. Your backpack must weigh 20 pounds or less.

> **Materials**
> • camping gear item list (on pages 14 and 15)

Twenty pounds is a constraint—a limit to possible solutions. Different problems have different limits. Often a limit is a certain amount of money or a due date. Here, the constraint is weight. A list of gear that totals more than 20 pounds is not acceptable.

Procedure

STEP 1 Look at the details about all of the gear in the table at the end of this activity. The constraint is listed below. What are the criteria you should also consider when planning what gear to get?

Constraint
The gear can't add up to more than 20 pounds.

Criteria

1. _____   3. _____

2. _____   4. _____

STEP 2 Study the information about the gear you have to choose from. The star ratings show how easy a product is to use. Take those ratings into account in your evaluation. Describe one item for which it is hard to address the criteria and constraints at the same time. Explain why that piece of gear presents such a challenge.

_____

_____

_____

_____

STEP 3 List the gear you chose. Explain why you chose these items.

_____

_____

_____

_____

Analyze Your Results

STEP 4 Now suppose you have a less money to spend. The dollar signs indicate price range—more means a higher price. Make a list of equipment that meets your needs while costing the least. How is it like your first list? How is it different?

_____

_____

_____

_____

Draw Conclusions

STEP 5 Suppose that your trip is in the summer. To be safe, your gear must include enough pure drinking water for three days. Is this one of the criteria or the constraints? Explain.

_____

_____

_____

_____

_____

Camping Supplies The star ratings show quality and ease of use. Take them into account. Dollar signs show price range.

Item picture	Details
	Rectangle Sleeping Bag **Weight:** 6 lb **Rating:** ★ ★ ★ **Price:** $$
	Barrel Sleeping Bag **Weight:** 4 lb **Rating:** ★ ★ ★ **Price:** $$
	Mummy Sleeping Bag **Weight:** 2 lb **Rating:** ★ ★ **Price:** $$$
	Dome Tent **Weight:** 6 lb **Rating:** ★ ★ ★ ★ **Price:** $$

Item picture	Details
	Ridge Tent **Weight:** 4 lb **Rating:** ★★ **Price:** $
	Tunnel Tent **Weight:** 2 lb **Rating:** ★★★★ **Price:** $$$
	Mess Kit **Weight:** 3 lb **Rating:** ★★ **Price:** $
	Dinnerware **Weight:** 2 lb **Rating:** ★★★★★ **Price:** $$$
	Picnicware **Weight:** 1 lb **Rating:** ★★★ **Price:** $$
	Poncho **Weight:** 1 lb **Rating:** ★★★ **Price:** $$
	Jacket **Weight:** 2 lb **Rating:** ★★★ **Price:** $$

Item picture	Details
	Coveralls **Weight:** 4 lb **Rating:** ✱✱✱ **Price:** $$$
	Portable Gas Cook Stove **Weight:** 1 ½ lb **Rating:** ✱✱✱✱✱ **Price:** $$$
	Camp Stove **Weight:** 1 lb **Rating:** ✱✱✱✱ **Price:** $$
	Propane Stove **Weight:** 2 lb **Rating:** ✱✱ **Price:** $

Exploring the Limits on Problem Solving

Finding the Limits

Part of an engineering problem is identifying the **constraints.** Constraints are the limits on the resources that you can use to solve a problem. People never have endless amounts of time, money, or other resources to solve a problem.

NASA engineers think about constraints to make decisions. Trips to the International Space Station (ISS) can carry only so much weight. Each item on board has an allowable weight. If an astronaut gains 1 kg before a flight, then 1 kg of something else must be left behind. Constraints are absolute limits, not just desirable features.

Space in Space

6. Is the space that an item takes up a criterion or a constraint? Circle the answer.

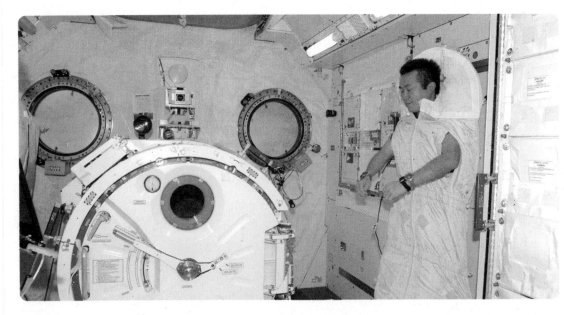

Astronauts don't have bedrooms on the ISS. They use small sleeping bags as shown. Is the amount of space for sleeping a criterion or a constraint?

Astronauts can't just buy groceries. Their food must last until the next delivery from Earth. So most of their food is freeze dried. Is how long food must last a criterion or a constraint?

Language SmArts
Ask and Answer Questions

7. Recall that criteria are the desirable features of a solution, and constraints are absolute limits. Then, describe a problem and how you solved it. The problem should have at least two criteria and at least one constraint. The constraint might be the amount of money you could spend, or a time limit to solving, or the materials you had. Be sure to use the words *criteria* and *constraint* in your answer.

_____

_____

EVIDENCE NOTEBOOK Identify some of the possible constraints on a classroom plant watering system.

Discover More

Check out this path . . . or go online to choose one of these other paths.

Careers in Science & Engineering

- **Phoning Home**
- **Solve Your Own Problem**

Interview an Engineer

Think about different jobs that engineers do in your community. Work with your teacher or parent to contact a local engineer.

You will need to:

1. Find the contact information for the engineer.

2. Prepare interview questions for the engineer. See the Tip if you need help.

3. After your teacher reviews it, send a neatly written letter or e-mail to the engineer. Be sure to include your mailing address at the school, and thank the engineer for taking time to answer your questions.

4. Give a report of the questions and responses to your classmates. Record the presentation and submit it to your teacher.

Explore Online

Engineers use science and math to solve problems.

Tip

When writing interview questions, use terms such as *problems, wants, needs, criteria,* and *constraints.* You might also ask about how the person became interested in engineering and what someone needs to study in school to become an engineer.

Lesson Check

Name _____

Can You Solve It?

1. Remember that the school will be closed for a long holiday break and no one can care for the plants.

   • Act as an engineer and define the problem in the photo.

   • What are the criteria for this problem?

   • What are the constraints for this problem?

📋 **EVIDENCE NOTEBOOK** Use the information you've collected in your Evidence Notebook to help you cover each point above.

_____

_____

_____

_____

_____

Checkpoints

Sometimes we encounter problems and have to design a solution.

2. Define *criteria* in terms of engineering solutions.

_____

_____

3. Define *constraints* in terms of engineering solutions.

_____

_____

4. Explain how criteria and constraints are used to define a problem.

_____

_____

5. Act as an engineer.

    a. Define the problem in the photo from the beginning of the lesson.

_____

_____

    b. Describe the needs or wants.

_____

_____

    c. List the criteria. Then list the constraints.

_____

_____

    d. Explain how you identified the problem, criteria, and constraints.

_____

_____

Lesson Roundup

7/10

A. Choose words that complete the sentences.

define the problem, want, or need	criteria measurement	problems constraints

a. Before engineers can do anything, they must _define the problem_.

b. After this, they must clearly state the _problems_ that the solution will address.

c. When engineers are testing a solution, they look for _constraints_ or desired features to show that the solution works.

d. Engineers also deal with _measurement_, because resources are limited.

B. Choose the words that complete the sentences.

criteria	constraints	needs
money	weight	time

a. When you are packing for a camping trip, you must think about how much _weight_ you can carry. You also may have a budget, or limited amount of _money_ to spend. These are examples of _criteria_.

b. For a camping trip, you have certain _needs_, like staying warm and having enough food. In order to meet your needs, you must plan solutions that meet both _constraints_ and _____.

How Can We Design a Solution?

In the last lesson, you learned about the problem of the plants needing water. What might a solution look like?

By the end of this lesson . . .
you'll be able to consider constraints and criteria and brainstorm to design a solution to a problem.

Can You Solve It?

Plants need light daily to survive.

Plants need a certain amount of water, too.

Remember from Lesson 1: school will be locked for a 2-week break. No one will be able to come to water your class's indoor garden.

1. How can you make sure that the plants are watered and healthy during the break? What steps would you take to solve this problem? What are some of the constraints? What are the criteria?

_____

_____

_____

_____

_____

_____

 EVIDENCE NOTEBOOK Look for this icon to help you gather evidence to answer the questions above.

Water Movers

Researching Solutions!

Think about a problem you have had. Did you ask others how they might solve it? Sometimes the best way to begin solving a new problem is to look at how others have solved similar problems.

When rain is scarce, people often use irrigation systems. Below are some of these watering systems. Solving the classroom garden problem will involve an irrigation system.

Some Irrigation Systems

2. Look at these irrigation systems. Circle the picture that probably uses the most water.

▷ **Explore Online**

a. Watering canals carry water to farm fields.

b. Sprinkler systems water large circular areas of farms.

c. Drip hoses let out tiny drips of water near the hose.

d. Watering spikes seep water into dirt over a long time.

3. Which irrigation systems on the previous page might be the most practical solutions to your problem? Circle all that apply.

   a   **c**

   b   **d**

4. Research other possible irrigation systems you might use to solve the problem. Take notes on the lines below.

_____

_____

_____

 Apply What You Know

Brainstorming Ideas

5. Use these prompts to help you think up ways to water the classroom plants.

   a. First, think about these questions: Where will you get water? How will you control the flow of water? What is safe and doable in a classroom?

   b. Now as a team, tell as many different ideas as you can in 5 minutes. Have one person record the ideas.

   c. Discuss the ideas in more detail. Vote or decide on the three you think are best.

   Which idea do you think would be the easiest to make work? The hardest? Tell why.

_____

_____

_____

Considering Constraints and Criteria

Think about each of the irrigation systems you saw and those you researched. Which systems might work well to solve your problem? Which systems wouldn't work as well?

Comparing Irrigation Systems

6. Enter Yes or No for each watering system.

Irrigation system	Criteria		Constraints	
	Provides water	Easy to control flow	Works for 2 weeks	Safe for classroom
Watering canal				
Sprinkler system				
Drip hose				
Watering spike				

 EVIDENCE NOTEBOOK In your notebook, add your own ideas to the chart. Which irrigation system idea would be best for the plants in a school? Record your choices in your Evidence Notebook.

Putting It Together

7. How does researching others' solutions help you solve a new problem? Why should you always keep constraints and criteria in mind when solving a problem?

_____

_____

_____

_____

 Tip

Criteria and Constraints
Criteria are the needs a system must meet. Constraints are limitations or obstacles.

© Houghton Mifflin Harcourt

How Dry Am I?

Detailed Water Needs

You know that plants need water to survive. Some plants need water more often than others. The amount of light and how moist or dry indoor air is also determine how much water is needed.

Water Me . . . More or Less

8. Compare the water needs of these plants in the indoor garden.

a. aloe Conditions Sunny and Dry: every 1-3 weeks; Cloudy and Damp: every 1-2 months

b. Boston fern Conditions Sunny and Dry: few times a week; Cloudy and Damp: every 1-2 weeks

c. Christmas cactus Conditions Sunny and Dry: every other day; Cloudy and Damp: every two weeks

d. fig tree Conditions Sunny and Dry: weekly; Cloudy and Damp: every two weeks

e. gerbera Conditions Sunny and Dry: daily; Cloudy and Damp: every other day

f. jade plant Conditions Sunny and Dry: every week; Cloudy and Damp: every 1-2 weeks

g. pothos Conditions Sunny and Dry: daily; Cloudy and Damp: weekly

h. snake plant Conditions Sunny and Dry: few times a week; Cloudy and Damp: every 1-2 weeks

Details, Details!

You now know about some irrigation systems and the general water needs of certain plants. But you still need to know how many times you'll need to water each plant over the break.

9. Use the data on the previous page to complete the chart.

Plant type	Number of waterings per 2 weeks for sunny and dry classroom
aloe	
Boston fern	
Christmas cactus	
fig tree	
gerbera	
jade plant	
pothos	
snake plant	

Putting It Together

10. How can learning more details about needs help you think about solutions to a problem?

_____

_____

Modeling Irrigation

Objective

With a team, **plan and build** a prototype irrigation system from the materials your teacher provides. The prototype should give at least enough water to keep a plant alive without rotting its roots. The prototype represents a full-size irrigation system for the classroom plants.

Possible Materials

- safety goggles
- plastic cups
- small, empty, clean plastic milk jugs
- plastic tubing with different diameters
- water
- balloons
- large and small containers for water
- tape
- tent stakes
- rubber bands
- aquarium pump

Procedure

STEP 1 Choose a plant from page 28 to build for. Then, consider the materials your teacher provides. Sketch your design. Tell how you plan to put it together. Submit your design to your teacher.

STEP 2 What constraints already exist for your plant irrigation system? What constraints do the materials you have to work with make for your system? List them.

_____

_____

_____

_____

_____

STEP 3 Build a plant irrigation system based on your drawing.

Record Your Results

STEP 4 What type of irrigation system did you make?

_____

_____

_____

STEP 5 Put some water into your system. Leave it overnight if you need to. Does it work as you expected? Explain.

_____

_____

_____

STEP 6 Evaluate your prototype. Does it meet all of the criteria and constraints?

_____

_____

_____

Analyze Your Results

STEP 7 Make a drawing of your irrigation system in the box below. Then describe how your plan for the system will work. Be prepared to explain your drawing to the class.

Draw Conclusions

STEP 8 Think about your prototype. What are some advantages of your proposed solution? What are some of its limitations?

_____

_____

_____

Testing, Testing

Test It!

Now that you have learned about the water needs of the plants, how more details needed to be considered in your solution, and designed an irrigation model; it is time to describe how you will test your model.

How will you know that your irrigation solution works? If you don't remember, look back at your list of criteria.

Can It Pass the Test?

11. Recall that most solutions to a problem are not perfect. Limitations of any solution often arise during testing. On the lines below, write a step-by-step plan to explain how you could test your solution with one plant. Use the Guide Questions and Writing Guide to help you.

Guide Questions

- Describe your test. What are the constraints and criteria?
- What will you observe or measure to show that your irrigation solution works?

Writing Guide

My Solution Summary: _____

_____

_____

Constraints: _____

_____

Criteria: _____

_____

a. The first step I would do to test my irrigation solution is . . .

_____

_____

_____

This would show me. . . _____

_____

This would demonstrate . . .

_____

b. The second step I would do to test my irrigation solution is . . .

_____

_____

_____

This would show me . . .

_____

This would demonstrate... _____

12. What types of evidence would support whether or not your system passed its test?

_____

_____

_____

EVIDENCE NOTEBOOK Why is it important to have a plan before you test a design? Write your answer in your Evidence Notebook.

Peer Review

Teamwork is an important part of most engineering and science work. Getting and giving advice can often lead to better solutions.

Exchange your test plan with another team. Review each other's plans. Tell what you think will work well with the team's plan and what might not. Be prepared to explain why!

Sharing ideas can help improve a solution to a problem.

13. Now enter the advice the other team shared with you about your test plan on the lines below. Explain what part of the other team's advice was most helpful.

_____

_____

_____

_____

_____

_____

Engineering Tests

Creating a solution design for watering plants requires attention to detail, constraints, criteria, and many other important aspects. Professional engineers make sure to do the same with their solutions. Look at each picture to learn more about some of the ways professional engineers plan and test their solutions.

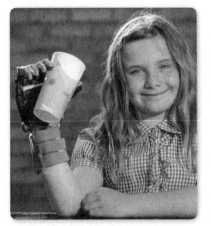

Engineers can use 3D printers to make prototypes to see what their ideas might look like and how they might move when finished.

Small-scale model testing is done to see if a solution will work. Often, these models don't include all the details of a solution.

Durability tests show whether an idea or object will work under certain conditions, such as high temperatures or severe weather conditions.

HANDS-ON Apply What You Know

Clipped!

14. Plan and carry out a test of how well a paper clip works. Think about what a paper clip is designed to do. Collect and analyze relevant test data. Below, tell how you would compare your results to those for a different paper clip size or design.

_____

_____

_____

Do the Math
Use Less Water

15. Many areas have a problem—not enough water. Traditional landscaping often uses plants that are not native to the area or that require a lot of water to stay alive. A Xeriscape® [ZEER•ih•skayp] is a landscape that focuses on using plants that do not require a lot of water.

Traditional landscaping often uses large volumes of water.

Xeriscaped yards save water.

Xeriscape Savings

Xeriscaping is a designed solution. Homes with Xeriscaped yards can use much less water than regular landscapes, especially in dry regions. The savings are greater in the summer. A certain type of home in Arizona with a traditional landscape spends an average $80 per month on water in spring, fall, and winter, and $100 a month in June, July, and August. A similar home with a Xeriscaped landscape spends half that cost.

Figure the Savings

The chart on the next page is a comparison of how much these two types of landscapes spend on water in the same area. Enter how much each landscape costs per month in the table. Now find the water costs for each landscape in a year. Subtract the yearly totals to find the savings.

© Houghton Mifflin Harcourt

Month	Traditional	Xeriscape®
January		
February		
March		
April		
May		
June		
July		
August		
September		
October		
November		
December		
YEARLY TOTALS		

Savings _____

Language SmArts
Comparing and Contrasting

16. Use the water needs of the plants in the classroom garden to decide which might be best for a Xeriscaped landscape in a dry area. Write your answer on the lines below.

_____

_____

_____

Tip

The English Language Arts Handbook can provide help with understanding how to compare and contrast.

Discover More

Check out the path . . . or go online to choose one of these other paths.

Watering for Sale

- **Large Scale Watering Plans**
- **People in Science and Engineering: Archimedes**

Think about all the different cereal packages at a grocery store. Some have bright colors on them. Others have cartoon characters or famous people on them. Even the colors and sizes of the words on the boxes are different. Some highlight the benefits of the cereal, such as added fiber. Others show a picture of the cereal in a bowl.

Product packaging can make a huge difference in whether or not an item sells.

With an adult, research examples of different product packaging. Find out how much work goes into them. Learn how people design product packages. Find typical criteria and constraints.

17. Use what you discover to create a package for your classroom irrigation system. Think about what the product package will look like and how the packaging will protect the irrigation system. Also consider what information you would need to provide for someone buying it.

Use the English Language Arts Handbook to help you design your product package. Show your package to your teacher.

Lesson Check

Name _____

Can You Solve It?

1. Now that you've learned more about the engineering design process, explain how a solution might not always be perfect. Be sure to:

▶ Explore Online

- Explain the importance of researching past solutions.

- Describe how you developed your proposed solution and explain why you communicated with others about your design.

- Understand what to consider when testing a possible solution.

EVIDENCE NOTEBOOK Use the information you've collected in your Evidence Notebook to help you cover each point above.

_____

_____

_____

_____

Checkpoints

2. One of the first steps in designing a possible solution to a

problem is _____.

a. testing the design

b. building the prototype

c. researching past designs

d. collecting test data

3. Choose words from the word bank to complete the sentences.

| strengths | weaknesses | durability | constraints | criteria |

   a. The desirable features of a solution or design

     are _____.

   b. A proposed solution is not acceptable if it fails to meet the

     _____.

4. One strength of a drip irrigation system is that it _____.

   a. uses little water

   b. is hard to design

   c. is an old design solution

   d. can only be used in dry areas

5. The most important part of testing a possible

   solution is to _____.

   a. finish the design project

   b. gather evidence that criteria are met

   c. change all of the design constraints

   d. develop the packaging

6. It is important to know as many _____ as possible
before planning a solution.

   a. outcomes

   b. details

   c. data

   d. teammates

Lesson Roundup

A. Which of these designs is best at giving small, controlled amounts of water? Circle all that apply.

B. Which pair of plants most likely need the same amount of water, the boxed or circled pair?

C. Which of these are important parts of a test plan after your design is built? Choose all that apply.

    a. choosing the materials for the design

    b. talking to others about the design

    c. researching past design problems

    d. making sure criteria will be tested

How Do We Test and Improve a Solution?

When testing solutions to a problem, it is not easy to think up every way a solution might fail. The real world often will find a way to break something.

By the end of this lesson . . .
you'll test and improve a solution.

Can You Solve It?

▷ Explore Online

The Tacoma Narrows Bridge collapsed on November 7, 1940. Engineers studied the wreckage. They found out that strong winds caused the bridge to flex, twist, and tear apart.

1. What are some adjectives you would use to describe the collapse of the Tacoma Narrows Bridge? How do you think new bridge designs were tested and improved?

_____

_____

_____

_____

_____

_____

 EVIDENCE NOTEBOOK Look for this icon to help you gather evidence to answer the questions above.

What Could Possibly Go Wrong?

Where Things Break?

Engineers work to design and test solutions. The Tacoma Narrows Bridge was a solution that was designed and tested but unfortunately didn't work as well as the engineers hoped. Engineers can learn from failures. Failures are a way to make better and safer solutions.

A Rube Goldberg Device

2. Look at Steps A–R of the garage opener below. What are some ways that it could break or not work properly? Use the table on the next page to explain three ways. Two examples are given.

Part	Why this part might fail
M cat	The cat might not wake up or might move in an unexpected way.
A bumper	It might not hit the mallet in the right spot.

Part	Why this part might fail

3. Choose one of the parts from your table. Explain a way to make sure that the part works correctly and doesn't fail.

_____

_____

_____

_____

HANDS-ON Apply What You Know

Plan a Test

4. With a team, review the irrigation system you designed in a previous lesson. Identify a possible improvement. With a team, plan and draw how you would test your improvement. Be prepared to share your test plan, drawing, and explanation.

Think It Through

The cartoon image from before showed a complex device with different things that could go wrong. Your irrigation solution won't be as complex. However, just like the Tacoma Narrows Bridge and this image of a broken yard sprinkler, failures can happen.

Revisit your irrigation plan. Analyze it in the same way that you analyzed the cartoon. Think of parts of the irrigation system that might not work properly.

5. List three potential problems that could occur in your irrigation system.

_____

_____

_____

EVIDENCE NOTEBOOK Explain how you could design and test your solution to make sure that these three potential problems won't happen.

Language SmArts
Planning

6. Engineers work hard to think ahead about any problems that could occur. By thinking ahead, they can make sure that their solutions are safe and work properly. How does thinking ahead help avoid different types of design problems?

_____

_____

_____

© Houghton Mifflin Harcourt • Image Credits: ©allaksei Putau/Shutterstock

Tip

The English Language Arts Handbook can provide help with understanding how to organize your thoughts and plan your writing.

Looking It Over

Collaborate to test your model. In Lesson 1, you learned about criteria and constraints, which help guide a solution. In Lesson 2, you learned that having a plan and checklist are important, too. When testing and redesigning your irrigation system, all of these things are going to be used. Now it's time to test your model and find out what works and what doesn't work with your irrigation system.

What question will your team investigate in this activity?

Possible Materials

- prototype irrigation system from Lesson 2
- safety goggles aprons, and gloves
- graduated cylinder
- plastic cups
- tubing
- large and small containers for water
- water
- balloons
- tape
- tent stakes
- rubber bands
- aquarium pump

Procedure

STEP 1 First, think about the criteria and constraints of your irrigation system. If there is anything you need to change, use the available materials to change your irrigation system.

What were the limits on what you could design and build?

_____

_____

_____

STEP 2 Engineers write out the steps they used so that others can duplicate and test their work. Think about the steps you used from the start of the idea to the creation of your model.

Write out and number your steps.

_____

_____

_____

_____

_____

STEP 3 Review the ways you recorded in the last lesson to test your plant irrigation system. When doing this, keep in mind the criteria that relate to the needs of the plants.

How will your device meet the plant's particular need for water? How will you test this?

_____

_____

_____

_____

_____

STEP 4 Look at your design and model. Think back to your list of things that might not work correctly. How will you avoid those problems?

_____

_____

_____

STEP 5 Test your plant irrigation system according to your plan. Record your information in the table below.

WATER IRRIGATION TEST (in mL)

	Expected amount	Actual amount	Difference	Changes to make
Test 1				
Test 2				
Test 3				

Analyze Your Results

STEP 6 After each test, consider your data and consider if any changes need to be made to your system. Make any one improvement you feel is necessary after each test. Record those changes below.

_____

_____

_____

_____

STEP 7 There might have been parts of your irrigation system that did not work as well as you expected. Analyzing results of a test shows you what went wrong and what went right.

When you tested your solution, what didn't work as well as you thought it would?

_____

_____

STEP 8 What parts of your irrigation system did you have to redesign before trying it again? Why these parts?

_____

_____

Draw Conclusions

STEP 9 Make a claim about testing designs. Cite evidence from your irrigation model to support your claim.

_____

_____

_____

_____

STEP 10 List at least one other question you would like to ask about testing engineering designs.

_____

_____

_____

_____

Fixing Failures!

Learning from Failure

Problems often happen. Even the best engineers can't predict every problem or failure that will happen. The best thing to do is to plan ahead to avoid as many problems as you can.

Part of being an engineer is learning to accept that things get better after a failure. Finding out what went wrong and why can help improve the design. Sometimes you only need to make small adjustments. Sometimes you need to redesign and test many different things before a design works well.

A lot was learned from the Tacoma Narrows Bridge failure. New bridge designs are tested more in wind tunnels like this.

7. How does analyzing failure help you succeed?

_____

_____

Failure Brings Improvement

The original Tacoma Narrows Bridge collapsed in 1940. Engineers built a new bridge in the same spot years later. Look at each image to see the difference between the original and the current Tacoma Narrows Bridge.

This is the original Tacoma Narrows Bridge that collapsed in 1940. There was very little to hold the bridge stiff when the winds blew.

The new Tacoma Narrows Bridge has a stiffer, wind-resistant design.

As you have discovered, many different things can happen to a design, system, or solution that cause it to fail. The Tacoma Narrows Bridge collapse was unfortunate, but engineers learned from the bridge's failures. Years later, a redesigned bridge was built in the place of the original bridge, one that holds up to the wind.

Putting It Together

8. What will engineers do if a bridge design fails during testing? Circle the best answer.

a. Give up on the project.

b. Analyze what went wrong and come up with solutions to fix it and then test again.

c. Build a different type of bridge altogether.

d. Try to test again without analyzing the bridge.

The Best . . . for Now

Getting Advice

You made your irrigation system. You tested it. It looks ready to go. As engineers, it is important to have other engineers and experts look at our work, too.

Think about your irrigation system and what makes the best design for the need. Now review at least three other classmates' irrigation systems. Evaluate their irrigation system designs. Enter the information in the table about the irrigation systems. Make sure to rate the designs on a 5-star rating with 1 star as the lowest rating and 5 stars as the highest rating. Give the reasons for your ratings in the table.

Team	5-star rating	Reason for rating

9. What did you learn from reviewing other classmates' designs?

_____

_____

_____

_____

Improving Together

Evaluating design solutions isn't as easy as riding a bike or following a recipe. There are many things to consider. Often the best design may come from looking at many different designs and taking the best ideas from each one. Sometimes doing this is the best way to meet the criteria and constraints.

It is important to always communicate and record information about your design. Also, keep track of any lessons you learned along the way. Even if you feel you have finished the design, you may still have work to do.

10. Think of the irrigation system you built. Now think of the classmate systems that you just evaluated. Describe an ideal design that combines the best features from all the systems.

_____

_____

_____

_____

Putting It Together

11. Write the words that complete the sentences.

past failures	future ideas	giving up
Different projects	Future designs	Others' successes

Lessons learned from _____ show you what to avoid.

_____ can help you improve your final design.

Discover More

Check out this path . . . or go online to choose one of these other paths.

People in Science & Engineering

- **Model Work**
- **Go Further**

Olivia Lum

People need clean water to live. Plants also need clean water. Many people live near oceans, but ocean water is too salty for drinking, bathing, or plants. A chemist in Singapore, Olivia Lum, saw the problem of not enough clean water.

Her solution was to start a company that develops ways to remove salt from ocean water as well as other kinds of water so that it can be used. Her company now builds new ways to make ocean water more usable. Because of her work, people in Central and South America, Europe, China, India, and Africa now have access to clean water.

Olivia Lum (above) and a water treatment plant

12. What type of problem did Olivia Lum identify? What are a constraint and some criteria of the problem?

_____

_____

_____

Desalination is a process in which excess salt and other minerals from water are removed. This is done to obtain fresh water suitable for drinking or irrigation.

When nearly all the salt is removed so that humans can drink the water, a by-product is table salt. This process occurs in a desalination plant. Desalination is much more affordable than developing a new fresh water source.

Salt filter tubes inside a desalination plant

13. What need does desalination meet?

_____

_____

_____

Lesson Check

Name _____

Can You Solve It?

1. Engineers thought the Tacoma Narrows Bridge was strong but it collapsed in November of 1940, when strong winds blew.

Explore Online

- How do failures help make designs better and safer?

- What are some important reasons for testing solutions?

- Looking back, what steps could the bridge designers have taken to better engineer the bridge?

- What key details from this lesson support your answer?

EVIDENCE NOTEBOOK Use the information you've collected in your Evidence Notebook to help answer these questions.

_____

_____

_____

_____

_____

Checkpoints

2. What are some ways that engineers improve their product, solution, or system? Circle all that apply.

   a. having other engineers

   b. stopping work when a problem comes up

   c. analyzing their work

   d. thinking ahead

   e. not learning from their mistakes

3. Write the words that correctly complete the sentences.

design solutions	materials	decrease	increase

Engineers test _____. They do this in order to

_____ safety.

4. Which of the following is a good thing to do when designing or redesigning an engineering solution? Circle the best answer.

a. overlook failures

b. keep ideas to yourself

c. combine the best ideas of different solutions

d. test lots of changes at once

5. Which of the following is helpful to keep in mind when redesigning an engineering solution? Circle the best answer.

a. past failures

b. the weather

c. only your designs

d. only your successes

solution	materials	communicate	increase	record

6. Choose the words that correctly complete the sentences.

When designing a _____, it is important to always

_____ and _____ information about

your design.

Lesson Roundup

A. Circle the best answer to complete the sentence.

When designing a new product, solution, or system,

engineers _____ to avoid design problems.

a. think backwards

b. stop when there is a problem

c. think ahead

d. ignore criteria

....

B. Write the word that correctly completes the sentence.

ignore	revise	analyze

It is helpful to get other engineers to _____ your

new product, solution, or system to get their opinion on it.

....

C. How many times should a solution be evaluated and redesigned and why? Write your answer below.

_____

_____

_____

ENGINEER IT!
The Benefits of Research

Your class will be divided into two groups. Both groups will need to solve a design problem. The problem is that the wheel on a skateboard keeps getting loose and falling off. Group A will try to solve the problem by doing research. Group B will try to solve the problem without doing research.

IDENTIFY THE PROBLEM: What problem do you need to solve?

_____

_____

Before beginning, look at the checklist at the end of this project to be sure you are meeting all the requirements.

RESEARCH: Group A will conduct research to solve the design problem. Group B will not conduct research. Summarize your research here.

_____

_____

BRAINSTORM: With your group, brainstorm three or more ideas to solve the design problem. Keep in mind the criteria and constraints.

Criteria	Constraints
☐ Skateboard rolls	☐ Shape of the skateboard cannot be changed
☐ Skateboard is fun to ride	☐ Cannot change the number of wheels

DESIGN: Design a solution to the problem.

COMPARE: Compare the solutions provided by Groups A and B by having a class discussion.

_____

_____

Are the solutions similar or different?

_____

_____

_____

EVALUATE: Weigh the benefits and drawbacks of doing research. Did Group A have better design solutions than Group B? Why or why not?

_____

_____

_____

☑ Checklist

Review your project and check off each completed item.

_____ Includes the identified problem.

_____ Includes a comparison of both solutions.

_____ Includes an evaluation of the benefits or drawbacks of doing research.

Unit Review

1. Look at the image. What is the unmet want or need presented in the scene?

   a. Having air in the tire to ride on safely

   b. Reducing the number of cars on the road

   c. Riding a bike instead of driving a car

   d. Not having someone around to help change the flat tire

2. Henry carries books to school, then to a math tutor's house in the afternoon. Henry's back is starting to hurt, maybe because of his heavy backpack. How might an engineer solve Henry's problem?

   a. Designing a backpack that can hold more books

   b. Making a backpack that takes pressure off his back

   c. Designing a backpack with separate compartments for books

3. Jody's family is planning a 9-hour trip. Each person can bring only one suitcase. Her parents will take turns driving. Snacks must fit inside lunchboxes. Which is a constraint? Select all that apply.

   a. The trip will take 9 hours.

   b. Each person can bring only one suitcase.

   c. Snacks must fit inside lunchboxes.

   d. Jody's parents are taking turns driving.

4. Complete the sentences using the words in the word bank.

Criteria   Constraints

   _____ are the desired characteristics of a solution.

   _____ are absolute limits on a solution, often the

   available money, time, or materials.

5. Based on this image, what is the best solution to the problem?

   a. Dig up the plant.

   b. Find a way to water the plant.

   c. Keep the plant away from animals that may eat it.

   d. Design a way to hold the plant up straight.

6. Write the words and phrases from the word bank in the correct columns to describe the type of irrigation.

Above ground	Water releases into soil
Sprays water	Trickles water directly to roots
Emitters	Releases water on its own

Sprinkler system	Drip hose	Watering globe

7. Using the word bank below, write the steps in order for a possible plan to design a solution.

1. _____

2. _____

3. _____

4. _____

5. _____

Think of possible solutions.
Test the solution.
Record results.
Perform research on solutions.
Identify the problem.

8. Look at the image. Identify the possible types of design failures that can occur. Select all that apply.

   a. Seats can come loose from the chains.

   b. The soil underneath can become loose.

   c. Connectors between the top bar and bottom poles can break.

   d. Chains can disconnect from the top bar.

9. What will engineers do if the design for a submarine fails during testing? Select all that apply.

   a. Give up on the project.

   b. Analyze what went wrong.

   c. Come up with solutions to fix it.

   d. Test it again.

10. Write a word or phrase from the word bank into the correct column to tell what you can study to improve designs and avoid problems. Terms may be used more than once.

Failures	Past designs	Others' successes

Improve the design	Avoid problems

Forces

Explore
Online

Unit Project: Balanced forces

How can you keep an object at rest when forces are changing all around it? Brainstorm ideas with a team. Ask your teacher for details.

Kicking a soccer ball is an example of how force and motion work. Force is a concept that can be applied to many daily and fun activities.

At a Glance

LESSON 1

What Are Forces? 68

LESSON 2

What Are Some Types of Forces? 88

LESSON 3

What Forces Act from a Distance? 108

Unit Review 130

Vocabulary Game: Concentration

Materials
- 1 set of word cards

Setup
- Place the cards face down on a table in even rows.

How to Play
1. Take turns to play.

2. Choose two cards. Turn the cards face up.
   - If the cards match, keep the pair. Go again.
   - If the cards do not match, turn them back over.

3. The game is over when all cards have been matched. The players count their pairs. The player with the most pairs wins.

force

A push or a pull, which may cause a change in an object's motion.

Unit Vocabulary

balanced forces: Forces that cancel each other out because they are equal in size and opposite in direction.

electricity: A form of energy produced by the flow of electric charges.

force: A push or a pull, which may cause a change in an object's motion.

gravity: A force that pulls two objects toward each other, such as the force between Earth and objects on it.

magnet: An object that attracts iron and a few other—but not all—metals.

net force: The combination of all the forces acting on an object.

static electricity: The buildup of electric charges on an object.

unbalanced forces: Forces that cause a change in an object's motion because they don't cancel each other out.

What Are Forces?

Running and kicking are forces in motion on the soccer field.

By the end of this lesson . . .
you'll be able to demonstrate how the strength and direction of a force can change the motion of an object.

Can You Explain It?

▶ Explore Online

Your dog sled is sliding along on the snow. The dogs are happy and eager to run. All the dogs together are strong enough to move the sled. You can signal your dogs to go faster or slower. You can turn the sled left or right.

1. Does it take a strong force or a weak force to move the dog sled? How do you turn the sled left or right?

_____

_____

_____

_____

_____

_____

 EVIDENCE NOTEBOOK Look for this icon to help you gather evidence to answer the questions above.

Forces Everywhere

I Like to Move It, Move It

You have probably made a swing move. How does a swing move when you push it? How does it move when you pull it?

A swing moves because a force acts on it. A **force** is a push or a pull. When you push or pull the swing, you add a force that makes the swing move. If you push or pull a moving swing, you can make it move more or even stop.

Swingin'

2. What makes a swing start or stop moving? Write your answer on the line.

▷ Explore Online

| air | force | rope | _____ |

© Houghton Mifflin Harcourt • Image Credits: (c) ©Morsa Images/Getty Images

When you pull something, you use force to move it toward you. When you push something, you use force to move it away from you. You might pull a closed door toward you to open it. Then you push the door away from you to close it again. Your arm provides the force that opens and closes the door.

3. Look at the park picture. Can you tell which actions most likely show a push and which actions show a pull? Identify each action as either a "push" or a "pull" to show what happened to the object. Write your answers on the lines:

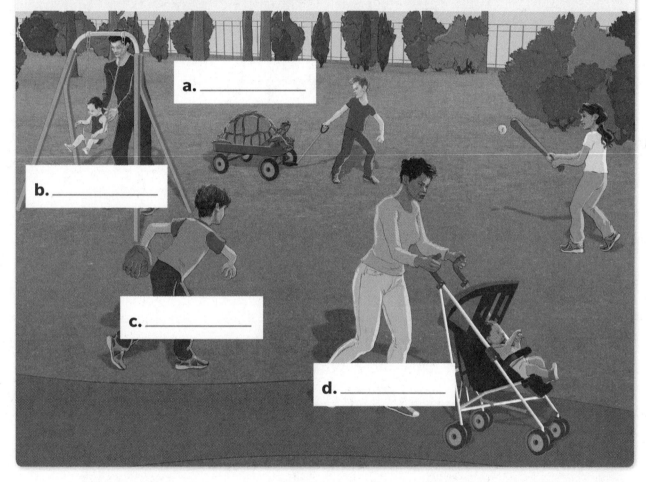

a. _____

b. _____

c. _____

d. _____

 HANDS-ON Apply What You Know

Playground Pushes and Pulls

4. Your teacher will arrange for you to observe another group of students on the playground or elsewhere in your school. Look for forces as you observe the students for 15 minutes. Record the number of times you see pulls and the number of times you see pushes. Use your data to make a graph comparing the number of pushes and pulls. Based on your observations, was there more pushing or more pulling? Cite your evidence.

Special Delivery

The dog sled team has a heavy load to deliver. It will take all of the team working together to move the sled. The whole team can push or pull with more force than if only part of the team helps.

If the dogs push the people, the sled may move, but not for very long.

If the people pull the sled, it may move, but not very fast.

If the dogs apply a force to the sled as a team, it will move far and fast.

5. Write your ideas about the best way for the dog sled team to move the sled. Explain whether they should push it or pull it.

_____

_____

_____

Engineer It!
Engineering a Dog Sled Race

It takes more than a team of strong dogs to win a modern dog sled race. Look at the pictures, and read about how engineering can increase a team's chances of winning a big race.

The dog sled must be made of lightweight materials to make it easy for the team to pull.

Dog sled races often go through wilderness areas. A GPS device helps racers find their way to the finish line.

6. Why would a large sled made of heavy materials be a poor choice for moving through the snow?

_____

_____

Language SmArts
Give an Oral Report

7. Do research to find out about some other technologies related to dog sled racing. Choose one technology. Prepare a one-minute talk that explains how or why it is used. Write the main idea of your talk on the lines below.

_____

_____

Tip

The English Language Arts Handbook can provide help with understanding how to give an oral report.

Strong Enough

Strong or Weak

A force can be weak or strong. You can tap lightly on a door by using your fingers to create a weak force. Or you can use your fist to apply a strong force to knock loudly.

The strength of any force can be changed. If your friend across the room doesn't hear what you say, you can put more force into your voice to make it louder.

Pizza Problem

8. Is a stronger force always better? Look at what happened when different forces were used to toss different objects.

Explore Online

In both pictures below, the pizza maker uses force to push the dough into the air. In which picture does the pizza maker use a weaker force? Put an X in the correct circle.

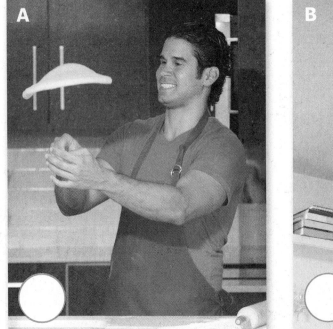

9. Put an *X* in the circle on the picture that shows the girl using a stronger force to throw the ball more accurately.

10. What would happen if you threw a basketball with too much force?

_____

_____

_____

EVIDENCE NOTEBOOK The amount of force you need changes. Sometimes you need to use less force. Sometimes you need to use more force.

Do the Math
How Many Dogs?

Why do dogs pull a sled as a team? Why can't just one dog pull the whole sled? When there are more dogs, they can pull with more force.

Pretend that you are a dog sled driver. You must carry big, heavy boxes on your sled. You know that each dog can pull ½ the weight of one box.

11. Fill in this table to show how many boxes can be pulled by 3 dogs, 4 dogs, and more.

Number of dogs on the team	1	2	3	4	5	6
Number of boxes that can be moved	$\frac{1}{2}$	1				

Putting It Together

12. How does changing the strength of the force change the amount of weight that can be moved?

_____

_____

_____

_____

Tip

Cause and Effect
When two things have a cause-and-effect relationship, changing one changes the other.
Reading and Writing in Science.

Demonstrating How Forces Affect Motion

Objective

Collaborate Apply a strong force and a weak force, and see how it affects the motion of an object. Fill in the data table in Step 4 as you do this activity.

What question will you investigate?

_____

_____

Materials
• toy truck
• masking tape
• meterstick
• stopwatch

Procedure

STEP 1 Mark start and finish lines 1 meter apart with tape.
Why do you think you will need a stopwatch?

_____

_____

STEP 2 Push with a very weak force, and time how long it takes the truck to cross the finish line. Repeat with a medium force.
What evidence do you have that you applied weak forces both times?

_____

© Houghton Mifflin Harcourt

STEP 3 Now push with a strong force, and measure how long it takes the truck to cross the finish line. Repeat this step with an even stronger force.

What evidence do you have that you applied a strong force both times?

_____

_____

Record Your Results

STEP 4 Fill in the data table as you do this activity.

Toy Truck Data		
	Time (seconds)	**Truck motion**
Weakest force		
Medium force		
Strong force		
Strongest force		

Analyze Your Results

STEP 5 Explain what you used to move the truck.

_____

_____

STEP 6 Explain what caused the differences in the way the truck moved from one trial to the next.

_____

_____

Draw Conclusions

STEP 7 What conclusions can you make about strong forces and movement?

_____

_____

STEP 8 State a claim that is related to your question at the beginning of this activity.

_____

_____

Cite evidence from your results to support your claim.

_____

_____

_____

STEP 9 Think of other questions you would like to ask about how forces affect motion.

_____

_____

_____

Which Way?

Toward or Away

The direction that a force is applied matters as much as how strong the force is. When you push something, you use force to move it away from you. When you pull something, you use force to move it toward you.

More than one push or pull often happens to an object at the same time. Also, different forces may be applied in different directions.

Explore Online

The dogs are playing a game like tug of war. The strongest pull wins!

13. Which statements about the photo are correct? Circle all that apply.

    a. Both dogs are applying force by pulling on the toy.

    b. Only the stronger dog is applying force by pulling on the toy.

    c. The motion happens in the direction of the stronger force.

    d. The dog pulling with the stronger force might also pull the other dog towards it.

Direction Matters

You know that the direction that a force is applied is important. In air hockey, pushing the puck in the wrong direction could make you lose the game!

 Explore Online

Players use mallets to apply forces to the puck.

The force of the mallet changes the direction of the puck and sends it into the other goal.

14. What force sets the puck in motion? Is that force a push or a pull? What force makes the puck change direction?

_____

_____

EVIDENCE NOTEBOOK Draw a diagram to show the force that puts an air hockey puck in motion. Also show a force that can make an air hockey puck change direction.

Language SmArts
Asking Questions

15. Think about two activities that you do. Write one question about the forces involved in each activity. Use the words weak, strong, push, pull, and direction in your question.

_____

_____

More Force or Less?

Now pretend that you have to choose between two paths for your dog sled. You could signal the dogs to pull the sled along a level path. The other choice is to take a path that goes up a steep hill. How will the dogs use force differently along these two paths?

16. You choose to drive the dogs up the steep hill. They move slowly.

Then you take them to the level path. They run quickly. It takes

_____ force to pull the sled uphill. It takes

_____ force to pull it over level ground.

© Houghton Mifflin Harcourt

Language SmArts
Compare and Contrast

17. Write a sentence about going uphill or walking on level ground. Use the terms *stronger force* and *weaker force*.

_____

_____

_____

Tip

The English Language Arts Handbook can provide help with understanding comparing and contrasting.

Discover More

Check out the path . . . or go online to choose one of these other paths.

Simple Machines

- **Predicting Motion: Golf**
- **Safety Engineer**

Simple Machines

Explore Online

Simple machines change the strength or direction of a force. A seesaw changes the direction of a force. When one person moves down, the other person moves up. A pulley also changes the direction of a force. You can pull down on a rope to raise a flag up a pole at school.

Pulleys change the direction of a force. The girls pulled the rope toward them. The pulley changed the direction of that force to pull the basket upward.

Some simple machines change the strength of a force you need to do something. A screwdriver is a simple machine called a wheel and axle. The handle is a wheel. The metal shank is an axle. The metal shank would be hard to turn without the handle. It takes less force to turn using the handle.

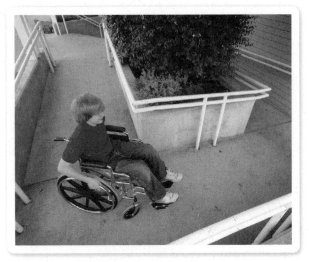

A ramp is a simple machine. This ramp reduces the force needed to move from one level up to another.

This girl is using a simple machine called a lever to reduce the force needed to pry open the paint can.

18. Circle the letter of the word that best completes the sentence.

A _____ is a simple machine because it

changes the strength or direction of a force.

a. thermometer

b. bookcase

c. hammer

19. When you pull down on curtain cords, the curtains move sideways to open or close. The curtain cord is a part of a pulley. How does this type of pulley change a force?

_____

_____

_____

Lesson Check

Name _____

Can You Explain It?

1. Think about the dog sled example in this lesson. Explain how forces are involved. Be sure to:

Explore Online

- Identify forces used to move the sled as either pushes or pulls.

- Describe how the strength and direction of forces on the sled can change.

- Explain how the direction and speed of the sled are affected. by forces.

EVIDENCE NOTEBOOK Use the information you've collected in your Evidence Notebook to help you cover each point above.

_____

_____

_____

_____

_____

Checkpoints

Forces change the speed of an object. They can change the direction of an object. Or they can change both.

speed

direction

speed and direction

2. Adding an extra dog to a dog sled team will

change the _____ of the sled.

3. Sort these actions as pushes or pulls.

| kick a ball | pick up a book from your desk |
| reel in a flying kite | put a box on a high shelf |

Push	Pull

4. Sort by whether the action will change the strength or the direction of a force.

| hit a tennis ball with a racket | blow harder into a horn |
| go around a curve on a skateboard | use brakes to stop a bicycle |

Change in strength	Change in direction

Write words from the word banks to correctly complete the sentences.

| pulls | pushes | changes | strong | medium | weak |

5. When a quarterback throws a long pass, his hand _____ the football with a _____ force.

| push | pull | stay in its path | change direction |

6. A defender's hand knocks the ball aside away from him. He uses a _____ to redirect the path of the ball. That force makes the football _____.

Lesson Roundup

A. Label each image with either *push* or *pull* and *strong* or *weak*.

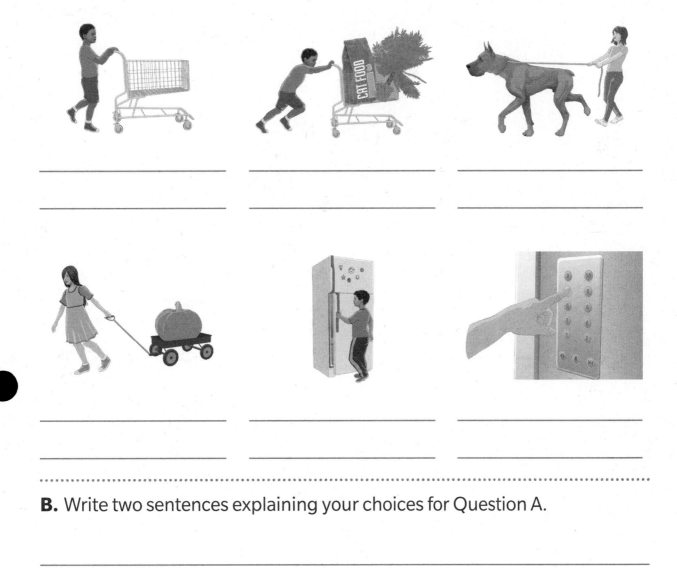

....

B. Write two sentences explaining your choices for Question A.

....

C. How will a force change an object that is not moving?
How can a force change the direction of a moving object?

What Are Some Types of Forces?

All motion is caused by forces. Changes in motion are caused by forces, too. Forces affect everything this skateboarder is doing.

By the end of this lesson . . .
you'll be able to plan and conduct an investigation about balanced and unbalanced forces.

Can You Explain It?

▷ Explore Online

The indoor skydiver "flies" because of forces acting on her. A cushion of air pushes her up. The instructor applies force to adjust her position.

1. Look at the picture. Can you identify the forces pushing or pulling on the indoor skydiver? Are those forces balanced or unbalanced?

_____

_____

_____

_____

_____

_____

_____

Tip

Learn more about pushes and pulls in What Are Forces?

EVIDENCE NOTEBOOK Look for this icon to help you gather evidence to answer the questions above.

Touchy, Touchy

Pushing Back

If you push or pull an object by touching it, you apply a **contact force** to it. When you use a contact force to push an object, the object pushes back. If you pull on an object, the object pulls you.

Push Play

2. Look at the picture. There are 4 pairs of contact forces. Label the forces by drawing arrows.

▷ Explore Online

3. Write the correct answers from the word bank to complete the sentences.

push	pull	toward	away from

When you _____ on an object, it moves farther

_____ you. When you _____ on an object, it

moves closer _____ you.

Carefully Balanced

Pairs of forces are either balanced or unbalanced. **Balanced forces** are the same size and strength but act in opposite directions, so there is no motion. When one force is stronger than the other and the forces act in different directions, they are **unbalanced forces**.

Tug of War

4. Look at the pictures. Draw an arrow showing the direction of the force in each picture.

The two dogs are evenly matched. They both pull with a force of 10. The X marks the center of the rope at the start. The rope hasn't moved, even though both dogs are pulling.

Now, one dog is playing tug of war with a big horse. The horse is stronger and pulls with a force of 40. The dog will be pulled over the X in the direction of the horse.

You can add all the forces that push or pull on an object. This sum is called **net force**. If the animals pull with equal force, the forces are balanced. This is zero net force. The motion does not change.

5. Predict who will win and whether the forces are balanced or unbalanced.

Force A	Force B	winner	Balance or Unbalanced?
big horse	big horse		
big horse	adult elephant		

EVIDENCE NOTEBOOK Consider a big, strong bird and a small, weak bird pulling on opposite ends of a stick to use in a nest. Use evidence to predict which bird will get the stick, and tell why you think so.

Funny Car Forces

A powerful force from the engine pushes these race cars down the track. The cars move so fast that the brakes alone can't stop them! To stop the motion before the cars run off the end of the track, another force needs to act on the cars, too.

Stop It!

6. Look at the pictures below. Describe how the forces acting on the cars change from balanced to unbalanced, or vice versa.

▷ **Explore Online**

This car goes from not moving to moving very quickly.

_____

_____

_____

_____

A parachute rapidly slows this car down.

_____

_____

_____

_____

_____

7. You can use math symbols to show balanced and unbalanced forces. There are six horses on this team. It takes a force of 80 or greater to move the farmer on the plow.

   a. Is the combined pulling force of all the horses >, <, or = 80?

_____

   b. Is the pulling force of a single horse >, <, or = 10?

_____

   c. Write a math sentence to show balanced forces for a team of four horses that cannot move the farmer and plow.

Putting It Together

8. What adds the force needed to slow and stop the speeding racecar? Describe how the forces acting on the car change from unbalanced to balanced.

> **Tip**
>
> When forces are balanced, there is no motion.

_____

_____

_____

What Are Everyday Forces?

Friction

On the slick wet surface of a water slide, you glide along easily and smoothly. If you sat down like that on a dry, hilly sidewalk, you wouldn't move at all. Friction against the sidewalk would stop you from sliding.

Friction is a force that opposes motion between objects that are touching. Rub your hands together quickly. They soon feel warm because of friction between them.

Explore Online

Friction on a zipline is low until you are near the end of the ride. Then the braking system makes high friction. That friction brings the rider to a comfortable, safe stop.

Friction is low when a bobsled speeds swiftly down its icy track. Only the blades of its four narrow runners touch the ice.

9. Here is a chart of items that are used for moving around. They are sorted by whether they have low or high friction against the surfaces on which they are used.

Add three items of your own to the table. Also list the surfaces on which they are used and the friction they produce.

Item	Surface	High or low friction
ice skates	ice	
hiking boots		
snow tires		

10. Write the correct answers from the word bank on the lines.

less easily	motion	more easily

Friction is a force that opposes _____ between

objects that are touching. You slide _____ when there

is low friction than when there is high friction.

 HANDS-ON *Apply What You Know*

Sliding Along

11. Gently push a few objects made of different materials across the surface of your desk. You could choose items such as a wood pencil, a plastic ruler, and a rubber eraser. Determine which material causes the most friction. Then discuss your observations with a partner. Compare the materials you both chose.

Birds of Prey

Gravity is the force that pulls things down toward the center of Earth. The eagle below can weigh 29 kg (63 lb). The kestrel weighs less than 1 kg (2 lb). The eagle can carry large prey and still fly, but the kestrel would not be able to carry more than 1 kg because of gravity.

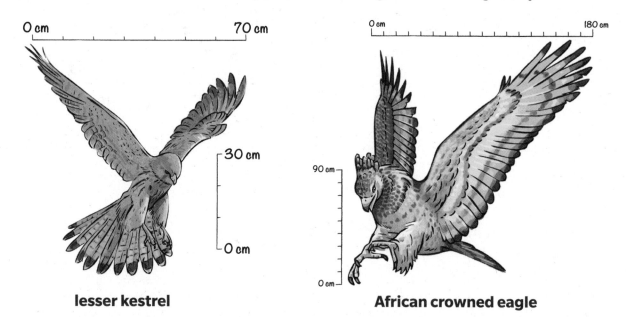

lesser kestrel

African crowned eagle

Who Will Carry It?

12. What can each bird carry? The combined weight of the bird and the object must overcome gravity. Fill in the chart.

lesser kestrel
500 g

mouse
28 g

grasshopper
.3 g

monkey
27 kg

branch
1 kg

Kestrel	Eagle

13. Look at your finished chart. Which flier can carry the least number of different items? Why do you think other fliers can carry more?

_____

_____

_____

14. Think of five things you do that involving lifting something up against the force of gravity.

_____

_____

_____

Gravity and Net Force

An object's weight is the strength of gravity's pull on it. A large rock is heavier than a pillow. Gravity pulls down on the rock more forcefully. The rock is hard to lift because you must apply an upward force against gravity's downward force.

A rocket is very heavy. It takes a huge unbalanced force to exceed gravity and move a rocket away from Earth.

▶ Explore Online

The force of the rocket's engines push up against gravity. The net force is in an upward direction.

15. Write the correct answer from the word bank on the lines below.

weight	push	force

A rocket's _____ is the

strength of gravity's force pulling

it down. The rocket's engines

_____ it upward strongly.

16. Write the correct answer from the word bank on the line below.

gravity	net	weight

The _____ force is upward, and the rocket leaves Earth.

Language SmArts
Rocket Research

17. Research a famous rocket launch. Gather information about the structure of the rocket and its engine. Find photos of the rocket launching, and label the forces. Share your research with a classmate, and turn it in.

Engineer It!

Sticky Stuff

When you place an object on a table, it stays in one place because of gravity. But, how do astronauts keep things from floating away?

To help materials stick together, scientists develop adhesives. Adhesives make objects that are in contact with each other stick together. Scientists at NASA developed an adhesive by watching geckos climb up walls. The new adhesive is strong enough to keep tools and other objects attached to the outside of the International Space Station. It can be used over and over again too.

This gecko has sticky pads on the bottom of its feet.

The adhesive holding this solar panel was inspired by gecko feet.

 EVIDENCE NOTEBOOK Write down your observations about how scientists use contact forces to develop useful tools.

Putting it Together

18. What other tools have been inspired by the natural world? How are these tools used today?

_____

_____

_____

_____

HANDS-ON ACTIVITY

Exploring Forces

Objective

Collaborate as a team to investigate forces and motion.

Procedure

STEP 1 Sometimes you want objects to move and sometimes you don't. Think about that statement. Ask questions about making something move or stay still. On a separate piece of paper, write down as many different questions as you can. Be ready to share them with the class.

Materials

- long flat piece of cardboard and books to form a ramp
- toy truck
- plastic canister
- washers
- strings
- chenille items
- other objects to complete your plan

_____

_____

STEP 2 With With your class, select the most important questions about objects that move or stay still. Write down the questions your class came up with here

_____

_____

_____

_____

_____

STEP 3 How can you investigate the questions your class picked as most important? Think about the materials your teacher shows you and what else you might need. Write your plan and show it to your teacher to see if you can get the other things you need. Attach your plan to this lab sheet. If you use other things than those shown by your teacher, be sure to write them in the list above.

_____

_____

_____

_____

_____

_____

_____

_____

_____

_____

_____

_____

_____

STEP 4 Carry out your plan and record your results. Present your data in a way that everyone can see what you did and what happened. You might choose a table or a graph as a presentation tool. Or you might choose to make a poster with photographs.

Make a **claim** that answers the question or questions your class decided to explore. You may need to have a claim for each question. Support your claim with **evidence** from your investigation and reasoning to explain how the evidence supports your claim. Record your claim, evidence, and **reasoning**, on a separate sheet of paper and attach it to this lab sheet.

Take It Further

After your investigation, what new questions do you have about forces and motion? You can start your question with "What happens if . . ." or "Is this always . . ."

Discover More

Check out this path . . . or go online to choose one of these other paths.

People in Science and Engineering

• Extreme Sports
• Birds of a Feather

People in Science & Engineering
Christine Darden & The Wright Brothers

Making objects fly has been a challenge for even the most talented engineers. Here you will learn about three very talented aerospace engineers.

Christine Darden was an aerospace engineer who worked with NASA for over 40 years. She was an expert in designing wings for aircraft that travel faster than the speed of sound. She also researched the sonic boom, which is a very loud noise produced at that high speed.

Explore Online

The Wright brothers invented the first successful airplane, which they flew for the first time in 1903. They faced the challenge of the different forces that act on an airplane while it flies.

Language SmArts
Do Research and Prepare a Presentation

19. Research the Wright brothers, and learn about the forces that affect a plane. Or find more information about Christine Darden and her work with the sonic boom. Use print and digital sources for information. Then prepare a presentation, and present your findings to other students.

20. Pretend you can interview the Wright brothers or Christine Darden. Write your interview questions about their work below.

_____

_____

_____

_____

_____

Lesson Check

Name _____

Can You Explain It?

1. Look at this picture from the beginning of the lesson. Explain what forces are at work. Be sure to do the following:

    • identify which objects are in contact with each other;

    • describe different forces;

    • identify whether multiple forces are acting at once;

    • describe forces as balanced or unbalanced.

Explore Online

EVIDENCE NOTEBOOK Use the information you've collected in your Evidence Notebook to help you cover each point above.

_____

_____

_____

_____

_____

Checkpoints

2. Write the correct number.

    John and Chris are moving a heavy table. John pushes it with a force of 20. Chris pushes it with a force of 30. Together they use a force of _____ to move the table.

3. To sort by whether the action uses a higher or lower friction strength, write the words in the correct column below.

sledding downhill	**walking uphill**
striking a match	**coasting on a bicycle**
sliding on ice	**using bicycle brakes**

Lower Friction   Higher Friction

_____   _____

_____   _____

_____   _____

4. Circle the correct answer. What do we call the strength of gravity's pull on an object?

a. the object's size

b. the object's weight

c. the object's motion

5. Write the correct answer from the word bank on the line below.

unbalanced	**gravitational**	**contact**

It takes an enormous _____ force to move a

rocket away from Earth.

6. Circle the correct answer. Why do you feel the handle's force against your hand when you pull a loaded wagon?

a. The wagon is pulling back on you.

b. Friction is pulling down on you.

c. Gravity is pushing up on you.

Lesson Roundup

A. Write the correct answers from the word bank on the lines below.

> **balanced**   **direction**   **force**

a. Most objects have more than one _____ acting on them at a time. When the forces are _____, the object's motion does not change.

b. _____ forces cause a change in speed or direction.

B. Write down each description in the correct column to sort it as a balanced force or an unbalanced force.

> **plate on table**   **rocket taking off**
>
> **chair on floor**   **book falling off shelf**
>
> **squirrel sitting in a tree**   **parked car**
>
> **bird flying to nest**   **ball hit by bat**

Balanced Forces   Unbalanced Forces

_____   _____

_____   _____

_____   _____

_____   _____

What Forces Act From a Distance?

This device produces a force that causes the girl's hair to stand up when she touches it. How does that force reach her hair?

By the end of this lesson . . .
you'll be able to ask and answer questions about forces between objects that are not in contact with each other.

Can You Explain It?

 Explore Online

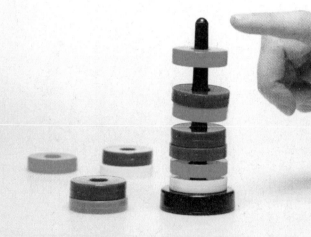

Magnetism is a force that acts from a distance. Magnetic forces surround magnets. These forces cause magnetic objects to push apart or pull toward each other without touching.

1. What do you see happening in the picture? Write what you observe. As you write, tell what you think might cause the effects you see.

_____

_____

_____

_____

_____

Tip

Learn more about forces in *What Are Forces?* **And** *What Are Some Types of Forces?*

 EVIDENCE NOTEBOOK Look for this icon to help you gather evidence to answer the question above.

Magnets Everywhere!

Stick to This!

A **magnet** is an object that attracts things made from certain metals. You may have seen or used magnets at home or at school. Can you find all the magnets in this house?

Speakers have magnets that help move sound waves into the air.

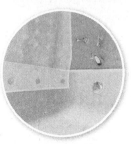
Magnets in some shower curtains pull the curtain toward the tub. This helps keep water inside the tub.

A magnetic knife holder pulls on knives to hold them in place.

Some purses and wallets use magnets to keep them closed.

A vacuum's motor has magnets in it. The magnets help turn the fan to create suction.

Refrigerators often have magnets in the doors to help keep them closed. This keeps cold air inside the fridge.

What Pulls to the Poles?

The shape of a magnet may be a horseshoe, a bar, a button, or another form. No matter the shape, every magnet has two poles: north and south. A magnetic force is strongest near a magnet's poles.

Force Field

2. Iron filings are small bits of iron. They can be used to show the area around a magnet in which the force pulls or pushes. The magnet has a magnetic field that exerts a force on the filings.

> Explore Online

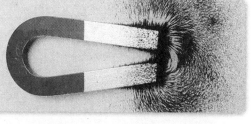

Compare the magnetic fields of the three magnets. Tell where the field is strongest.

_____

_____

_____

_____

_____

_____

3. Choose the words from the word bank that correctly complete each sentence.

| middle | poles | more | fewer |

Many iron filings collect near the ___poles___ of a magnet.

The farther from the magnet, the ___fewer___ filings collect.

Pushing Away or Pulling Toward

4. Magnets can pull on, or attract, each other. Or they can push away, or repel, each other. Read the questions to complete a caption for each set of pictures.

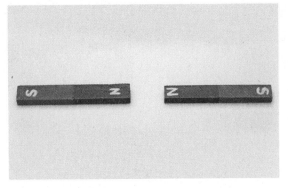

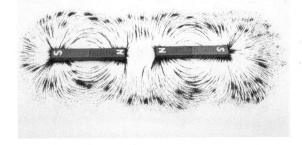

The north poles are alike. Do they repel or attract each other? What do the filings show?

_____

_____

_____

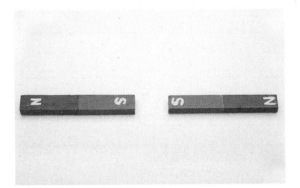

The south poles are alike. Do they repel or attract each other? What do the filings show?

_____

_____

_____

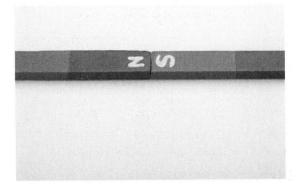

The north and south poles are opposite. Do they repel or attract each other? What do the filings show?

_____

_____

5. Look again at the pictures of the bar magnets. How did the magnetic poles interact with each other? Write your observations in the chart below.

Poles	Attract or repel
N to N	
S to S	
N to S	

6. In which test(s) did the magnets push apart? In which test(s) did the magnets pull together? What can you conclude about how the two poles of magnets interact? Write a paragraph to explain what happened and the reasons for your conclusions.

_____

_____

_____

_____

 EVIDENCE NOTEBOOK How are iron filings evidence that shows the relationship between a magnet's poles?

HANDS-ON Apply What You Know

Compass

7. Without allowing them to touch, move a compass around a bar magnet. What do you observe about the magnetic poles? What can you tell about how the compass works from this activity?

Does Distance Matter?

From what distance do magnets attract the most paper clips?

| 20 cm away | 10 cm away | 5 cm away |

8. In which picture are the paper clips most attracted to the magnet? In which picture are the fewest clips attracted to it?

_____

9. Predict what would happen if you changed the height of the magnet to 25 cm from the paper clips.

| **more** | **the same number of** | **fewer** |

At 25 cm, the magnet will pick up _____ paper clips than it did at 20 cm.

Putting it Together

10. Define _magnetic force._ Tell how magnets attract or repel one another and how distance affects a magnetic force.

Tip

Refer Explicitly to Text
Refer to words and ideas from what you have read. Reading and Writing in Science.

_____

_____

Electricity

It's Electric!

Electricity can make things move! **Electricity** is a form of energy. It comes to your home from energy-generating stations. It travels through wires to electrical outlets in your building, ready to be used.

Coal is a fossil fuel that can be burned to produce electricity.

At this energy-generating station, heat from burning coal provides the force to spin a generator.

Electrical lines like these carry electricity from the generating station across great distances.

Electrical lines like these carry electricity short distances to homes and businesses.

An electrical meter measures the amount of electricity used by the people inside buildings.

Electrical wires inside a building carry electricity to each light switch and outlet in the building.

11. Choose the best answer to complete the sentence below.

| electrical meters | generators | high-voltage lines |

Electricity travels long distances through _____.

EVIDENCE NOTEBOOK Suppose a storm knocks out one of the electrical lines in your neighborhood. What evidence from the pictures on pages 115 and 116 explains why you would lose electricity?

HANDS-ON Apply What You Know

Meter Reader

12. With an adult, find an electrical meter. Are the numbers on it changing slowly or quickly? Write down the current number.

_____

What is the number after 1 minute?

_____

If energy usage stays the same, predict the number in 10 minutes.

_____

Engineer It!
Foot Energy

Did you know you can use energy from your own body to power small electrical devices? You can! A bike such as this can change the energy from pedaling motion into electrical energy that can charge the battery in a device such as a cell phone. This is one small way to save natural resources and get some exercise at the same time!

Language SmArts
Body Power

13. Research other methods that allow people to convert energy from their own bodies to power small electrical devices. Describe one device, and explain how it works.

_____

_____

_____

Zap! Static Electricity!

Remember the picture of the girl whose hair stuck out in all directions? At that moment, her hair had an electrical charge, or static electricity. **Static electricity** is a charge that builds up on an object. It is a type of electricity.

Sometimes an electrical charge builds up inside a cloud. When the charge releases suddenly, what happens? Lightning!

Your hair stands up after a slide ride on a dry day. Your clothing rubs against the slide, causing a static charge to build.

Like magnetic force, static electricity also can work across a distance. Recall how magnets can pull or push, attract or repel. Static charges also attract or repel. In magnets, two like poles repel each other. In static electricity, two like charges will repel each other, too. In magnets, two opposite poles will attract each other. If two objects have opposite static charges, they will attract, or stick to, each other.

14. Select as many answers as are true.

Static electricity _____

a. can be caused by objects rubbing together.

b. moves in all directions.

c. is a charge that builds up on an object.

d. has two poles.

Jump, Spark!

Like magnetic force, electric force can act across a distance. And like a magnet, electricity can produce a field—an electrical field. An electrical field is strongest nearest the charged object. Van de Graaff machines such as the ones shown below make a field of static electricity. The attraction is strong enough to pull a charge across the gap. You see (and maybe feel) a spark!

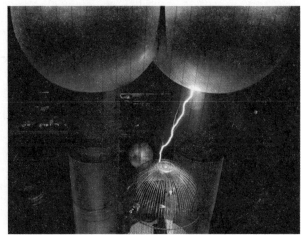

A spark jumps across an electrical field when the static charge reaches a certain distance away.

How does the electrical field made by this machine differ from the field generated by the other machine?

15. Fill in the blanks using the word bank below.

charged	repel	spark	static electricity

A Van de Graaff machine causes _____ to

build up on an object. When opposite charges come

into contact, you may see a _____ as the

charges cross the gap.

Making Magnetism

Recall how some magnets in your home are electrical. Such magnets are called electromagnets. Electromagnets are a kind of temporary magnet. When electricity passes through wire wrapped around a piece of iron, it causes the metal to become magnetic. When the electricity is turned off, the magnetism goes away.

16. What causes an electromagnet to pick up scrap metal?

_____

_____

_____

Putting it Together

17. Explain how magnetic and electric forces act across a distance. Use two examples in your answer.

_____

_____

_____

_____

© Houghton Mifflin Harcourt • Image Credits: ©worradirek/Shutterstock

> **Tip**
>
> **Recount Details**
> Examples are details that help prove your information is correct.
> Reading and Writing in Science.

Build an Electromagnet

Objective

Collaborate with a partner to build an electromagnet and test its strength.

What question will you investigate to meet this objective?

Procedure

STEP 1 Gather your materials. Wrap the wire around a large nail or bolt so there are 20 coils.

Why do you think you must use a nail or a bolt in the electromagnet? Is there another object that would work?

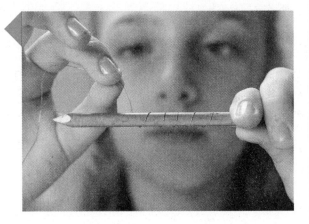

STEP 2 Connect the wire to the two ends of a battery holder.

What happens if one end of the battery has a wire attached to it but the other does not?

STEP 3 Insert one battery into a battery holder. The electromagnet should start to work. How many paper clips does the electromagnet attract with 20 coils? Record your observations in the data table.

STEP 4 Add a second battery holder to the loop. Insert another battery. How many paper clips get attracted to the electromagnet with 20 coils and two batteries? Record your observations in the data table.

How are your wires arranged now that you have a second battery in the system?

_____

_____

_____

_____

_____

STEP 5 Add 20 more coils of wire around the nail (40 coils total). How many paper clips get attracted to the electromagnet with 40 coils? Record your answer in the data table.

STEP 6 Use this data table to record your results.

Strength of Electromagnet

	Coils	Batteries	Paper clips attracted
Test 1	20	1	
Test 2	20	2	
Test 3	40	2	

Analyze Your Results

STEP 7 How can you change your electromagnet to pick up even more paper clips? Make a plan to modify your electromagnet and test it. Write your plan in the box. Record your results in the data table at the bottom of the page.

Modifications to Electromagnet

Results—Predicted and Actual

	Coils	Batteries	Prediction	Result
Test 4				
Test 5				

Draw Conclusions

STEP 8 Study your results. Describe the math pattern among the number of coils, the number of batteries, and the number of clips the electromagnet will pick up.

_____

_____

_____

_____

STEP 9 Why is it important not to change the number of batteries at the same time you change the number of coils?

_____

_____

_____

STEP 10 How do the results of your modifications relate to what you know about magnetic fields?

_____

_____

_____

_____

STEP 11 Make a claim about factors that affect the strength of an electromagnet. Cite evidence from the data you recorded to support your claim.

_____

_____

_____

_____

Discover More

Check out this path . . . or go online to choose one of these other paths.

Careers in Science & Engineering

- **Maglev Train**
- **Make a Compass**

Careers in Science & Engineering

Explore Online

Electrician

Electricians help get electricity to where it is needed. They help design, install, and fix problems with electrical systems. They may work at an energy generating station. Or they may set up and check on electrical lines. Electricians also fix transformers, poles, and electrical lines damaged by storms.

Electricians can set up the wiring, light fixtures, outlets, and switches in buildings. They always practice safety when working with electricity.

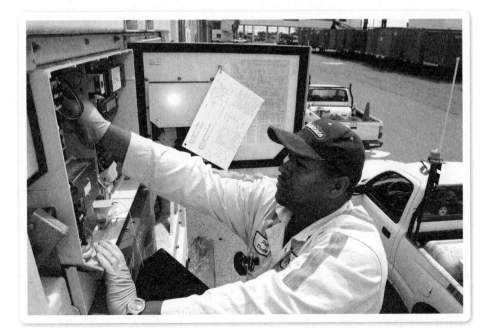

Electricians must know about electrical forces to do their jobs safely and correctly.

125

18. Investigate where the electricity for your school is produced. Research how energy is generated. Make a presentation to show the sequence of steps in which electricity gets generated and then delivered to your school. You may use photos, drawings, maps, and diagrams in your presentation.

Try to answer all these questions in your presentation:

- Where is the energy generating station in your area?

- What is the name of the company that provides the electricity to your area?

- What is the path of the large transmission lines leading to your neighborhood?

- Where is the closest local substation?

- Where is the electrical line that leads into your school?

- Where is the electrical meter in your school?

Draw or take notes about your findings in the box below.

Turn your presentation in to your teacher.

Lesson Check

Name _____

Can You Explain It?

Explore Online

1. Now that you've learned more about forces that act at a distance, explain what you observed about the donut magnets shown. Be sure to do the following:

• Identify the force involved.

• Identify factors that can affect the strength of this force.

EVIDENCE NOTEBOOK Use the information you've collected in your Evidence Notebook to help you cover each point above.

_____

_____

_____

_____

_____

Checkpoints

2. Which sentence best explains how a magnetic door latch works?

   a. Static electricity creates a magnetic field.

   b. Static electricity charges the magnets.

   c. Like poles of two magnets repel each other.

   d. Opposite poles of two magnets attract each other.

3. Draw a line to match the questions on the left with the correct answers on the right.

What happens if you attach an electric source to a wire coiled around a metal bolt?	The attracting force becomes weaker.
What happens if you place the N and S ends of two magnets near each other?	You make a temporary magnet.
What happens when lightning strikes or a spark jumps?	They will attract each other.
What happens if you move a magnet farther from some metal clips?	Built-up electric charges move from one object to another.

4. Circle the choice or choices from the word bank that tell what two objects must be for electric and magnetic forces to act.

> **not touching**   **touching**   **uncharged**

5. Fill in the blank using the word bank below.

> **opposite poles**   **like poles**   **static charges**

Some ring magnets attract each other because their

 are facing each other.

6. How many poles does a magnet have?

  a. none

  b. one

  c. two

  d. four

Lesson Roundup

A. Look at the pictures. Decide whether the objects are attracting or repelling each other. Write what you observe in the correct column.

Objects Attracting   Objects Repelling

_____   _____

_____   _____

_____   _____

B. Select all the answers that are true.

How do you know electrical force works from a distance?

a. An electrical transformer changes the force of the electricity.

b. Objects charged with static electricity repel or attract.

c. Sparks sometimes jump between a charged object and another object.

C. Select all the answers that are true.

How do you know magnetic force works from a distance?

a. Metal objects are pulled toward magnets.

b. Like poles push each other apart.

c. Unlike poles pull together.

ENGINEER IT!
Moved without Touching

In small groups, design and build a maze through which you can move an object. The goal is to move the object through the maze without touching the object. Work with materials provided by your teacher.

FIND A PROBLEM: What problem do you need to solve?

_____

_____

Before beginning, look at the checklist at the end of this project to be sure you are meeting all the requirements.

RESEARCH: Study the various forces that cause objects to move. Use online or library sources for research. Use multiple sources and cite them.

_____

_____

_____

BRAINSTORM: Brainstorm three or more ideas with your group to solve the problem. Keep in mind the criteria and constraints.

Criteria	Constraints
☐ Object must move through the full maze.	☐ You cannot touch the object.
☐ The maze must use some form of force.	☐ Use only the materials provided by your teacher.

MAKE A PLAN: Make a plan by considering the questions below.

1. Which force or forces will you use to move the object through the maze?

2. How will the force or forces affect the type of design for the maze?

Present a step-by-step plan here.

_____

_____

DESIGN, BUILD, AND EXPERIMENT: Draw out a design of the maze, and build the maze using the materials provided by your teacher. Conduct the final experiment to move the object through the course of the maze without touching it.

EVALUATE AND REDESIGN: Did you meet the criteria and constraints? What are ways you could improve the design of the maze? Make changes to your design to improve it.

_____

_____

_____

☑ Checklist

Review your project and check off each completed item.

_____ Includes a list of materials used.

_____ Includes the force or forces used to move the object.

_____ Includes a design of the course or maze.

_____ Includes a physical, built course or maze.

Unit Review

1. Identify the examples in the word bank as examples of a push or a pull.

soccer kick	putting on socks
tug of war	rolling a mat

Push	Pull

2. Look at the scene. What would happen if the person uses strong force to put the books away? Select the best answer.

a. The books could fall off the shelves.

b. The books would be fine.

c. The books would make a small sound.

3. Emily's ice cream cone tips over. Her ice cream falls to the floor. Which force caused it to fall?

a. gravity

b. friction

c. magnetism

d. static electricity

4. Soojinn and Michael are playing tug of war. The game is about even, meaning Soojinn and Michael are not moving the rope too much. Which concept of force describes what would happen if Soojinn had two friends to help her pull? Select the best answer.

a. The pulling force is faster with more people.

b. The pushing force is stronger with more people.

c. The pulling force is stronger with more people.

d. The pulling force is slower with more people.

5. Write if the force used is more or less to move the box.

   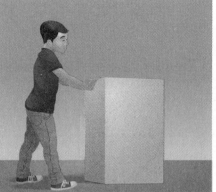

_____   _____

6. Imagine there is a puppy sitting in a wagon. Describe the forces on the puppy. Are they balanced or unbalanced? A girl comes along and pulls the wagon. Have the forces changed? Are they balanced or unbalanced?

_____

_____

_____

7. Using the word bank below, complete the table about friction.

Water slide	Snow	Sneakers
Skis	Gym floors	Inner tube

Item	Surface	Friction (High or Low)
		Low
		Low
		High

8. Which concept of force is being shown in the image?
Select all that apply.

   a. The seesaw has contact force.

   b. The forces are balanced.

   c. Forces are moving in opposite directions.

   d. There is no motion.

9. Put the correct phrase into the table to decide if the two objects will attract or repel.

> **north pole to south pole**
> **north pole to north pole**
> **south pole to south pole**

Attract	Repel

10. Which concept of force is shown in the image?
Select the best answer for the question.

   a. static electricity   **b.** magnetism

   c. gravity   **d.** friction

Motion

Explore Online

Unit Project: Motion Detectives

Can you figure out what an object is from clues about its motion? Investigate with your team. Ask your teacher for details.

How could you describe the motion of this pinball in a pinball machine?

UNIT 3

At a Glance

LESSON 1

What Is Motion? 138

LESSON 2

What Are Some Patterns in Motion? 158

Unit Review 176

Vocabulary Game: **Bingo** (for 3–6 players)

Materials
- 1 set of word cards
- 1 bingo board for each player
- Counters for game markers

speed

position

Setup
- Choose one student to be the caller. The caller will call out the words but not play.
- To make bingo boards, players write words from the unit in the squares. Students can use words more than once to fill out the board.

Directions
1. The caller chooses a word card and reads the word, the caller then puts the word card in a second pile.
2. Players put a marker on the word each time they find it on their bingo boards.
3. Repeat steps 1 and 2 until a player marks five boxes in a line going down, across, or on a slant and calls "Bingo." Check the answers.
4. Have the caller check the word cards in the second pile against the bingo board.

© Houghton Mifflin Harcourt • Image Credits: (l) ©Agencja Fotograficzna Caro/Alamy

Unit Vocabulary

frame of reference: A background that remains the same, allowing you to determine if an object is changing position.

motion: A change of position of an object.

position: The location of an object in relation to a nearby object or place.

speed: The measure of an object's change in position during a certain amount of time.

What Is Motion?

The world's fastest animal is the cheetah, which clocks in at about 112 km/h (about 70 mph). The average adult man runs about 13 km/h (about 8 mph).

By the end of this lesson...

you'll be able to describe ways that unbalanced forces affect the motion of an object.

Can You Explain It?

▷ Explore Online

With the help of a rocket engine, the Bloodhound SSC will attempt to break the land speed record for the fastest car ever built. It should travel nearly 1,000 mph (about 1,600 km/h).

1. What forces act on the Bloodhound SSC car to make it speed up or slow down? Are forces different at super-high speeds than at slow speeds?

Tip

Learn more about forces in Forces and What Are Some Types of Forces?

_____

_____

_____

_____

_____

_____

_____

_____

EVIDENCE NOTEBOOK Look for this icon to help you gather evidence to answer the questions above.

Here or There

Changes in Position

You are waiting for the bus. You see your friend walking on the sidewalk. Is your friend moving toward you or away from you? How can you tell?

Your friend's **position**—place or location—changes. If your friend comes closer, he or she is walking toward you. **Motion** is the change in position of an object.

Scientists study animals' movements to learn more about them. They track and record an animal's position to see what direction, how far, and how fast it moves over time.

The map shows the positions of a monk seal observed over several weeks around Hawai'i. Each change in position shows how far it moved and in which direction.

The tracking device communicates an animal's position.

EVIDENCE NOTEBOOK Describe your position in your classroom. Then describe your position in the school. You can use direction words, such as *north, south, east,* and *west.* You can also use position words, such as *next to, behind,* and *in front of.*

Shark on the Move

2. Complete the chart of a shark's movements in the Atlantic.

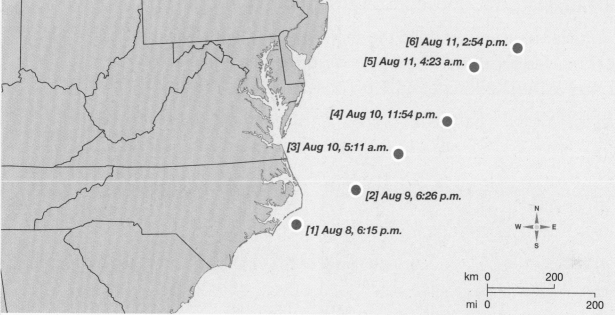

[6] Aug 11, 2:54 p.m.

[5] Aug 11, 4:23 a.m.

[4] Aug 10, 11:54 p.m.

[3] Aug 10, 5:11 a.m.

[2] Aug 9, 6:26 p.m.

[1] Aug 8, 6:15 p.m.

km 0   200
mi 0   200

Explore Online

Position points	Date	Time	Motion description
1	Aug. 8	6:15 p.m.	northeast, 200 km
2			
3			
4			
5			
6			

3. How can you tell whether the shark was in motion?

a. The points on the map did not move.

b. Its position changed.

c. Its position was observed six times in two days.

Describe how the shark moved.

Moving or Still

Look at the photos of a balloon race. To see a change in position, you also need to see things that do not move. You see how one object moves by comparing its position to an object that is still. The things in view that do not move are called a **frame of reference.**

Recall how you mapped the shark's movements. The map and grid stayed the same. The map and grid form a frame of reference to observe the shark's motion. Now observe things that form a frame of reference in the balloon photos.

Explore Online

The colorful balloon is to the left of the rocks.

The colorful balloon has moved. It is to the right of the rocks. The rocks provide a frame of reference.

HANDS-ON Apply What You Know

Frame of Reference Flipbook

4. Make a flipbook that shows a stick person moving past a tree. Then flip the pages to see how the stick person's position changes. Hint: On each page of your flipbook, the tree is your frame of reference. It should always be in the same spot. Share your flipbook with a classmate, and then turn it in to your teacher.

5. The pictures below show a boat race. Find a frame of reference in the pictures to put them in the correct order from one to four.

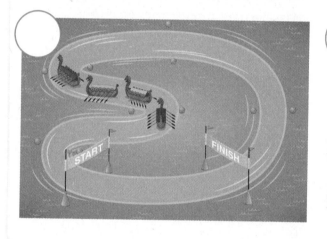

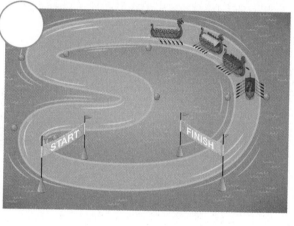

Language SmArts
Making Inferences

6. Which boat had the fastest motion from start to finish? Which boat moved the slowest? How could you tell? Write your answers below.

_____

_____

_____

_____

© Houghton Mifflin Harcourt

Tip

Making Inferences
The English Language Arts Handbook can provide help with understanding how to make inferences.

143

Speed It Up!

How Fast Is It?

Speed is a measure of how far something travels in a given amount of time. If your car is moving at 60 miles per hour (mph), it will take 1 hour for your car to travel 60 miles.

Do the Math
Animals Off to the Races

Speed can be slow or fast. Things move at different speeds. The speed of these animals is described in the number of meters the animals move per second.

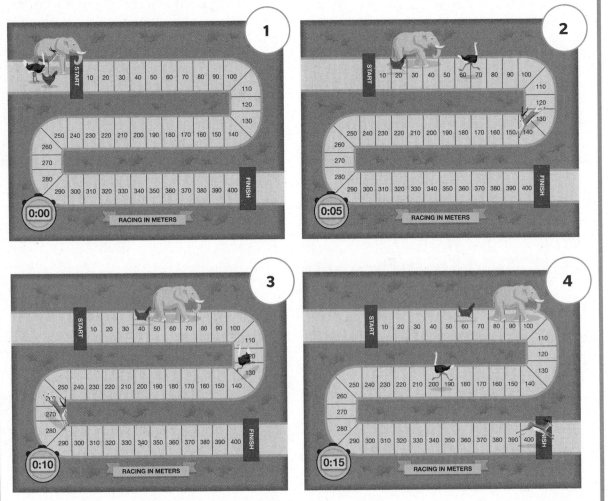

7. Look at the pictures. How far did each animal travel at 10 seconds in the race? How far at 15 seconds? Complete the chart.

	Chicken	Elephant	Antelope	Ostrich
5 seconds	20 meters	30 meters	135 meters	65 meters
10 seconds				
15 seconds				

8. Which animal has the fastest speed?

_____

9. Write the correct answer from the number bank below.

4,000	400	40

The winner ran about _____ meters (m) in 15 seconds (sec).

10. Write the correct answer from the number bank below.

600	60	6

To calculate speed, divide the distance traveled by the time it

takes. If an elephant runs 60 meters in 10 seconds, its speed

would be _____ meters per second (m/sec).

11. Write the names of the animals from slowest speed to fastest speed.

_____

© Houghton Mifflin Harcourt

Speed and Direction

Speed is a measure of time to move a distance. When things move, they also move in a direction. Suppose you want to go from your home to the library. You want to go to the library as quickly as possible. A bus, a subway, and a train all go to the library. To find which one gets to the library the fastest, you must consider how fast it goes, but also in which direction.

Which subway to take in a large city depends on how fast it gets you to your distance. A subway that goes in the wrong direction won't get you to your destination very fast!

In large cities, cars are not always the fastest form of transportation. During rush hour, cars move very slowly or not at all. Sometimes cars are stopped at traffic lights also.

 8. Language SmArts

12. Explain how two cars traveling to the same place and at the same speed could get there at different times.

_____

_____

_____

_____

_____

_____

 Tip

Cause and Effect The English Language Arts Handbook can provide help with understanding how to determine cause and effect.

Transportation Map

13. Complete the chart with data from the map to help decide which vehicle would get you from home to the library fastest. Each circle represents one stop.

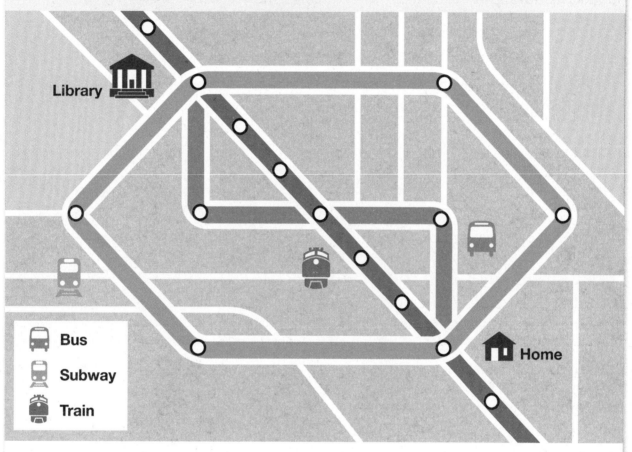

Vehicle	Number of stops	Speed (slow, medium, or fast)	Distance (short, medium, or long)
Bus		slow	
Subway	3		
Train			short

14. Which vehicle do you take and why? Write your answer below.

Speed and Unbalanced Forces

To change his speed, a dirt bike rider applies a force to the pedals. To change his direction, the rider applies a force to the handlebars. The sum of the forces becomes unbalanced. Unbalanced forces cause a change in motion.

Faster pedaling applies greater force to turn the wheels faster. The dirt bike speeds up. Pressing the brakes causes a sudden increase in friction. The dirt bike slows. Steering the handlebars applies forces that change the dirt bike's direction.

One dirt bike is going faster than the other. A stronger forward force is applied to it.

Forces change the direction of the dirt bike's motion.

15. How did the rider use forces to cause a change in speed? How did the rider use forces to cause a change in direction?

_____

_____

_____

_____

Engineer It!
Going Even Faster

Surveyors use equipment with lasers to determine how big or flat an area is.

Here are the results of the laser survey.

BLOODHOUND SSC TRACK - HAKSKEEN PAN, SOUTH AFRICA

Before the Bloodhound SSC can be tested, engineers must prepare the test track. A car that can move 1000 mph can't race on just any road. The track is being built on a dry lakebed. The ground may look smooth, but it actually has many small bumps and dips.

Bumps and dips can cause friction, which would slow the car. Surveyors used lasers to measure the ground. These measurements helped produce a three-dimensional map of the lake bed's surface.

Putting it Together

16. What is the Bloodhound SSC team likely to do with the information they gather from the laser survey?

_____

_____

_____

Tip

Answer Questions
Refer to words and ideas from the text. Reading and Writing in Science.

HANDS-ON ACTIVITY
Slow Walk, Fast Walk

You think you are walking quickly. Your friends think you are walking slowly. No one can agree on what it means to walk fast or walk slow. How can you all agree about a person's speed?

Objective

Collaborate with a team to measure and describe walking speeds.

Procedure

STEP 1 Use a meterstick and masking tape to mark off a distance of 10 meters (m).

Why do you think 10 meters is a good distance to select? Why not 1 meter or 100 meters?

_____

_____

STEP 2 Use a stopwatch. Measure how long it takes each of you to walk 10 m. Each person should walk slowly. Write each person's time in seconds (sec) and distance in meters (m) in the data table.

Why does each member of the team walk? Isn't having the data for one person enough?

_____

_____

STEP 3 Now time each person walking the same 10 m as fast as possible. Use the stopwatch again to measure the time. Record each person's time and distance in your data table.

STEP 4 Calculate the speed of each person's slow walk, in meters per second (m/sec).

_____

What other units could you convert your data to?

_____

_____

STEP 5 Calculate the speed of each person's fast walk in m/sec. Enter your results in the tables below.

DATA TABLE: SLOW WALK

	Distance (m)	Time (sec)	Speed (m/sec)
Person 1			
Person 2			
Person 3			

DATA TABLE: FAST WALK

	Distance (m)	Time (sec)	Speed (m/sec)
Person 1:			
Person 2:			
Person 3:			

Analyze Your Results

STEP 6 What is the average fast walk in your investigation?

_____

_____

STEP 7 What is the average slow walk in your investigation?

_____

_____

STEP 8 What is the average difference between a fast walk and a slow walk?

_____

_____

Draw Conclusions

STEP 9 Discuss the results with your investigation team. Can you now agree on what a slow walk and fast walk are? What is your conclusion as a team?

A slow walk is a speed of _____.

A fast walk is a speed of _____.

STEP 10 Why is it helpful to know an object's actual speed instead of just saying that it moved fast or slowly? Enter your answer below.

_____

_____

_____

Discover More

Check out this path . . . or go online to choose one of these other paths.

People in Science & Engineering

- Movie Making
- Robots Race

People in Science & Engineering

Explore Online

Mark Fuller and Megan Leftwich

Have you ever played with a garden hose? Did you notice that if you close most of the opening with a thumb, you can force the water to move farther and in a controlled direction? That's the basis behind what Mark Fuller and his company, WET, have been doing around the world for years. He is an expert in laminar flow, the ability to "squeeze" water or other fluids and force its direction one way or another.

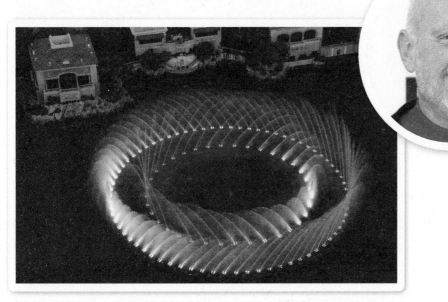

Mark Fuller studies how forces move water so he can design ways to make water look like it is dancing.

Dr. Megan Leftwich studies how sea lions move in water. She is developing a robot flipper to mimic the motion of sea lions. Sea lion motion is unlike that of other sea mammals. Her robot will allow observations of motion that are not possible in the wild.

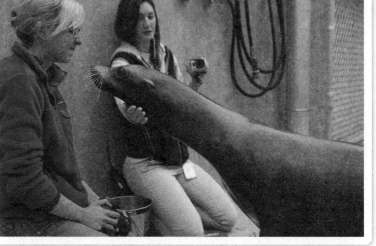

Dr. Leftwich studies sea lion motion in aquariums. Sea lions are hard to observe in the wild.

© Houghton Mifflin Harcourt • Image Credits: (t) ©William Atkins/George Washington University, MAE Department; (c) ©William Atkins/George Washington University, MAE Department

Language SmArts
Interview Questions

17. Research to find out more about either Mark Fuller or Megan Leftwich. Create an interview with questions you would ask the person, and then answer each question as if you were the person being interviewed.

When you have finished, turn in your interview to your teacher.

Lesson Check

Name _____

Can You Explain It?

1. Think back to the photo of the fastest car in the world.

   • Describe how forces affect its motion.

   • Explain how its speed is determined.

 EVIDENCE NOTEBOOK Use the information you've collected in your Evidence Notebook to help you cover each point above.

_____

_____

_____

_____

_____

_____

_____

Checkpoints

2. Which of these can cause an object to change position?

   a. force

   b. distance

   c. speed

   d. direction

Speed It Up

3. Enter data from the map for tracking point 3 in the chart. Now enter the missing time, location, distance, direction, and time elapsed.

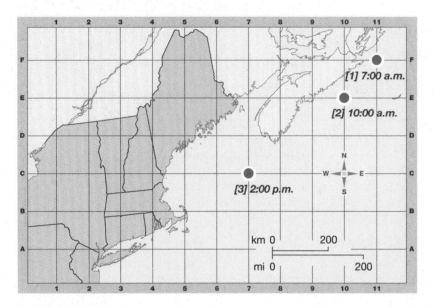

Tracking Mimi the Whale

Tracking points	Time	Location on grid	Distance from last sighting	Time elapsed since last sighting
1	7:00 a.m.	F11		
2	10:00 a.m.			
3				

4. Write the correct answer from the word bank.

> **she swam quickly**   **she had three sightings**
> **her position changed over time**

a. We can conclude that Mimi was in motion because

_____

b. The time of Mimi's third sighting was

_____ hours after the first sighting.

Lesson Roundup

A. Write the correct words or phrases that complete the sentence.

speed	forces	gravity

a. Unbalanced forces cause changes in the _____ of an object in motion.

remain at rest	start to move	slow down

b. If forces are balanced, an object at rest will _____.

any number	zero	less than zero

c. Balanced forces means that the forces acting on an object

add up to _____.

B. Read each situation in the center column. Decide whether the forces are balanced or unbalanced.

Balanced	Are the forces balanced or unbalanced?	Unbalanced
	A pilot starts a plane's jet engines. The jet speeds up and takes off.	
	Two teams pull against each other in a tug of war. Neither team pulls the other over the line.	
	A strong wind causes a tree's branches to sway.	
	You hold a ball and let it go. The ball drops.	
	Your bike is headed downhill. You apply the brakes, and it slows down. Then you steer the bike around a corner.	
	Your friend threw a snowball at you. It missed. Now it is on the ground and not moving.	

What Are Some Patterns in Motion?

Some motions occur in patterns. Others don't.

By the end of this lesson . . .
you'll be able to provide evidence that patterns can be used to predict future motion.

© Houghton Mifflin Harcourt • Image Credits: ©arnaudbertrande/Getty Images

Can You Explain It?

▷ Explore Online

There are many types of motion at a carnival. A merry-go-round always repeats its motion. You can predict when you'll see each horse again. A bumper car's direction and movement changes randomly with every bump. You cannot predict the next motion.

1. Look at the photos of the carnival games above. What motion can you predict in each game? What motion can't you predict in each game?

Tip

Learn more about motion in What Is Motion?

_____

_____

_____

_____

_____

_____

 EVIDENCE NOTEBOOK Look for this icon to help you gather evidence to answer the questions above.

Back and Forth, Up and Down

Patterns, Patterns Everywhere

Patterns of motion happen when the same motion repeats itself. A rabbit hops up and down. A merry-go-round spins in a circle. A skier zigzags down a hill. A swing goes back and forth.

Patterns of Motion

2. Circle the pattern of motion in each set of pictures.

▷ Explore Online

 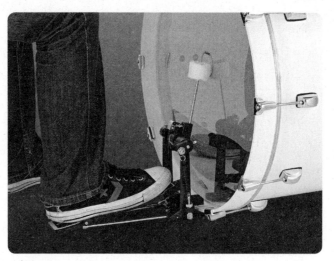

a. back and forth   spinning   up and down   zigzag

b. back and forth   spinning   up and down   zigzag

c. back and forth   spinning   up and down   zigzag

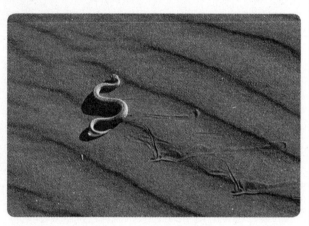

d. back and forth   spinning   up and down   zigzag

3. Write or draw an example of each type of motion in the chart.

back and forth	spinning	up and down	zigzag

EVIDENCE NOTEBOOK Think of objects that can move in more than one way. In your Evidence Notebook, describe how they move.

Moving Many Ways!

An elevator only moves up and down, but often an object moves in more than one way. When you walk somewhere in school, you may go upstairs, walk back and forth along the hall, zigzag around people in front of you, and circle around the room to get to your seat.

Ways of Moving

4. Draw arrows on each picture of medicine bottles to show the patterns of motion.

▷ Explore Online

pills dropping into the bottles

traveling to get put in boxes

preparing bottles for filling

moving through the factory

5. Choose the best words or phrases to complete the sentences.

| circular | back and forth | up and down | zigzag |

When luggage is taken out of a plane and lifted onto a cart, it has a(n) _____ pattern of motion. The bag's motion pattern is _____ on the moving luggage carousel. To avoid banging into other people in the crowded airport, the owner walks with the bag in a(n) _____ motion pattern. While leaving the airport on level ground, the bag's movement follows a(n) _____ motion pattern.

HANDS-ON Apply What You Know

Engineering Motion

6. Think about materials you could use to make a path for a marble to roll along. How could you cause the marble to move in different ways? Design a path to make a marble move in several different patterns. Make a detailed drawing of your design. Be sure to label the materials in your drawing. If your teacher provides the materials to do so, build and test your design.

7. Language SmArts When you roll a ball down a hill, what do you expect it to do? When you roll a ball up a hill, what do you expect it to do?

_____

_____

_____

_____

Tip

The English Language Arts Handbook can provide help with understanding cause and effect.

How Will it Move?

When you see a pattern of motion, you can predict how an object will move next. You can predict that the hands of a clock continue to move in a circle. But you cannot predict a butterfly's next movement.

8. For each image, make a prediction of what you think will happen next. Enter your answer in the table. Then circle the motions that do not have a pattern.

▷ Explore Online

Situation	What motion will happen next?
A Ferris Wheel	
Window washer on a platform at the top of a tall building	
An adult rocking a baby in a rocking chair	
A snow skier moving down a hill, ma king a wavy path	

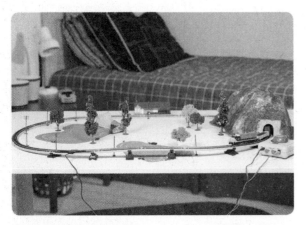

The toy train's motion is easy to predict because it will go where the track is. You can see exactly where it will go next.

Divers bounce to go up, and then they fall into the pool. They may twist or flip. That part of their motion is not predictable.

A scuba diver's movements are random. You can't predict if he or she will move up and down, back and forth, in a circle, or in a zigzag motion.

The only real thing you can predict about the way an animal chases its prey is that there will be many changes in direction.

In everyday life, you make predictions about motion all the time. You notice whether or not your predictions are correct.

9. Predict each next motion to tell whether or not it is a pattern.

Situation	Pattern	No pattern
A piece of toast is lowered into the toaster.		
The wheels on the bus move the bus.		
You are playing soccer.		
You dribble a basketball.		

 10. Language SmArts Think of some predictable motion in games and sports. Write an example of a way that predicting motion can help you win a game.

_____

_____

_____

Tip

The English Language Arts Handbook can provide help with understanding how to use details to support your ideas.

Engineering Art in Motion

Engineering can be used to create devices that do useful tasks. It is also used to make wonderful pieces of moving art. Theo Jansen is an artist who uses engineering to build Strandbeests. His newest versions have taken many years to make. He builds each new sculpture using what he learned from the ones he built before. Engineers use this same method of trial and error and improvement.

This Strandbeest can move in many different ways. Some parts move in a zigzag

Some parts move in a circular motion. Others move back and forth and up and down.

11. Theo Jansen calls his creations animals. He has even given them Latin names, the way real animals are named, and refers to a group of them as a herd. How do the motions of Strandbeests remind you of the ways animals move? Explain your answer.

_____

_____

Motion Inside Motion

Earth is in motion all the time. It moves around the sun. It also rotates. It spins around one complete turn every 24 hours. You can't watch Earth rotate, but you can observe one effect of it turning. You see day and night every 24 hours because where you live on Earth turns toward and away from the sun.

The motion of Earth slowly changes the direction of a Foucault pendulum's swing. In 24 hours, a Foucault pendulum's swing makes a complete circle. This picture is from a time-lapse video. That makes the pendulum look like it swings much faster than it really does. Think about the patterns of motion that you see.

12. Choose the words or phrases that best complete the sentences.

in a circle	back and forth	up and down	zigzag

Every few seconds, the Foucault pendulum swings

_____. However, over the course of a day, the Foucault

pendulum moves _____.

Putting It Together

13. Describe two kinds of motion that happen at once when you pedal a bike.

_____

_____

_____

© Houghton Mifflin Harcourt

Tip

Sequence
Think about what happens first and at the same time.
Reading and Writing in Science

Tick Tock

Objective

Collaborate to investigate variables in pendulums. The length can be short or long. The weight can be heavy or light. Do they move at the same speed or different speeds?

What question will you explore to meet this objective?

Materials
• scissors
• string
• meterstick
• small metal washer
• large metal washer
• timer

_____

_____

Procedure

STEP 1 Be careful using scissors. Work with a partner. Cut two pieces of string, each about 40 centimeters (cm) long. Knot one end of each string to a washer, forming two pendulums.

Why are you preparing two pendulums?

_____

_____

STEP 2 Hold the string of the smaller pendulum so that the pendulum length is 10 cm.

How do you think the motion of the pendulum with the smaller washer will differ from the one with the larger washer?

_____

STEP 3 Pull the washer to the side and release it. Count the number of swings it completes in 5 seconds. One partner should hold the pendulum while another uses the timer. Record your data in the table below.

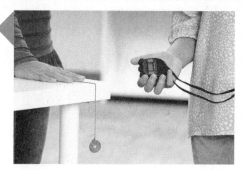

STEP 4 Predict how using the larger washer will affect the pendulum swing rate. Write your prediction here, and then repeat Steps 2 and 3 using the larger washer.

_____

_____

STEP 5 Predict how making the string longer will affect the swing rate. Choose a distance between 10 and 30 cm. Write that number on the data table. Hold the string so the small washer's pendulum length is that distance and repeat Step 3. Do the same using the large washer. Record your data in the data table below.

_____

_____

Record your Results

STEP 6 Repeat Step 5 holding the string so the pendulum length is 30 cm. Record your data in the data table below.

	Time to Complete Five Swings		
	10 cm	_____ cm	30 cm
Small washer			
Large washer			

Analyze Your Results

STEP 7 Which pendulum produced the greater number of swings? Was this true for all string lengths?

_____

_____

_____

STEP 8 Which string length produced the least number of swings? Was this true for all washer sizes?

_____

_____

_____

Draw Conclusions

STEP 9 Describe what makes a difference in how many times a pendulum swings in five seconds. Enter your answer in the box below.

_____

_____

_____

STEP 10 How would observing the pattern of motion of the pendulum help you predict its future motion? Enter your answer below.

_____

_____

_____

Discover More

Check out the path . . . or go online to choose one of these other paths.

Careers in Science & Engineering

- **Where Does Earth Go Every Year?**
- **Well-Oiled Machines**

Careers in Science & Engineering

Biomechanist

▶ Explore Online

A biomechanist studies patterns of body movements. Biomechanists help athletes move in more effective ways. They also study how to have fewer injuries in some sports. Observe the ways that biomechanists study patterns of motion and work to change those patterns.

How might studying the movements in a golf swing help a golfer improve?

What patterns of motion do swimmers have?

Biomechanists study motion. Changing the motion of a baseball swing, a runner's pace, or swimmer's breathing patterns can help improve performance.

Biomechanists also help improve products for athletes. Watching how a shoe performs on a treadmill tells engineers how to improve a design.

Language SmArts
Interview a Biomechanist

14. Suppose you were going to interview a biomechanist. Enter the questions you would want to ask in the box below. Include a question about a sport you enjoy.

_____

_____

_____

Do the Math
Improving Speeds

15. A biomechanist analyzes a long distance runner's race times. First, the runner could run a mile in 12 minutes. After the analysis, the runner made changes and her speed improved by 75 seconds. Is her new time greater or less than 11 minutes? _____

Lesson Check

Name _____

Can You Explain It?

Explore Online

1. Think back to the photos of the carnival game at the beginning of this lesson.

   • What motion was the same all through the game?

   • What motion did not stay the same during the game?

   • Explain whether a pattern makes it able to predict motion in the game.

EVIDENCE NOTEBOOK Use the information you've collected in your Evidence Notebook to help you cover each point above.

_____

_____

_____

_____

_____

Checkpoints

2. What does observing the patterns of motion of an object help you do? Choose all that apply.

   a. predict its future motion

   b. predict its past motion

   c. measure the motion

3. Sort each description by the type of motion in it. Write the letter of the item under the type of motion that describes how it will move.

a. broom sweeping floor

b. opening a jar lid

c. jack-in-the-box

d. crossing guard helping students

e. lightning

f. microwave turntable

g. teeth chewing food

Circular/ around	Back and forth	Up and down	Zigzag

4. Choose the words or phrases that best complete the sentences.

cannot	can

a. If you observe the repeating pattern of a fan's motion, you

_____ predict how the fan will move next. You

_____ predict the next random motion of a flag fluttering in the wind.

zigzag	up and down	circular
around	back and forth	

b. When you go on a swing, you move both _____ and

_____.

5. A Foucault pendulum makes a complete circle in

_____ hours.

6. You watch a gray pendulum and a red pendulum. In 8 seconds the gray pendulum swings more times than the red one does. Is the gray pendulum shorter or longer than the red one?

_____

Lesson Roundup

A. Ann rides her bike on the sidewalk. As she does that, different parts of the bike move in more than one way. Read each activity. Write any types of motion that describe the motion in the chart.

pushing on the bike pedals	rolling wheels	turning the bike at the corner	swerving the bike around a crack

B. Choose the words that best complete the sentences.

cannot	can	no	random	repeating

After watching the motion pattern of a squirrel playing with

another squirrel in a tree, you _____ be sure of the next

motion of the squirrel. In contrast, you go to a factory that uses

machines to make parts and you notice the machines use

_____ patterns of motion.

C. Choose the best answer to the question.

A brown pendulum and a blue pendulum just started swinging. Each has a weight of 1 kg. The brown pendulum is 40 cm long. The blue pendulum is 60 cm long. Which of these will complete more swings in 10 seconds?

a. The brown pendulum will complete more swings.

b. The blue pendulum will complete more swings.

c. Both pendulums will complete the same number of swings.

ENGINEER IT!
Hunting for Treasure!

You and a partner will send each other on a treasure hunt. First, you will learn about using a compass. Then, you will each hide something and write instructions on how to find it. Finally, you will use each other's instructions to go on your hunt.

This compass shows the four main directions and four more besides.

DEFINITIONS: For this task, use the word *direction* ONLY to name a direction of movement. Call the written guidance for your partner *instructions* instead of *directions*.

STATE YOUR GOAL: What skills will you develop in this project?

_____

RESEARCH: Research how to use a magnetic compass. Find and write down definitions for the terms: *cardinal directions* and *ordinal directions*. Cite the sources you use.

_____

_____

BRAINSTORM: What information does a good set of instructions have? Remember movement involves both direction and distance.

Criteria	Constraints
☐ The instructions must be clear.	☐ You use instructions to tell where the treasure is located.
☐ Your partner must be able to locate the hidden treasure.	☐ You use directions and some type of measurement in your instructions.

MAKE A PLAN: Examine your brainstorming ideas as you prepare. Consider these questions:

1. What supplies will you need?

2. How will you use cardinal and ordinal directions?

3. How will you show distance?

4. How will you describe how and when to change direction?

Below, write instructions that show how to get to the main office.

_____

_____

_____

ON WITH THE HUNT: Go to your playground or gym. Hide a small object. Then write step-by-step instructions telling how to find it. Measure your distances, and use at least two ordinal directions. Give the instructions to your partner, and let the treasure hunt begin!

COMMUNICATE: After your partner has found the "treasure," discuss your instructions. Could they have been clearer? How?

WRAPPING UP: Now it's your turn to "hunt treasure." Use your partner's instructions, and bring back your prize. As a class, discuss your project and what you've learned.

✓ Checklist

Review your project and check off each completed item.

_____ Includes a list of materials needed.

_____ Includes ordinal and cardinal directions in instructions.

_____ Includes accurate measurements in instructions.

Unit Review

1. What best explains the cause of the motion shown here? Circle the correct answer.

   a. gravity

   b. magnetism

   c. balanced forces

   d. unbalanced forces

2. Which statements about speed are true? Circle all that apply.

   a. It is affected by forces.

   b. It is calculated using time.

   c. It is calculated using distance.

   d. It makes objects change direction.

   e. It applies only to objects on the ground.

3. Sort the following movements. Write "Z" for zigzag, "U" for up and down, "B" for back and forth, or "S" for spinning in circles or around a curve.

   ____ a mall escalator

   ____ a race car on an oval track

   ____ an adult rocking a baby

   ____ a helicopter blade

   ____ a playground swing

   ____ a skier on a snowy hill, following a path of flags scattered

   on a course

4. Indicate whether each action taken by the person shown here affects the car's speed, direction, or both.

Driving around a bend in the road	Driving downhill
Driving uphill	Stepping on the accelerator
Stepping on the brakes	Turning the steering wheel

Affects speed	Affects direction	Affects both

5. Speed is equal to _____ divided by _____.

6. At the airport, Sam and Jose are trying to get to their gate on time. They are moving at the same speed. Sam takes the moving sidewalk escalator, but Jose chooses to walk alongside. How can you tell that Sam is in motion even though he is standing still on the moving sidewalk.

_____

_____

_____

7. Which choices help describe the motion of the object shown here? Circle all that apply.

  a. back and forth

  b. up and down

  c. in a circle

  d. zigzag

8. Which of the following most directly results from Earth's yearly pattern of motion? Circle the correct choice.

  a. four seasons

  b. high and low tides

  c. sunrises and sunsets

  d. twenty-four hour days

9. A group of engineers has designed a high-speed train that will travel from New York to Indianapolis. Think about gravity and friction. Identify how these two forces could affect the motion of the train.

_____

_____

_____

_____

10. A pendulum on a _____ string swings faster than a

  pendulum on a _____ string.

Life Cycles and Inherited Traits

Explore Online

Unit Project: Life Cycle Model

Use your prior knowledge to make a model of a plant or animal life cycle. Ask your teacher for details.

White Bengal tigers lack the ability to produce red and yellow coloring. It is an example of an inherited trait.

At a Glance

LESSON 1

What Are Some Plant Life Cycles? 184

LESSON 2

What Are Some Animal Life Cycles? 208

LESSON 3

What Are Inherited Plant and Animal Traits? 234

Unit Review 254

Vocabulary Game: **Guess the Word**

Materials
- Kitchen timer or online computer timer
- Cards with vocabulary and science words

Directions

1. Choose a word card. Do not tell the word to the other players. Set the timer to 1 minute.

2. Give a word clue about your word to another player who has one chance to guess your word.

3. Repeat step 2 with a different one-word clue until a player guesses the word or time runs out.

4. The first player to guess the word gets 1 point and 1 more point if they use the word in a sentence. Then that player gets the next turn.

5. The first player to score 5 points wins.

organism

A living thing.

trait

A physical characteristic of a person, animal, or plant

Unit Vocabulary

life cycle: Changes that happen to an animal or a plant during its life.

metamorphosis: A series of changes that some animals go through.

organism: A living thing.

pupa: The stage of complete metamorphosis in which an insect changes from a larva to an adult.

trait: A physical characteristic of a person, animal, or plant.

What Are Some Plant Life Cycles?

It looks as if the flower is providing food for this bee. What is the bee doing for the plant?

_____

By the end of this lesson...
you'll be able to develop a model to describe a plant's life cycle.

Can You Explain It?

▷ Explore Online

The field starts out with a single dandelion. But over time, the field is filled with yellow dandelions. Think about how this happened.

1. Think about the dandelions in the field. How did the field end up with so many flowers?

_____

_____

_____

_____

_____

_____

_____

_____

 EVIDENCE NOTEBOOK Look for this icon to help you gather evidence to answer the questions above.

So Many Stages!

Seeds on the Go

Living things experience a **life cycle,** or changes that happen in order from the beginning of their lives to the time they die. Plants have life cycles with certain stages. You'll learn about these stages and then build a model of a flowering-plant's life cycle.

Flowering Plant Life Cycle

Read about the life stages of a dandelion. On the next page, you will place these stages in the correct order.

 Explore Online

Germination
During germination, the dandelion sprouts from a seed.

Adult
Eventually, the dandelion becomes an adult plant. It begins to develop a flower.

Reproduction
The flower produces seeds. A strong wind can blow the seeds off.

Seed
A seed begins the life cycle of a new dandelion plant.

Young adult
After the dandelion seed germinates, it grows into a young adult plant.

Death
The adult plant may reproduce many times. At the end of its life cycle, the plant dies.

2. Now that you have learned about the different stages in the life cycle of plants, it is your turn to put the stages in the correct order. Draw or write the stages in order.

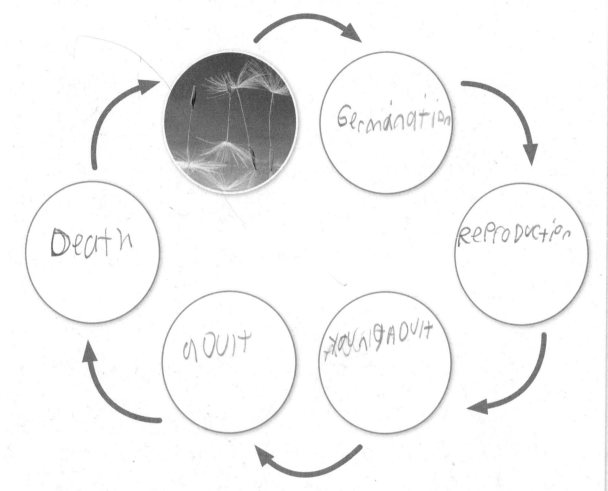

(circles, clockwise from top: photo of dandelion seeds; Germination; ReproDuction; xavniqaoult; aoult; Death)

With the right soil, water, and light, the dandelion seeds will germinate, and the life cycle will start again.

3. Language SmArts Does the flowering plant's life cycle always happen in the same order? Explain your answer.

_____

_____

EVIDENCE NOTEBOOK Draw and explain the stages of the dandelion life cycle. How does your diagram provide evidence for how dandelions can begin to grow in places where they didn't appear before?

Producing More Plants

Pollen is the sticky, yellow powder you see on a plant. Pollination occurs when pollen is moved from one plant to another. Pollinators are animals that move pollen. Pollen can also be moved in other ways.

When bees land on a flower, pollen sticks to the bee's legs or body. When the bee lands on other flowers, the pollen is moved to the new flower.

Hummingbirds get pollen on their beaks and faces. Then they carry the pollen to other plants.

Seeds need room to grow. Birds eat the seeds. Then they release the seeds in their droppings as they move.

Some seeds have winglike shapes that allow them to travel when the wind blows.

Do you like to blow on dandelion seeds? The seeds of dandelions are like parachutes, which help them travel in the wind.

This tumbleweed is on the move. Its seeds may break away, and new plants may germinate where the seeds land.

4. What are some ways seeds and pollen are carried from one place to another?

_____

_____

 Engineer It!
Flow Hive

Bees use nectar from flowering plants to make honey. Getting the honey from the bees can be hard, though. Beekeepers use hives with panels that pull out so they can get to the honey. This disturbs the bees. It also puts beekeepers at risk for stings!

Imagine turning a handle on a beehive and squeezing the honey out of a tap. Father and son Stuart and Cedar Anderson are beekeepers in Australia. They spent ten years inventing this new kind of beehive. Not having to open the hive to get the honey out is much easier for beekeepers and less stressful for bees. It's so simple. Honey on tap!

Stuart and Cedar Anderson

Flow hive

5. What problems does the Flow Hive solve for beekeepers and for bees?

_____

_____

_____

© Houghton Mifflin Harcourt • Image Credits: (r) ©Rex Features/AP Images; (l) ©Rex/AP Images

In Full Bloom Layered Flipbook

6. Make a flipbook to model each part of a flowering plant's life cycle. Fold three sheets of paper to make a booklet with six pages. Use each section to describe the stages of a flowering plant's life cycle. Include drawings or pictures to illustrate your flipbook.

Compare your flipbook with your classmates' flipbooks. Look for similarities and differences between your books and theirs. Describe the key differences and similarities below.

_____

_____

_____

_____

_____

_____

Putting It Together

7. Plant life cycles can differ a bit, but they all have some stages in common. What stages do they all have in common?

_____

_____

_____

_____

How Do Plants Grow?

Materials

- clear plastic cup
- 3 seeds
- soil
- water
- gloves

Objective

Collaborate with a team to plant some seeds and observe the life cycle as they germinate and grow.

What question will you investigate to meet this objective?

_____

_____

Procedure

STEP 1 Place the seeds in a plastic cup near the edge of the cup. Cover the seeds with soil. Moisten the soil.

Why do you think you planted the seeds against the edge of the cup?

_____

_____

STEP 2 Place your seeds in a sunny spot.

What do you think would happen if you placed your seeds in a place with little light?

_____

STEP 3 Plan to add water as needed for the next 10 days.

What do you think would happen if you did not water the soil?

_____

_____

STEP 4 Make a prediction. When do you think your plant will sprout?

_____

STEP 5 Observe your seedlings each day for 10 days, and measure their height in centimeters.

Record your observations every other day for 10 days.

Day	Plant Height (cm)	Drawing
2		
4		
6		
8		
10		

Analyze Your Results

STEP 6 How did your seeds change over 10 days? Compare and contrast your data table with a classmate's table.

_____

_____

Draw Conclusions

STEP 7 Make a claim about plant life cycles based on what you have observed. Cite evidence from your data to support your claim.

_____

_____

_____

STEP 8 Think of other questions you would like to ask about plants and how they grow and change.

_____

_____

How Do Life Cycles Differ?

Non-Flowering Plants

Luis and Hillary are surrounded by plants. What are they doing in the field?

a. This field has many wildflowers growing in it.

b. Luis and Hillary pick flowers from around the field to take to their teacher.

c. Hillary and Luis notice an apple tree covered in flowers and flat leaves.

d. Next, they notice a pine tree that has needle shaped leaves and cones.

e. They notice how different the pine and apple trees are. Luis and Hillary look closely at the apple tree.

f. Then they look closely at the pine tree. Why doesn't it have any flowers?

 8. Language SmArts How are the apple tree and pine tree different? Describe the differences you see.

_____

_____

_____

9. Read the descriptions. Draw lines from the descriptions to the pictures to show whether the words describe only apple trees, only pine trees, or both apple and pine trees.

has flat leaves

grows fruit

grows into an adult tree

has needle-shaped leaves

does not grow fruit

does not flower

has flowers

apple trees

pine trees

Flowers and Cones Galore

Apple trees flower and pine trees don't. Look at these pictures to learn about other plants that either flower or don't flower.

A tomato plant is another kind of flowering plant. Inside the tomato are new seeds. This is how the tomato plant reproduces.

Cacti are also flowering plants. The flowers have a scent to attract pollinators like birds, bees, and bats.

Redwood trees don't flower. They make seeds inside of cones, like pine trees.

Maple trees are flowering plants. The seeds are wing shaped. When they fall from the tree, the seeds spin and sail in the air.

Coconut palms are flowering plants that make coconuts. The coconuts bounce when they fall off the palm and can float in water.

Cedar trees produce cones. Like redwoods, they rely on the wind to transport their pollen.

10. What are two ways the different types of seeds pictured here get to new places?

_____

_____

11. Explain the differences between a flowering and a non-flowering plant.

_____

_____

12. What other plants can you think of? Are they flowering or non-flowering? Make a list.

_____

_____

_____

_____

Non-Flowering Plant Life Cycle

The life cycle of a plant that produces cones is similar to the life cycle of a flowering plant. But instead of having a stage where flowers produce seeds, it has a stage where cones produce seeds. Read about the life stages of a pine tree. On the next page, you will place these stages in the correct order.

 Explore Online

Germination
A new plant sprouts from a seed under the right conditions.

Adult
The adult tree forms the parts needed to produce new plants.

Reproduction
Seeds form inside cones.

Seed
Seeds will germinate to grow into new plants.

Young tree
Young trees do not produce cones until they mature.

Death
Trees can live and reproduce for many years. Eventually, they will die.

13. Starting with a seed, draw or write the stages of a non-flowering plant in the correct order.

Reproduction

Germiation

Youngtree

adult

Death

EVIDENCE NOTEBOOK Explain how a pine tree can begin to grow in new places where there wasn't one before?

Tip

The English Language Arts Handbook can provide help with understanding how to determine the main idea and details.

Language SmArts
Compare and Contrast

14. How is reproduction the same for both plants with flowers and plants with cones? How is it different?

_____

_____

_____

Broken Cycles

What If?

Many factors can interrupt a plant's life cycle.

15. Look at the pictures to identify what could interrupt a plant's life cycle.

▶ Explore Online

a. Without bees to pollinate them, plants will not produce seeds. What happens if plants can't make seeds?

_____

_____

b. Pollution can damage plants when harmful chemicals are added to the air or water. How might polluted air or water interrupt a plant's life cycle?

_____

_____

c. Too much or too little water can interrupt a plant's life cycle. What happens if seeds get too little water?

_____

_____

d. Human activity affects plant life cycles. What happens to the life cycle of a tree that is cut down?

_____

_____

Life Cycle Cause and Effect

Many things can happen in a plant's environment that cause changes in the way the plant develops.

16. What would happen if all dandelion life cycles didn't contain the adult and flowering stage? Choose all the answers that apply.

    a. Dandelions would reproduce more quickly.

    b. Dandelions would grow without stopping.

    c. Dandelions would not make seeds or reproduce.

    d. Dandelions would eventually die out.

Read each question and write your answer below.

17. A farmer planted seeds, and then there was not enough rain. What do you think happened to the seeds?

_____

_____

_____

18. What do you think happened to the rest of the plant's life cycle?

_____

_____

_____

 **EVIDENCE NOTEBOOK** Think about a field of yellow dandelion flowers. What life cycle stages must have occurred for the field to be full of flowers? Record your ideas in your Evidence Notebook.

Lights, Camera, Time to Take Action

19. Language SmArts Think back to the different things that could impact a plant's life cycle. If you need to, go back to the "What If" section of the lesson and look at the images again.

With a group of classmates, choose one topic from the lesson, or select another problem that can interrupt a plant's life cycle. Write four topic ideas below.

_____

_____

a. Research the topic. Learn more about how it harms plants and interrupts their life cycles.

b. Based on what you know and what you learn, make a presentation teaching classmates about the problem. Show them what they can do to help.

c. Present the presentation to classmates.

d. Turn in the presentation to your teacher.

Putting It Together

20. Write the words that correctly complete each sentence.

| die | reproduce | life cycle | germination |

If something causes a plant to skip a stage in its

___life cycle___ , the later stages might also be skipped.

This can cause the plant to not ___germinate___ or even

___reproduce___ . If you know about the life cycles of

different types of plants, you can better care for them.

Discover More

Check out this path . . . or go online to choose one of these other paths.

X-treme Plant Engineering Group

- The Germinators
- Careers in Science & Engineering

Engineer It!

X-treme Plant Engineering Group

Problem:

You are a botanist for the company X-treme Plants. You have been given the task of creating a new species of plant that can be transported to different places during its life cycle.

Criteria	Constraints
☐ Plant must go through all four stages (birth, growth, reproduction, and death). ☐ Must be a flowering plant.	☐ Your plant must include pollen that falls off as the plant is transported.

21. Find a Problem: What do you need to solve?

_____

_____

22. Brainstorm: Make a plan by brainstorming ways you can solve the problem and meet criteria and constraints.

23. Plan: Sketch out your design and then answer the questions below. How does your plant move?

_____

_____

_____

24. Explain the life cycle of your plant.

_____

_____

_____

25. Build and Test: Make a model of your plant in the adult stage of its life cycle when it is ready to reproduce with pollen. Use materials provided by your teacher. Your model should show how the pollen will drop off as the plant moves.

26. Evaluate and Redesign: Write down two ways you could improve your plant.

_____

_____

_____

_____

27. Communicate: Discuss your plan with your classmates.

Lesson Check

Name _____

Can You Explain It?

1. Look again at the picture from beginning of the lesson. How did the field end up with so many flowers? Be sure to do the following:

- Explain the steps in the life cycle of the plants.

- Describe the parts of the plants that allow it to reproduce.

EVIDENCE NOTEBOOK Use the information you've collected in your Evidence Notebook to help you cover each point above.

_____

_____

_____

_____

_____

Checkpoints

Answer the questions about the life cycles of flowering plants and plants that make cones.

2. Choose all the life cycle stages shared by flowering plants and plants that make cones.

a. germination   **d.** reproducing

b. forming seeds   **e.** young adult

c. flowering adult   **f.** dying

3. Put the stages of the life cycle of a flowering plant in order by writing the numbers 1–6 on the lines below.

_____5_____ reproducing   _____2_____ germination

_____4_____ young adult   _____6_____ dying

_____1_____ seed   _____3_____ flowering adult

4. Farmers and other growers are concerned about the drop in the number of honeybees. Why is this a concern for people working with plants?

   a. They use honey from the bees to feed the plants.

   b. The bees pollinate the plants to help form seeds.

   c. The bees keep problem insects away from the plants.

   d. They plant the seeds near where the bees live.

5. What part of the plant's life cycle most depends on flowers and cones?

   a. reproduction

   b. growing larger

   c. dying

   d. becoming a young adult

6. What part do some non-flowering plants have that flowering plants do not have?

   a. pollen

   b. flowers

   c. seeds

   d. cones

Lesson Roundup

A. Choose the correct answers from the word bank.

flowering	non-flowering	pollination	cones

Some _POllenation_ plants make fruit. An insect can carry pollen

from flower to flower through _cones_. Plants that don't

make flowers are called _non Flovering_. They reproduce with

Flowering.

B. Number the stages of the life cycle of an apple tree in the correct order.

C. What happens if one stage of a plant's life cycle is skipped?

_____

_____

What Are Some Animal Life Cycles?

Like many animals, adult birds take care of their babies so that they can survive.

By the end of this lesson . . .
you'll be able to develop a model to describe the stages of an animal's life cycle.

Can You Explain It?

 Explore Online

This animal is in an early stage of its life cycle. It does not look like the adult it will become. It has just hatched from an egg. Now it is eating to prepare for its next stage in its life cycle.

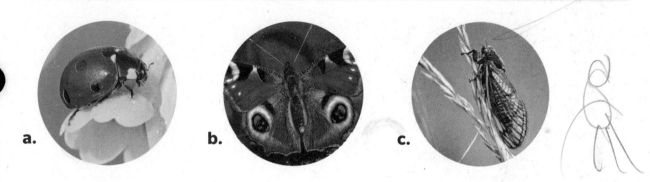

a.

b.

c.

1. Which photo shows the adult stage of the animal above? What makes you think this is the adult stage of the larva?

_____

_____

_____

_____

Tip

Learn more about life cycles in What Are Some Plant Life Cycles?

EVIDENCE NOTEBOOK Look for this icon to help you gather evidence to answer the questions above.

Stage by Stage

It's a Dog's Life!

In Lesson 1 you learned that dandelions and other plants go through life stages. The life stages of plants happen in a certain order. Animals also have life cycles that happen in a certain order.

Bow Wow!

2. Look at the pictures of dogs in different life stages. Read the captions, too. Then use the word bank to put the stages in correct order.

This puppy has just been born. Birth is the first stage in the life cycle of some animals.

This dog is near the end of its life cycle and will eventually die. Death is the end of a life cycle.

The adult dog has just completed the reproduction stage of life and is shown here with her puppies.

This puppy is in the growth stage of its life cycle.

| birth | death | growth | reproduction |

birth → groth → reqoswe → death

Engineer It!
I think We're Being Followed!

Explore Online

Scientists often use a GPS, or Global Positioning System, devices to study animals. A GPS uses satellites to help track the animals as they move or migrate to new areas. Some penguins migrate to a new location when it is time to reproduce. The tracking devices help scientists follow the animals to learn more about their life cycles.

Scientists can place GPS radio collars on animals to track their movement.

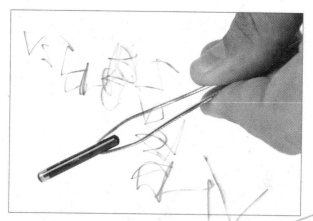

Some animals are tracked with a chip that is injected under their skin.

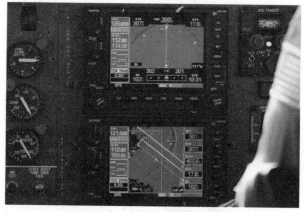

These scientists are tracking marine animals after an oil spill.

This penguin is wearing a satellite tag. The wire is an antenna that sends information to the satellite.

3. What can scientists learn about penguins tagged with tracking devices? Circle all that apply.

 a. where the animals are located   **c.** how tall the animals are

 b. what the animals eat   **d.** how long the animals stay in one place

Year by Year

Timelines can be used to show changes over a period of time. These timelines show and compare the life cycles of a dog and a penguin. View both timelines to learn more about the stages in each animal's life cycle.

4. On the lines at the bottom each page, tell how the stages are alike and different.

Birth is the first stage of a dog's life cycle. Dogs give birth to live young. Like most mammals, puppies depend on their mothers to feed them milk.

birth

Growth is the second stage in many animals' life cycles. During the growth stage, a puppy will increase in size, grow more hair, and learn new skills.

growth

Birds, such as penguins, are born when they hatch from eggs. They cannot take care of themselves at this stage. They depend on adults to feed and protect them.

Alike they need a some one to protect them.

Different a puppy is not born from an egg.

During its growth stage, a young penguin will increase in size and weight. Adult feathers replace fuzzy down. Young penguins learn to hunt for food.

Alike they will grow bigger

Different penguins hunt for food.

EVIDENCE NOTEBOOK What stages of a life cycle do most animals go through? Write the answers in your Evidence Notebook.

Reproduction is the third stage of most animals' life cycles. Adult animals such as dogs reproduce, and females give birth to live young. Mother dogs care for their pups.

reproduction

Death is the end of an animal's life cycle. Small dogs can live 15 or more years. Medium dogs average about 12 years. Large dogs usually only live about 7 or 8 years.

death

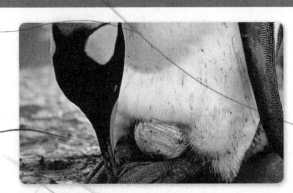

Female penguins reproduce by laying eggs. The young penguin develops inside the egg while an adult guards the egg and keeps it warm.

Alike the mothers protect there babys.

Different Penguins lay eggs and dogs don't.

Many types of penguins, on the other hand, can live for up to 20 years! But like all animals, eventually elderly adults will die.

Alike they can live very long.

Different they don't die the same time

213

A Different Start

The Everglades is mostly under water and covered in tall grasses. The animals on these two pages live in the Everglades. They have the same life cycle stages, but not every stage looks the same!

Alligators

5. Write the words from the word bank that make the statments true.

a. During the _____ birth _____ stage, alligators hatch from eggs.

| growth | birth |
| reproduction | death |

b. During the _____ stage, alligators get longer and heavier.

c. During the _____ stage, female alligators lay eggs.

d. Alligators can live up to 50 years. The end of their life cycle is

_____.

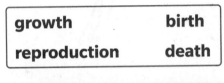

Read below to find out about other animals that live in the Everglades.

White-tailed deer give birth to live young. The deer grow and learn new skills. As an adult, they will reproduce. They can live up to 20 years before they die.

Fish hatch from eggs. They will grow to full-sized adults. The female adults lay hundreds of eggs during reproduction. Like all animals, fish will one day die.

© Houghton Mifflin Harcourt • Image Credits: (tr) ©JAMES ROBINSON/Getty Images; (bl) ©Tom Brakefield/Getty Images; (br) ©Robert S. Michelson/Animals Animals/Earth Scenes

6. Write the following words under the correct image:
growth, death, reproduction, birth

Egrets hatch from eggs with their eyes open.

Birth

Adult feathers replace downy feathers. Birds learn to hunt and fly.

Growth

A female egret lays up to 6 eggs. Eggs hatch after 23 to 27 days.

reproduction

Egrets live for about 15 years.

death

7. Select the way each of these animals is born.

| a. **live birth** |
| b. **hatches from eggs** |

_____ egrets   _____ alligators

_____ white tailed deer   _____ fish

Design a Nest

8. How can you design a nest to keep eggs or young animals safe, dry, and warm? Draw your design below, and label each of the materials you would use. Tell a classmate how your nest is designed to protect eggs or young and keep them dry and warm.

Language SmArts

Comparing and Contrasting

9. What stages do all of the life cycles you have learned about so far have in common? How are they different?

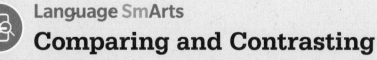

_____

_____

_____

Major Changes

What About Amphibians?

Amphibians are animals that live part of their lives in the water and part of their lives on land. How do you think that is possible?

Spotted Salamanders

A salamander hatches from an egg during its birth stage.

A young salamander lives in water and has gills for breathing. It also has a tail. When it develops full legs and lungs, it leaves the water to live on land.

Eventually, the salamander dies. This marks the end of its life cycle. All of these events in a salamander's life are called a metamorphosis.

When it is ready to reproduce, an adult salamander returns to the water to lay eggs.

10. Research other amphibians with life cycles similar to that of a salamander. Compare them below.

_____

_____

_____

Insect Metamorphosis

A **metamorphosis** is a major change that some animals go through to become adults. During metamorphosis, an animal looks very different in each of its life stages.

11. Compare and contrast the life cycles of a ladybug and a cicada on the lines below.

A cicada undergoes an incomplete metamorphosis. The first stage is the birth stage.

birth

During its nymph stage, a cicada grows and becomes too large for its covering. When this happens, the insect *molts*, or sheds its covering. Insects can molt many times.

growth

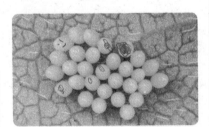

Ladybugs undergo complete metamorphosis. The first stage of this process is the birth stage.

In the second stage of its life cycle, a ladybug is a worm-like larva that eats a lot as it grows!

The third stage of complete metamorphosis is the **pupa** stage. The larva makes a protective covering for itself and becomes a pupa.

Alike _both are a metamorphosis._

Different _they both doint comefrom eggs_

Alike _____

_____

Different _____

_____

Insects can go through a complete metamorphosis or an incomplete metamorphosis. A *complete metamorphosis* has the following stages: egg, larva, pupa, and adult. *Incomplete metamorphosis* has the following stages: egg, nymph, and adult.

In their final molt, cicada adults grow wings. The adult reproduces by laying eggs in holes made in branches.

reproduction

Like all animals, the last stage of the cicada's life cycle is death. In the wild, a cicada can live up to 17 years.

death

When the ladybug comes out of the pupa, it looks very different. In the adult stage, ladybugs reproduce and lay eggs underneath leaves.

This ladybug is nearing the end of its life and will eventually die. A ladybug in the wild can live up to 3 years.

Alike _____

_____

Different _____

_____

Alike _____

_____

Different _____

_____

Compare and Contrast Poster

Step 1: Collaborate with one other student to research the life cycle of your assigned insect or amphibian.

Step 2: Research your assigned animal. Fill in the chart below with your findings.

Step 3: Your teacher will pair you up with a group that has researched a different animal. For example, an amphibian team will be paired up with an insect team.

Step 4: Compare a life cycle of the amphibian and the insect. Discuss similarities and differences.

Step 5: Design a poster that compares and contrasts the insect and the amphibian life cycles.

Step 6: Present your poster to your class.

Stage	Animal Name: _____

Putting it Together

14. How are the life cycles of amphibians and insects the same?

   a. Both begin life as eggs.

   b. Both have a larva stage.

   c. Both end their lives as pupae.

15. Which of these is true of insects?

   a. They all have a nymph stage.

   b. They all go through incomplete metamorphosis.

   c. They all lay eggs.

   d. They all develop into larvae.

16. What is the difference between complete and incomplete metamorphosis?

_____

_____

_____

HANDS-ON ACTIVITY

Observing Mealworm Metamorphosis

Objective

Mealworms are the larvae of mealworm beetles, a black insect. Many animals eat them.

Collaborate to observe and record the changes in a mealworm as it goes through its life cycle.

What question will you investigate to meet this objective?

_____

_____

Materials

- mealworms
- clear container with lid
- uncooked oatmeal
- baby carrot or slice of a raw potato
- magnifying glass
- camera

Procedure

STEP 1 Research the types of living conditions that a mealworm needs to survive. Record your findings on the lines below.

_____

_____

_____

STEP 2 Use your materials to make a living space for the mealworms. Make sure to ask your teacher for guidance.

STEP 3 Observe changes in the mealworms as they grow over several weeks. Record the changes in the data table below. In your journal, draw the mealworms close to the same time each day. Or take pictures of them, and paste the pictures in the journal. Make sure to put the date on each picture or drawing.

Weekly Changes in My Mealworms	
Week	**Observations**
1	
2	
3	
4	
5	
6	

STEP 4 Was the mealworm life cycle similar to the cicada or the ladybug?

_____

_____

_____

STEP 5 Choose your best pictures that represent each stage of the mealworm life cycle. Use your pictures to create a timeline in your Evidence Notebook that shows how the mealworms changed.

Analyze Your Results

STEP 6 Name three ways in which the mealworms used the oatmeal and the carrot or potato.

_____

_____

_____

STEP 7 What differences did you observe between your mealworms and those of others? How were all of the mealworms the same?

_____

_____

_____

Draw Conclusions

STEP 8 State a claim that is related to your question at the beginning of this activity. Cite evidence to support your claim.

_____

_____

_____

STEP 9 As an adult, what life cycle stages would you expect your mealworm to complete?

_____

_____

_____

Step by Step

You Look Just Like Your Parents!

When most animals reproduce, they have babies with characteristics similar to those of their parents. The newborn animals will eventually grow to be adults and also reproduce.

Mommy, Mommy!

17. Draw a line to match each photo of the young animal to its parent.

18. Choose one of the animals above. Explain what would happen if that animal did not reproduce

if they did not reproduce they will not have kids

Leapin' Lizards!

Eggs have been laid by a female lizard that has gone through the reproduction stage of her life cycle. These eggs are the start of a new life cycle.

19. What do you think would happen to the life cycle of the lizard if a snake ate the egg before it hatched?

20. Write words from the word bank to correctly complete the sentences.

Word Bank
increase
hatch
decrease
egg
reproduction

a. A lizard begins its life cycle as a(n) _egg_. If a snake eats a lizard before she lays her eggs, the eggs will not _hatch_.

b. Adult lizards lay eggs in their _reproduction_ stage. If an adult lizard lays fewer eggs, the number of offspring that become adults will _decrease_.

c. If an adult lizard lays more eggs, the number of future generations of lizards will _increase_.

EVIDENCE NOTEBOOK In your Evidence Notebook, record reasons an animal's life cycle could be disrupted. What situations can change an animal's life cycle?

Death Defying

You know that all animals go through life cycles. You also know that the end of any animal's life cycle is death. What would happen if animals never died?

Do the Math
Population Explosion

21. What could happen to a population of ten animals over 15 years if none of the animals ever died. Do the math to find out!

Year	Adult	Young	Offspring Population
2015	10	× 10	200
2020	100	× 10	
2025	1,000	× 10	
2030	10,000	× 10	

22. What do you think would happen in the animals' community if none of the plants or animals died?

    a. There would not be enough space.

    b. There would not be enough rain.

    c. There would not be enough seeds.

23. Language SmArts Research some problems caused by over population. Can you think of some solutions to the problem?

_____

_____

_____

_____

_____

_____

Putting It Together

24. Read each statement. Then write a *T* if the statement is true or an *F* if it is false.

a. _____T_____ All animals go through a complete metamorphosis.

b. _____T_____ All animals grow.

c. _____F_____ Animals reproduce during their growth phase.

d. _____T_____ All animals end their life cycles when they die.

e. _____F_____ All animals hatch from eggs.

f. _____T_____ All insects have a nymph stage in their life cycles.

g. _____F_____ All animals go through an incomplete metamorphosis.

h. _____T_____ All amphibians have a pupa stage.

i. _____T_____ The order of stages in all animals' life cycles is birth, growth, reproduction, and death.

© Houghton Mifflin Harcourt

Discover More

Check out the path . . . or go online to choose one of these other paths.

People in Science & Engineering

- **Careers in Science & Engineering**
- **Comparing Plant Life Cycles to Animal Life Cycles**

Steve Irwin

Have you been to a zoo? Zoos are places where people can see and learn about different types of animals and plants. They also can be used to protect certain plants and animals.

Steve Irwin was known as "The Crocodile Hunter". He lived in Australia, where he ran the Queensland Reptile and Fauna Park, which later became the Australia Zoo. Steve and his family dedicated their park to rescuing a wide variety of animals. The park was most famous for its reptiles.

Steve Irwin worked with a variety of wild life.

25. Research what zoologists do. Write your findings below.

_____

_____

_____

Visit My Zoo!

26. In this activity, you will design a model of a zoo you would like to visit.

Your zoo should include at least three animals and one plant. For the animals, include one insect, one mammal, and your choice of one of the following: a fish, a bird, an amphibian, or a reptile. Draw your zoo on a separate sheet of paper.

a. After you have chosen the animals and plant for your zoo, find out more about each of their life cycles. Write your findings below.

_____

_____

_____

_____

b. Now make a 3D model of your zoo. Make a separate section for each animal. Display a card in each section that tells about the life cycle of the animal or plant for the visitors to read. Compare your zoo with those of your classmates. What was similar, and what was different?

_____

_____

_____

_____

Lesson Check

Name _____

Can You Explain It?

1. Now that you've learned more about animal life cycles, explain what you see in this photo. Be sure to do the following:

Explore Online

- Identify this life stage.

- Describe the stages in this animal's life cycle.

- Explain the importance of reproduction.

EVIDENCE NOTEBOOK Use the information that you've collected in your Evidence Notebook to help you cover each point above.

_____

_____

_____

_____

_____

Checkpoints

2. Look again at the picture at the top of the page. Use what you know to draw each stage of the animal's life cycle in order. Label: adult, eggs, larva, pupa.

eggs   pupa   larva   adult

3. List the four main stages, in order, that all animals go through in their life cycles.

birth, growth, reproduction, adult

4. Write the correct life cycle stage under each image.

reproduction   _growth_   _birth_

| birth | growth | reproduction |

5. Think about animal life cycle patterns. If a bird eats a mealworm, which stage(s) of metamorphosis will the mealworm not complete? Circle all that apply.

a. adult

b. larva

c. egg

d. pupa

6. Look at the picture. What is happening to the brown horse at this stage of its life cycle? Circle the correct answer.

a. It is increasing in size.

b. It is nearing the end of its life.

c. It has just reproduced.

Lesson Roundup

A. If a fox eats a young mole, which stage of the mole's life cycle will not occur?

    a. birth   **c.** growth

    (**b.**) reproduction   **d.** death

B. Which are the stages of an animal's life cycle? Circle all that apply.

    (**a.**) birth   (**d.**) growth

    (**b.**) death   **e.** pollination

    c. germination   (**f.**) reproduction

C. Write the words from the word bank that make the statements true.

birth   growth   death

The _growth_ stage follows the birth stage in an animal's life cycle. All animals end their life cycles with _death_.

D. All animals go through the same four life stages. Why do the stages look different in some animals?

because of how they look.

E. Explain why reproduction is important for animals.

What Are Inherited Plant and Animal Traits?

What makes these flowers look the way they do? Why does their appearance differ?

_____

By the end of this lesson . . .

you'll be able to recognize plant and animal traits and where they come from.

Can You Explain It?

Kittens have certain traits that make them look like their father or mother. *Traits* are features, such as fur color, size, and ear shape. This mother cat has had a litter of kittens. Look closely at their traits.

1. Do you think all of these kittens are the offspring of this mother cat? Why or why not?

_____

_____

_____

_____

_____

_____

 EVIDENCE NOTEBOOK Look for this icon to help you gather evidence to answer the question above.

Plants Have Parents

We Are Family

You might be able to match parent plants and trees with young plants by looking closely at traits, like color or shape. When an **organism** or living thing reproduces, the new organisms are called offspring.

Parents and Offspring

2. Draw lines to match parents to their offspring.

3. What sort of characteristics did you use to figure out which offspring and parent went together?

_____

_____

_____

Family Tree

Where do offspring get their traits? **Traits** are features that offspring inherit, or get passed down, from their parents.

Pass It On

4. Look at the images of the offspring. Draw lines to connect the offspring to both parent flowers.

5. Choose the words or phrases that best complete the sentences.

> **parents**   **siblings**   **petals**

Because traits are passed from _____ to offspring,

offspring often look like their parents. An example of an observable

trait the offspring share with their parents is the color of their

_____.

Do the Math

Hello Up There!

Plants inherit traits from their parents. Height is an inherited trait. Tall plants usually produce tall offspring. Short plants usually produce short offspring.

To record observations of data, you can use tally tables and line plots. Each sunflower height has been measured for you.

274 cm   304 cm   365 cm

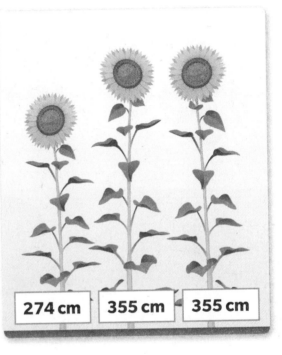

274 cm   355 cm   355 cm

274 cm   304 cm   355 cm

243 cm   304 cm   304 cm

6. Place a tally in the tally column to represent each sunflower height. Then total the tallies and place the total in the Number column.

Plant height (cm)	Tally	Number
243		
274		
304		
355		
365		

7. Now use your tally to create a line plot. Place an X to represent each plant height on the graph.

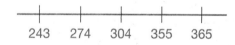

8. Which plant heights had the same number of tally marks? Choose the best answer.

a. 243 cm and 274 cm   **c.** 274 cm and 355 cm

b. 274 cm and 304 cm   **d.** 304 cm and 365 cm

9. Which height had the most number of plants? Choose the best answer.

a. 243 cm   **c.** 355 cm

b. 304 cm   **d.** 365 cm

Similar But Different, Too

If you have a brother or sister, you are a sibling! Siblings have at least one parent in common. Both plants and animals can have siblings. If a rose plant produces two or three new rose plants, the new offspring are all siblings. If a mother dog has a litter of puppies, all of those puppies are siblings. In both plants and animals, offspring get some traits from each parent. This is true of siblings, too. This is why siblings often look like each other.

Look at the two different pea plants. Do you notice any differences?

Language SmArts
Compare and Contrast

10. Use the chart to compare the two siblings. Decide if the trait listed is the same or different, and color in the matching box. The first one is done for you.

Trait	Pea Plant Siblings	
Leaf shape	⬭same⬭	different
Leaf color	same	different
Petal color	same	different
Overall shape	same	different
Height	same	different

Use the chart to write a compare and contrast paragraph about the similarities and differences in the two siblings.

_____

_____

_____

_____

_____

_____

_____

 EVIDENCE NOTEBOOK List the different types of shared traits you have seen so far in the examples of plant parents and offspring.

Putting it Together

11. Choose the words or phrases that best complete the sentences.

inherits	different	parent
unrelated	gives	similar

When offspring have at least one _____

in common, they are siblings. Each sibling

_____ traits from both parents. Most of

the time, siblings look _____.

Do Animals Look Like Their Parents?

Help, I'm Lost!

The pictures show four sets of parents. Each set of parents has lost its offspring!

Parents and Offspring

12. Look at the traits. Draw a line from each offspring to its parents.

Elk have thick fur to keep them warm. The males have large antlers.

Nyala have brown and white fur. They have long legs and can run 40 mph.

Moose have thick fur. The males have huge antlers that are almost 2 meters long.

13. In what ways are the parents and offspring from the activity above similar? Circle all that apply.

a. Both the parents and offspring have fur.

c. Both are the same height.

b. Both the young and the adult have antlers.

d. Both have a similar shape.

Different But Similar

Some animals can seem very different. But when you compare them more closely, they have many similarities. A falcon and sparrow are both birds and both have feathers. Their feet are a similar shape, although the falcon's feet are much larger and are better for catching prey.

Moose and Nyala are two different animals. If you compare their traits, you will notice that they share some similarities. Use the chart to notice the similarities and differences between an adult male moose and an adult male nyala.

Moose

Nyala

	Weight	Shoulder height	Total length	Ears	Head
Moose	816 kg	152–198 cm	243–304 cm	large, furry, pointed at tip	very long snout, low forehead; males have huge antlers
Nyala	40–75 kg	83–99 cm	229–259 cm	upright, pointed at tip, not furry	long snout, low forehead; males and some females have horns

14. Which statements are true about moose and nyala? Circle all that apply.

a. Both have similar foreheads.

b. Both have large, furry ears.

c. Both weigh about 816 kg.

d. Both have pointed ears.

© Houghton Mifflin Harcourt • Image Credits: (l) ©Jeff Vanuga/Corbis; (r) ©EcoPic/Getty Images

Family Portrait

Take a look at the Texas Longhorn cattle parents. Notice some characteristics of the parents, such as fur, ear shape, and color. How can this help you find their offspring? If you said that the offspring will look similar, you are right!

Down on the Farm

15. Use what you know about traits to decide which of the calves are most likely offspring of the Texas Longhorn parents. Circle all that apply.

male parent

female parent

16. How are these parents and offspring similar? Give an example that explains how they are similar.

_____

_____

_____

Pick a Hand

17. Which hand you write with is an inherited trait. Take a survey of your classmates. How many are left-handed? How many are right-handed?

Make a graph that compares the number of students in each group. Which is the more common inherited trait?

Show your graph to your teacher. Look at graphs prepared by other classes. How does the data for your class compare to the data for other classes of students?

EVIDENCE NOTEBOOK List the different shared traits you have seen so far in the examples of animal parents and offspring.

Language SmArts
Main Idea

18. What are the main ideas of this lesson? Circle all that apply.

a. Animal parents care for their young.

b. Animals inherit traits from their parents.

c. Animal siblings usually dont look alike.

d. Animal siblings often look similar.

HANDS-ON ACTIVITY
Monster Traits

Objective

Collaborate to create the offspring from two monster parents based on the traits of each parent.

Write a question about what you will investigate?

_____

_____

Materials
- monster parent traits table
- coins
- Monster Trait Handout Sheets (2)
- crayons or colored pencils
- scissors
- glue

Procedure

STEP 1 You will determine which traits the baby monster inherits from each parent by flipping two coins for each trait listed below. After flipping the coins, use your results to find the inherited trait in the chart below. Repeat this for each trait, and complete the table.

Monster Parent Traits

Body Part	Mom (2 heads)	Dad (2 tails)	Blended (1 heads, 1 tails)	Baby
Arms	6	4	5	
Face	square	round	try again	
Eyes	3	1	2	
Mouth	lots of big square teeth	3 sharp teeth	3 square teeth	
Hair style	lots of curly hair	short spiky hair	short curly hair	
Hair Color	green	purple	try again	

STEP 2 Cut out the traits your monster inherited from his or her parents.

STEP 3 Glue your baby monster together. Don't forget to color and decorate your monster.

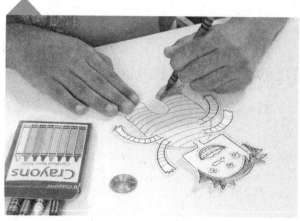

STEP 4 Describe your finished monster. Be sure to list its inherited traits.

_____

_____

_____

Analyze Your Results

STEP 5 What traits did the monster baby inherit from its mom?

_____

_____

_____

STEP 6 What traits did the monster baby inherit from its dad?

_____

_____

_____

STEP 7 Did the monster baby inherit more traits from its mom or its dad?

_____

_____

Draw Conclusions

STEP 8 How might a sibling of the monster baby look? Why?

_____

_____

STEP 9 Because all the monster babies in the room have the same parents, they are siblings. Compare your monster baby with its siblings. How are they similar? Explain why they are similar.

_____

_____

STEP 10 How are the siblings different? Explain why they look different?

_____

_____

_____

STEP 11 Make a claim about inherited traits based on what you observed. Cite evidence to support your claim.

_____

_____

_____

Discover More

Check out this path . . . or go online to choose one of these other paths.

| Careers in Science & Engineering | • Scavenger Hunt
• Hot Diggity Dog! |

Genetics Specialist

Dr. Rick Kittles is an American biologist, or a scientist who studies living things. He has looked at parents, grandparents, and earlier generations of African Americans using genes. His studies also focus on how learning about family history can help us learn more about inherited diseases and an individual's ancestors.

Dr. Rick Kittles

Just as plants and animals inherit traits from their parents, so do humans. Children inherit traits from their parents. Their parents inherited traits from their parents (the children's grandparents).

19. What questions would you ask a genetics specialist like Dr. Rick Kittles?

_____

_____

_____

All in the Family

20. The illustration shows three generations of a family tree. Study the family tree, and then answer the questions.

21. Which physical traits did child B inherit from his family? Circle all that apply.

  a. freckles

  b. wavy hair

  c. brown eyes

  d. blue eyes

22. Child C inherited her eye color from which family member?

  a. dad

  b. grandfather

  c. grandmother

  d. mom

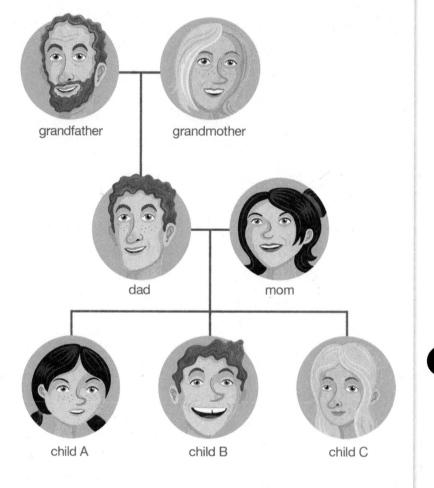

grandfather   grandmother

dad   mom

child A   child B   child C

23. Pick one of the children. List their traits, and then write who they inherited those traits from. An example is that child C inherited her hair color from her grandmother.

_____

_____

_____

_____

Lesson Check

Name _____

Can You Explain It?

1. Think again about the mother cat and kittens in the picture. Study their traits. Do you think they are all related? Be sure to do the following:

Explore Online

- Discuss the traits you observe.

- Identify where the traits come from.

- Explain how you know which cat did not belong.

📖 **EVIDENCE NOTEBOOK** Use the information you've collected in your Evidence Notebook to help you cover each point above.

_____

_____

_____

_____

_____

Checkpoints

2. What is true about siblings? Circle all apply.

   a. Siblings share at least one parent in common.

   b. Plants can have siblings.

   c. Siblings often look like each other.

   d. Siblings inherit traits from their parents.

3. A female elk gives birth to an offspring. What would you expect the offspring to look like? Circle the best answer.

  a. The offspring would look exactly like its mother.

  b. The offspring would look exactly like its father.

  c. The offspring would look similar to both the mother and the father.

  d. The offspring would not look like either the mother or the father.

4. Choose the words or phrases that best complete the sentences.

_____ pass traits to their _____.

Siblings often look similar because they

share inherited traits from _____.

siblings	parents
offspring	a parent

5. A white pea plant and a purple pea plant reproduce. What colors would you expect the offspring to have? Circle all that apply?

  a. red   **b.** purple   **c.** yellow   **d.** white

6. If these dogs reproduced, what traits would you expect their offspring to have? Circle all that apply.

  a. blue eyes

  b. brown eyes

  c. pointed ears

  d. floppy ears

Lesson Roundup

A. Look at the parent photos and the offspring photos. Draw a line between the parents and the correct offspring.

parent   offspring

....

B. Choose the correct words to complete the sentence.

Plant offspring _____ traits

_____ their parents.

inherit	pass down
to	from

....

C. Look at the photos of the cattle. Draw a line between one of the cattle and the correct sibling.

....

D. Choose the correct words to complete the sentence.

Animal parents _____ traits

_____ their offspring.

inherit	pass down
to	from

Cool Beans! (And Warm and Hot Ones, Too!)

You have been asked to design an experiment to see how temperature affects life cycles.

STATE YOUR GOAL: What question are you trying to answer?

_____

_____

Before beginning, look at the checklist at the end of the next page. Remember that list as you perform your task.

What temperatures make this happen the best?

STEP 1: Look online or in books for ways to make things cooler or warmer. Which ways would work for soil? Search the Internet for experiments about plants and temperature. What good ideas do they have? Note them and cite your sources.

_____

_____

STEP 2: Brainstorm ways to make the soil cool and warm. Discuss how long your experiment should run and why.

MAKE A PLAN: Use these questions to help plan your experiment. List the equipment you will need. Then explain how you will set it up and use it. Finally, describe how you will record your results.

1. What equipment will we use to heat and cool our soil?

_____

_____

2. What steps will our experiment have?

_____

_____

_____

3. How long will we run our experiment?

There are lots of great sources for information online.

_____

_____

4. How often should we examine our plants?

_____

5. What results should we write down?

_____

_____

PERFORM AND RECORD: Setup your experiment and follow your schedule. Don't forget to keep track of your results.

COMMUNICATE: Prepare and give a short presentation that describes your team's experiment. Tell what you did and what you learned. Don't forget to tell about the answer to your goal question.

✓ Checklist

Review your project and check off each completed item.

_____ Answered all the questions on this page.

_____ Kept track of your results in a data table.

_____ Presented the project to the class.

Unit Review

1. What is the plant shown here doing?
Circle the correct answer.

   a. It is dying.

   b. It is growing.

   c. It is germinating.

   d. It is reproducing.

2. Which statements will happen to all plants? Select all that apply.

   a. They will eventually die.

   b. They are eaten by animals.

   c. They germinate and grow.

   d. They will freeze during cold weather.

   e. They all develop flowers.

3. Fill in the blank with the correct phrase to complete each sentence.

   > **get pollen on their bodies**
   > **release them in their droppings**

   Hummingbirds help the life cycle process when they drink

   nectar from flowers and _____

   _____.

   Birds help the reproduction process when they eat seeds and

   _____.

4. Circle the correct description of each organism inside the table.

   a. Hatches from egg, begins life cycle in water, goes through metamorphosis, then lives on land

   b. Born live, has growth and adult stages on land

   c. Hatches from egg, has larva, pupa, and adult stages on land

| a, b, c | a, b, c | a, b, c |

5. Fill in the blank with the correct word to complete each sentence.

| flowers | cones | flowering |

An apple tree produces seeds using _____ and fruit.

A pine tree is a non-_____ plant that produces seeds in cones.

6. Using the numbers 1–4, arrange the statements to describe the general life cycle of an animal.

_____ It dies.

_____ It grows.

_____ It is born.

_____ It reproduces.

7. Which choices are steps in the incomplete metamorphosis of this cicada? Circle all that apply.

   a. egg

   b. larva

   c. pupa

   d. nymph

   e. adult

8. From which of these do plants and animals inherit traits? Circle the correct choice.

   a. from siblings

   b. from parents

   c. from offspring

   d. from environment

9. Fill in the blank with the correct word to complete each sentence.

offspring	sibling	traits	parent

A litter of kittens is a mother cat's _____.

Siblings have at least one _____ in common.

10. Fill in the blank with the correct word to complete each sentence.

mother	cousin	father	uncle

Offspring from animal parents will usually resemble both their

_____ and their _____.

Organisms and Their Environment

Explore Online

Unit Project: Lucky Layers

Why do some animals have thicker body fat than others? You will develop a model to investigate this question. Ask your teacher for details.

Geese migrate to a warmer climate to meet their needs.

© Houghton Mifflin Harcourt • Image Credits: ©Myotis/Shutterstock

At a Glance

LESSON 1

How Does the Environment Affect Traits? **262**

LESSON 2

What Are Adaptations? **282**

LESSON 3

How Can Organisms Succeed in Their Environments? **302**

LESSON 4

What Happens When Environments Change? **320**

Unit Review **340**

Vocabulary Game: Picture It!

Materials • Timer or clock • sketch pad

How to Play

1. Choose a word. Do not tell the word to the other players. Set the timer for 1 minute.

2. Draw pictures on the sketch pad to give clues about the word. Draw pictures only.

3. The first player to guess the word gets 1 point. Then that player gets a turn to choose a word. The first player to score 5 points wins.

habitat

mimicry

Unit Vocabulary

 **adaptation:** A trait or characteristic that helps an organism survive.

 **camouflage:** An adaptation that allows an organism to blend in with its surroundings.

 **environment:** All of the living and nonliving things that surround and affect an organism.

 **habitat:** A habitat is the place where an organism lives and can find everything it needs to survive.

 **mimicry:** An adaptation that allows an animal to protect itself by looking like another kind of animal or a plant.

 **population:** All of the members of a certain kind of plant or animal in an environment.

How Does the Environment Affect Traits?

Traits are features that an organism inherited from its parents. This zebra finch has characteristics that are similar to those of other birds. It also has traits that make it unique.

By the end of this lesson . . .

you'll be able to explain how the environment may affect organisms.

Can You Explain It?

▷ Explore Online

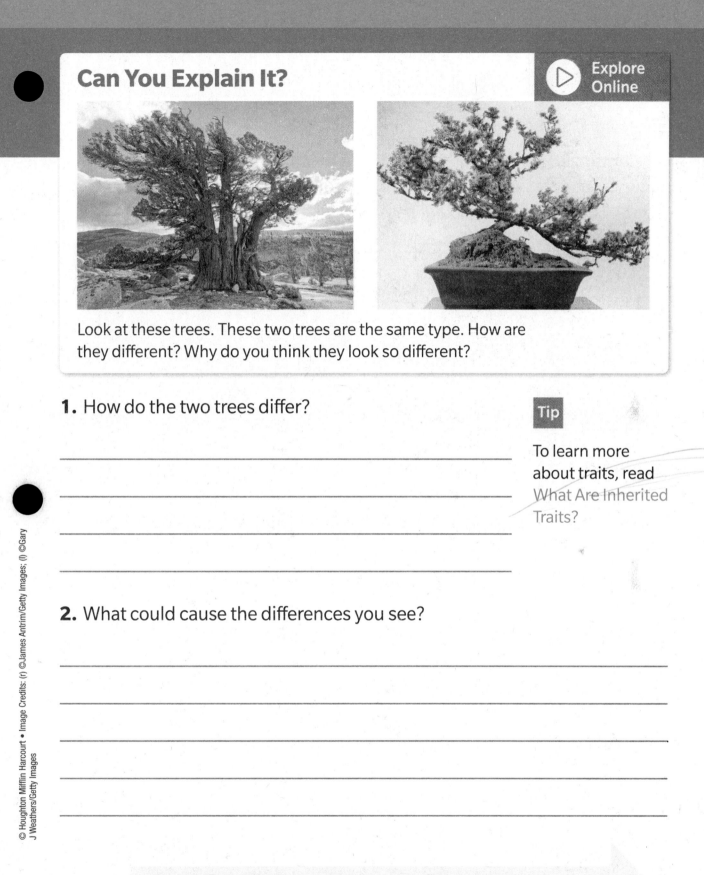

Look at these trees. These two trees are the same type. How are they different? Why do you think they look so different?

1. How do the two trees differ?

_____

_____

_____

_____

Tip

To learn more about traits, read *What Are Inherited Traits?*

2. What could cause the differences you see?

_____

_____

_____

_____

_____

 EVIDENCE NOTEBOOK Look for this icon to help you gather evidence to answer the questions above.

Plants and the Environment

Seeing the Light

Plants need air, light, water, and nutrients to be able to live and grow. Sometimes a plant gets too much or too little of something it needs. This can affect the plant's growth and how it looks.

| Morning | Evening |

3. Look at the pictures of the flowers. What is different about these flowers in the morning and evening? Write your answer below.

_____

_____

These flowers, called Arctic poppies, "follow" the sun. In the morning, the flowers face east, where the sun rises. By evening, the flowers turn to face the sun's location in the west.

Scientists are not sure why the poppies do this. Some think that the flowers need the heat from the sun to grow more seeds. The sun causes other plants to react in a similar way, too.

4. In what ways have you seen plants react to the sun?

_____

_____

Plants and Their Environments

Factors in the **environment** may affect plant structures or traits. The environment is made up of all the living and non-living things that affect an organism. If a plant that needs more sun is planted in the shade, it may not grow as tall.

Causes and Effects

5. Look at the photos of the plants. Underline the cause and effect in each caption.

Explore Online

These plants were affected by the amount of light they got. Too little light can cause plant leaves to turn yellow and fall off. Too much light may burn leaves.

Sometimes nutrients in soil affect the color of flowers. These plants grow different colored flowers with more or less of certain nutrients in the soil.

People or animals can change plants when they cut off or eat plant parts. Cutting some plants keeps them small or makes them grow back bushier.

What Happened?

6. Write the letter for each cause in the circle for the photo that shows its effect.

a. hot temperatures
b. nutrients in the soil
c. too much light
d. cutting leaves

7. Choose one of the images above. Describe how the effect on the plant could be changed again.

_____

_____

_____

EVIDENCE NOTEBOOK Water is one factor that can affect a plant. In your Evidence Notebook, describe how other environmental factors affect plants.

Plan a Garden

8. Design a greenhouse to grow plants in. Label the parts of your design. Write how the parts will help plants grow healthy.

 Language SmArts
Making Inferences

9. Your friend's parents have poppies in their garden. Your friend has noticed that the flowers turn throughout the day. Explain to your friend why this happens. Also explain other ways that the environment can affect plants.

Tip

The English Language Arts Handbook can provide help with understanding how to make inferences.

How Much Water Do Plants Need?

Objective

Collaborate to investigate how environmental factors, such as amount of water, can influence the traits of plants. Use evidence to support your explanations.

What question will you investigate to meet this objective?

_____

_____

_____

Materials

- 3 plants of the same height
- tape
- permanent marker
- metric ruler
- measuring cup
- plastic cups

Procedure

STEP 1 Obtain three plants of the same height from your teacher. Label the plants A, B, and C.

STEP 2 Measure the height of each plant. Record your observations in the data table.

What other observations did you make? How are your three plants alike? In what ways are they different?

_____

_____

_____

STEP 3 Water each plant every other day for the next 2 weeks. Each time you water Plant A, use 50 mL of water. Each time you water Plant B, use 100 mL of water. Each time you water Plant C, use 200 mL of water.

Why are you using different amounts of water for each plant?

_____

_____

Do you think your results give enough data or should you collect more data from other groups? Why or why not?

_____

_____

_____

STEP 4 Each time you water the plants, record their heights in the table.

Day	Plant A height (cm)	Plant B height (cm)	Plant C height (cm)
Day 0			
Day 2			
Day 4			
Day 6			
Day 8			
Day 10			
Day 12			
Day 14			

Analyze Your Results

STEP 5 Use the data in your table to draw a graph.

STEP 6 Which plant had the most growth? Which plant grew the least? Why?

_____

_____

_____

_____

_____

Draw Conclusions

STEP 7 What other things did you notice about the plants as they grew?

_____

_____

_____

STEP 8 How did your results compare with those of other groups? Were they the same? Why or why not?

_____

_____

_____

_____

STEP 9 Make a claim about the effects of too much and too little water on a plant?

_____

_____

_____

_____

STEP 10 Cite evidence to support your claim.

_____

_____

_____

_____

STEP 11 What other questions could you ask about how the environment can affect traits?

_____

_____

_____

_____

_____

Animals and the Environment

Birds of a Feather

Flamingos are birds that live in and near shallow water. Flamingos also live in many zoos. These are called captive flamingos. In the wild, flamingos eat small shrimp and algae. Captive flamingos eat special pellets. The pellets have the nutrients the birds need to stay healthy.

Pink or Pinker

10. Why do you think the wild flamingos look different from the captive flamingos?

▷ Explore Online

Wild flamingos

Captive flamingos

_____

_____

_____

_____

_____

Can the Environment Affect Animal Features?

You have learned that factors in the environment may affect features and traits of plants. Some factors may also affect features or traits in animals. These factors may include temperature and nutrients.

Temperature determines gender in many reptiles, such as alligators.

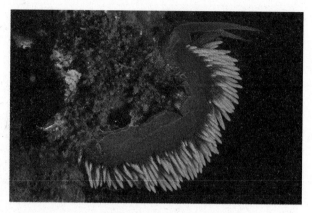

Like plants, animals need certain nutrients to develop certain colors.

Animals may gain weight because they eat but don't exercise enough.

Animals may have certain behaviors as traits. Orcas hunt in different ways depending on what they eat.

11. What can you infer about the amount of food and exercise that the cat in the photo gets?

_____

_____

 EVIDENCE NOTEBOOK List some of the factors in an environment that may affect animal traits or features. Tell how each factor affects an animal. List other factors that you think might also affect an animal.

12. Language SmArts Based on what you have learned about animals, do you think the environment can affect the traits of people? Explain your answer.

_____

_____

_____

Observe the Outcome

13. Match each photo of an effect on an animal with its cause.

▷ **Explore Online**

a. amount of food _____

b. air temperature _____

c. chemicals or nutrients in food _____

Lucky Lizards

Lizards are often pets. Their environment can be a cage, a terrarium, or some other container. The pet's owner controls certain factors in the environment to keep the lizard healthy.

a. A lamp provides heat the lizard needs to keep warm.

b. A rock can provide a shady place to hide if it gets too hot.

c. Pet lizards must be provided food so they get the nutrients they need.

d. The lizard needs a source of water.

Putting It Together

14. Think about the flamingos from the previous pages. What factors in the environment influences a trait that they have? What other factors in the environment could affect traits in flamingos?

_____

_____

_____

Discover More

Check out this path . . . or go online to choose one of these other paths.

People in Science

• **How Can Animal Growth Be Tracked?**
• **Human Traits and the Environment**

Dr. Charles Henry Turner and Dr. May Berenbaum

Explore Online

Cockroaches are survivors. It turns out that they are pretty good at learning and communicating, too.

Dr. Charles Henry Turner was a scientist who studied insect behavior. In one set of experiments, he trained cockroaches to stay away from an unlit portion of a small container. He also found that when cockroaches went through a maze and reached a dead end, they would not take the same path when placed in the maze again. Charles Henry Turner was one of the first scientists to show that insects could learn behavior.

Dr. May Berenbaum is another scientist who studies insects. She has discovered ways that plants change to keep insects from eating them. She has also discovered ways that insects change so they can eat the plants again. These are not behaviors that are learned. They are changes inside the insects. Plants and insects can make these changes to improve their chances of survival.

15. Design an experiment or a device that you can use to find out if and how organisms change their behaviors. You can design it to test how they respond to changes in things such as light, food, and water.

16. Explain your design and how it will work.

_____

_____

_____

_____

Lesson Check

Name _____

Can You Explain It?

Explore Online

1. Think back to the plants pictured at the beginning of the lesson. Even though these are the same type of plant, they look different.

- Why is one of the plants so much smaller than the other?

- How are the plants similar?

- What factor(s) in the environment do you think made the smaller plant smaller?

_____

_____

_____

_____

📋 **EVIDENCE NOTEBOOK** Use the information you collected in your Evidence Notebook to help you cover each point above.

Checkpoints

Answer each question about how the environment affects traits in plants and animals.

2. What are some traits of a pet dog that might be affected by the dog's environment?

_____

_____

Answer each question about how the environment affects features and traits in plants and animals.

3. Your friend has a female pet turtle. What is the most likely reason that it is not a male? Circle your answer.

   a. The mother turtle had more nutrients.

   b. The egg was at a certain temperature during development.

   c. The female turtle had its mother involved while developing.

4. Write the letter of the environmental factor that is most likely to affect a trait on the line.

> **a. learned behavior**   **b. nutrients in food**   **c. temperature**

A scientist places a heating pad on a reptile nest. _____

When birds called cardinals eat berries from a dogwood tree, their

feathers turn a brighter red than normal. _____

Young crows learn to avoid humans from adult crows.

_____

5. Circle your answer. This grass is dry and brown because it has...

   a. been cut too short.

   b. received the right amount of water.

   c. not received enough light.

6. Complete the sentence. The environmental factor that caused this change to the grass is...

_____

_____

LESSON 1
Lesson Roundup

Review what you have learned about how the environment affects traits in plants.

A. Match each cause with the photo that shows its effect.

   a. not enough light

   b. kind of nutrients

   c. cutting or eating stems or leaves

   d. not enough water

B. Match each cause with the photo that shows its effect.

   a. temperature

   b. chemicals in diet

   c. behavior

C. What is one way people are affected by their environment?

_____

_____

What Are Adaptations?

Watch out! The alligator snapping turtle has a strong jaw it uses to catch prey and to defend itself. The turtle blends well with its surroundings to hide from threats.

By the end of this lesson . . .

you'll be able to explain how adaptations help organisms survive.

Can You Explain It?

▷ **Explore Online**

All organisms have physical characteristics—how they look. Their behaviors are also a characteristic. Look at the images of this octopus. What is different between the two pictures?

1. What characteristic of the octopus changed? How does this change help the octopus?

Tip

Learn more about traits in *What Are Inherited Traits?* and in *How Does the Environment Affect Traits?*

_____

_____

_____

_____

_____

_____

_____

_____

EVIDENCE NOTEBOOK Look for this icon to help you gather evidence to answer the questions above.

Organisms Adapt

Berry Interesting!

Blackberry bushes are hearty plants. They can grow nearly anywhere. But this is just one adaptation of the plant. An **adaptation** is a trait or characteristic that helps an organism survive. Look at the picture to learn about more about this plant's adaptations.

Blackberry Adaptations

2. Write the letter on the picture to label the adaptations this plant uses to survive.

▷ Explore Online

a. When animals eat a berry, its seeds are scattered after passing through the animal.

b. Blackberry branches have many sharp thorns.

c. The leaves and stems grow back quickly even after very cold weather or after a wildfire.

d. Blackberries also spread from roots underground.

Plants aren't the only organisms that have adaptations—animals do, too! An organism's adaptations are related to its **habitat.** A habitat is where an organism lives and can find everything it needs to survive. To survive animals need food, shelter, water, and a place to raise their young. Earth has many different habitats within oceans, forests, rivers, and wetlands.

© Houghton Mifflin Harcourt • Image Credits: (tl) ©Insights/Getty Images; (tr) ©TORSTEN BLACKWOOD/Getty Images; (bl) ©Christian Vinces/Shutterstock; (br) ©Bernhard Richter/ Shutterstock

Parrots have strong wings because they need to be able to fly from tree to tree in their natural habitat to find food.

Emus are birds that have small wings and strong legs. They run quickly in their habitat because they can't fly.

Vampire fish live in rivers in South America. They have a mouth full of very sharp teeth to catch the smaller fish that make up their diet.

Look at this wild goat's teeth. Wild goat teeth are flat for grinding up the plants it eats in its habitat.

 EVIDENCE NOTEBOOK Make inferences about these animals' habitats. Make a list, and then do research to confirm your observations.

Armadillo Lizard Adaptations

3. Fill in the blanks with the letter that matches the adaptation.

a. spiny covering
b. strong jaw
c. drops tail
d. period of inactivity

_____ saves energy when food is not available

_____ discourages predators from eating it

_____ distracts predators

_____ used to attack when threatened

HANDS-ON Apply What You Know

Match It!

4. Develop a matching game that includes animals and their adaptations. These can be physical or behavioral adaptations. Conduct research to help you find out more about adaptations. Share your game with your classmates, and see if they can match the animals and their adaptations.

On Their Best Behavior

Explore Online

Physical characteristics are not the only adaptations that help animals survive in their environments. Animals also have useful behaviors.

Naked mole rats live in narrow tunnels. Sometimes predators get in the tunnels. So naked mole rats can run as fast backward as they can forward!

Lizards can't warm or cool themselves. At night, their body temperature drops in the night air. In the morning, they find a patch of sunlight to warm up in.

Some animals survive by living near each other. This frog and tarantula don't seem like typical neighbors. But both animals survive better with the other. The frog eats ants that prey on the spider's eggs, and the spider protects the frog.

 Language SmArts
Gather Information

5. Use evidence to explain the differences between physical and behavioral adaptations. Then give an example of each.

_____

_____

_____

Tip

The English Language Arts Handbook can provide help with understanding how to gather information.

Adaptation and Environment

Survival of the Fittest

Organisms have traits that allow them to survive in their habitat. They also have adaptations that make them very successful living in their environments. This leopard seal lives in the Antarctic. It has traits and adaptations to survive in this extremely cold habitat.

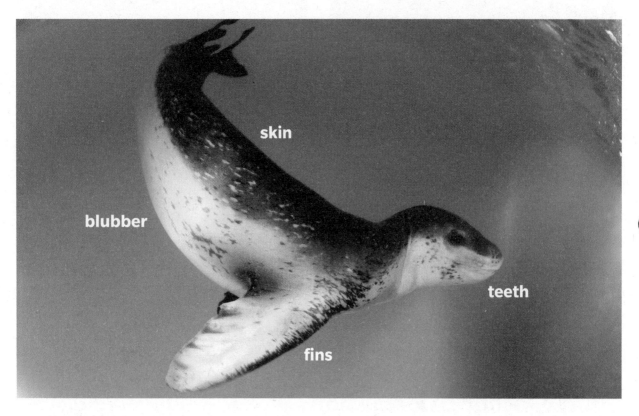

A leopard seal's fins enable it to swim in water. The spots on the seal's skin help the animal hide from predators.

6. List how other characteristics of the leopard seal make it well adapted to its environment. Write your answer below.

_____

_____

_____

Fun Ways To Fit In

Organisms have different kinds of adaptations. These adaptations help them survive in their habitats.

 Explore Online

When opossums become very scared, they pretend to be dead and give off a smelly odor. This makes predators think that the opossum is really dead.

The sweet pinesap grows under oak and pine trees. Its flowers are protected from animals with **camouflage**, or blending in with its surroundings. In this case, it blends in with dead leaves.

Monarch butterflies are poisonous to many animals. Viceroy butterflies are not. Viceroys mimic, or copy, the colors of the monarchs. This type of adaptation is called **mimicry**.

The bee orchid has markings on its petal that mimic a female bee. The flower gives off a scent that attracts male bees to the flower. This improves the flower's chances to reproduce.

 EVIDENCE NOTEBOOK Choose an adaptation that is mentioned above. List as many other plants or animals that you can think of with a similar adaptation.

7. Read the paragraph. Choose the words that make the sentences correct. Write them in the blank spaces.

| physical | behavioral | adaptations | habitat(s) |

Organisms have _____ to survive in their

_____. Some adaptations are _____

characteristics of the organism's structure. Other adaptations

are _____ characteristics of how an animal acts.

 HANDS-ON Apply What You Know

Illustrated Adaptations

8. Draw four animals in their natural habitats. Show one way each animal is adapted to protect itself. Write two sentences telling about the adaptation of each animal. Turn in your drawings and descriptions to your teacher.

Language SmArts
Describe Relationships

9. Describe the relationship between the leopard seal's environment and its spotted top coat and light belly. Write your answer below.

_____

_____

_____

_____

_____

© Houghton Mifflin Harcourt • Image Credits: (c) ©Andrew Darrington/Alamy

> **Tip**
>
> The English Language Arts Handbook can provide help with understanding how to describe relationships.

Surviving and Thriving

Adapt To It

Similar organisms that live in different environments will have different adaptations to better enable them to survive in their specific environments. Look at each pair of organisms. They are similar but live in different places.

Changing Places

10. Look at each picture, and read each paragraph. Write the words that make the sentences correct.

▷ Explore Online

| mangrove tree | sand live oak tree |

| wet |
| dry |
| would |
| wouldn't |

a. The mangrove tree on the left grows in _____ soil. The sand live

oak tree on the right grows in _____ soil.

The mangrove tree _____ survive well in a swamp habitat.

| camel | vicuña |

| mountains |
| desert |
| fur |
| hump |

b. Vicuñas and camels are related. The camel on the left lives in the

_____, while the vicuña on the right lives in the _____.

The vicuña's thick _____ protects it from cold temperatures.

The Same but Different

Just because two habitats have something in common doesn't mean that organisms there have the same adaptations. Compare the purple tansy and the bearberry that both live in dry environments.

Purple tansy grows in places that get little rain for long periods. Their seeds do not sprout until the rainy season, when the plant can get the moisture it needs.

11. Choose the word that best finishes the sentence. Write it on the line.

| pests | dry weather | little sunlight | cold temperatures |

One of the ways that the purple tansy is adapted to

_____ is having seeds that don't sprout until it rains.

Language SmArts
Survival Skills

12. Polar bears live in a very cold habitat. Use what you have learned to predict what would happen if a polar bear were in a hot rainforest environment. Use adaptations to explain whether the polar bear would survive. Do research if you need help.

_____

_____

_____

© Houghton Mifflin Harcourt • Image Credits: (t) ©JeniFoto/Shutterstock

EVIDENCE NOTEBOOK Think about the habitat of the octopus at the beginning of the lesson. How might another animal be adapted differently to that same environment?

Bearberry plants have thick, leathery leaves that keep moisture inside the plant during dry seasons with little rain.

13. Choose the word that best finishes the sentence. Write it on the line.

| pests | dry weather | little sunlight | cold temperatures |

Thick leaves are one of the bearberry's adaptations to

_____.

Putting it Together

14. The purple tansy flower and the bearberry live in similar environments but have different adapatations. Describe an environment where neither of the plants would be able to survive.

_____

_____

_____

_____

Just Pecking?

Materials
- straws
- plastic spoons
- chopsticks
- clothespins
- toothpicks
- bowl of water
- paper plate
- marbles
- foam packing noodles
- cup of colored water
- timer

Objective

Collaborate to model how different types of bird beaks are adapted for getting different types of food.

What question will you investigate to meet this objective?

_____

_____

Procedure

STEP 1 Gather a full set of materials.

Which of these materials do you think will be used to model types of bird beaks?

_____

STEP 2 Prepare the model food for your investigation. Place some marbles and packing noodles in the bowl of water.

How do the materials behave in the water? In what ways is this similar to sources of food for some birds?

_____

STEP 3 Place some marbles and packing noodles on the paper plate. In what ways is this similar to sources of food for some birds? In what ways is the colored liquid in the cup similar to sources of food for some birds?

_____

_____

_____

STEP 4 Use the remaining materials to model bird beaks adapted for getting different types of the model food. Work with a partner, and time each other for intervals of 10 seconds. Record your observations in the table.

STEP 5 Complete the table with your observations.

Model Beak	packing noodles in water	marbles in water	packing noodles on plate	marbles on plate	water in narrow cup

Analyze Your Results

STEP 6 Which beak was best able to pick up food at the bottom of the water? Which beak was best able to pick up food floating on water? Which beak was able to collect liquid food?

_____

_____

_____

STEP 7 Which beak was best able to pick up harder food from the plate? Which beak was best able to pick up softer food?

_____

_____

Draw Conclusions

STEP 8 This is a hummingbird beak. Hummingbirds drink nectar from flowers. Look up other bird beaks and compare them to your models. How did the models represent beak adaptations well? In what ways did they not model beaks well? Make sure to support your claims.

_____

_____

_____

STEP 9 Did other groups use their models in ways that were different from your group's? Explain how other investigations were the same as yours and ways they were different.

_____

_____

STEP 10 What else could you investigate about beak adaptations that help birds survive?

_____

_____

Discover More

Check out this path . . . or go online to choose one of these other paths.

Robotic Adaptations

- **Build a Super Organism**
- **Hide and Seek**

 Engineer It!

Robotic Adaptations

When robotics engineers plan their designs, they think about the environments their robots will work in. The engineers develop their designs so that the robots work in the most successful way in that environment. Much like organisms have adaptations to live successfully in their habitats.

Research an extreme environment, such as the surface of another planet, the deep ocean, inside a volcano, or a desert—there are lots of places to choose from!

Ask five questions about how a robot might work in the environment you chose. One question might be, "What is the surface like?" Find the answers to the question in your research.

Explore Online

The surface a robot must move around on determines how the robot will be able to move.

15. Think about how you could design a robot to operate in the environment you chose. Make sure the robot has at least three adaptations that address the extreme conditions and specifics you learned about in your research and a purpose for its work. Describe your robot and adaptations in the box below.

16. A classmate says that your robot is not well adapted to its environment. Give evidence to support your design and the purpose of your robot. Write your answer below.

_____

_____

_____

_____

Lesson Check

Name _____

Can You Explain It?

1. Think back to the beginning of the lesson.

Explore Online

- Why does the octopus change color to blend in with the environment?

- How is changing color both a physical and behavioral adaptation?

- How is camouflage an adaptation?

EVIDENCE NOTEBOOK Use the information you've collected in your Evidence Notebook to help you cover each point above.

_____

_____

_____

_____

_____

Checkpoints

2. Read the adaptations below. Then write whether each one is behavioral or physical on the line after it.

Opossum playing dead _____

Polar bears' thick fur _____

Lizard moving towards sunlight _____

Ducks' webbed feet _____

Select the choice that best answers the questions.

3. Which is an example of a adaptation that helps with reproduction?

   a. a cactus covered with spines

   b. a pinesap that looks like dead leaves

   c. a bee orchid flower that looks and smells like a female bee

   d. blackberry branches that grow 10 feet long

4. Which best describes an example of camouflage?

   a. Blackberries are segmented.

   b. Parrots have strong wings to fly.

   c. Viceroy butterflies look like monarch butterflies.

   d. Leopard seals have dark coats on their backs to blend in.

5. Which animal is less likely to survive in a cool mountain environment than a vicuña?

   a. goat　　　　**c.** bearberry

   b. octopus　　　**d.** blackberry

6. Which tree is adapted to live in a wet swampy environment, a mangrove or sand live oak? _____

Lesson Roundup

A. Choose the words that make the sentences correct.

Plants and animals have _____ that determine how they look and behave. An organism's traits determine how well it will survive in a _____. If an organism has _____ suited to its habitat, it is more likely to _____. For example, an armadillo lizard has a spiny covering, making it hard for its predators to eat. This is a _____ adaptation. Naked mole rats run backward as fast as they do forward because they live in very narrow tunnels that are hard to turn around in. This is a _____ adaptation.

> **traits**
> **adaptations**
> **habitat(s)**
> **survive**
> **physical**
> **behavioral**

B. Match each type of adaptation to the description.

_____ Sea slug spits out chemicals to distract predators.

_____ Anole skin changes color with conditions.

_____ Lithops is a plant that looks like a rock.

> **a. defense**
> **b. mimicry**
> **c. camouflage**

C. Choose the words or phrases that make the sentences correct.

Where organisms usually live depends on whether the environment can provide for the organisms' _____. If the environment provides for all of the needs, or the organism has adaptations suited to the environment, it will survive _____.

> **wants**
> **needs**
> **prey**
> **well**

How Can Organisms Succeed In Their Environments?

These giraffes work as a group to look out for predators while finding food. How does this behavior help it survive?

By the end of this lesson...

you'll be able to explain how an organism's characteristics and how being a member of a group may help an organism survive and reproduce

Can You Explain It?

▷ Explore Online

Look at each nest. They were made by the same kind of bird. How are they different? What do you think caused these nests to differ?

1. Male bowerbirds build nests to attract a mate. Female bowerbirds like nests with decorations. Which male bowerbird do you think is more likely to find a mate? Why?

_____

_____

_____

_____

_____

_____

_____

Tip

Learn more about the characteristics of living things in What Are Inherited Traits? and in How Does the Environment Affect Traits?

 EVIDENCE NOTEBOOK Look for this icon to help you gather evidence to answer the questions above.

Differences That Win

Characteristics for Survival

Animals and plants have many characteristics that help them survive and reproduce. This pitcher plant grows in soil that doesn't have a lot of nutrients. To survive, it is able to get nutrients from insects, such as flies. Because the plant can't move to get the flies, it has specialized characteristics to help it trap the insects it needs.

Plant Parts

2. Write the missing letters in the circles to label the characteristics on this plant.

▶ Explore Online

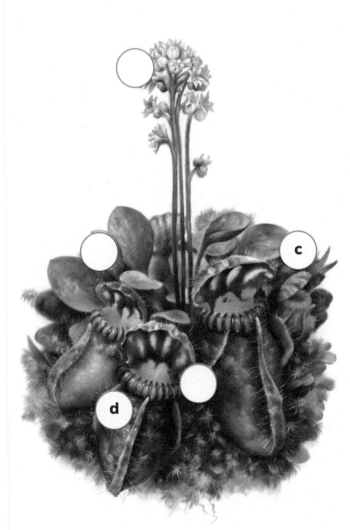

a. Flowers attract insects. Pitcher plants produce flowers before the "pitchers" form. The plant would not reproduce if the pollinators were trapped and consumed by the plant!

b. A lid hangs over the opening of the plant to keep the plant moist, rain out, and the insects in.

c. Translucent patches on the lids confuse insects and make it hard for them to find a way out.

d. If the plant grows in the shade, it is green. However, if it grows in direct sunlight, it is red.

e. Spikes line the opening of the plant. These make it difficult for the insects to climb out of the plant once inside.

© Houghton Mifflin Harcourt

Traits That Make It

You know that animals have different traits. Traits such as color, size, and body parts make animals look different, but these traits may also affect survival. These animals are both jaguars. How do the characteristics of jaguars differ?

Jaguars

3. Write letters in the circles to label the characteristics of these animals.

 Explore Online

a. Jaguars can be either black or tan. Both black and tan jaguars have spots. You just have to look closely to see them on the black fur.

b. Black jaguars are usually smaller and live in trees. Their black color makes them harder to see in the shadows.

c. Tan jaguars are larger and live on grasslands. They tend to eat larger prey. Their tan color and spots make it easier for them to blend in to the grassland.

d. Tan jaguars have larger, stronger jaws they use to crack bones and bite through tough reptile hide.

These sparrows have different traits. They differ both in physical traits and in behaviors. The differences affect their chances of reproducing. As you read, think about which traits help with survival and reproduction.

Sparrows

4. Write letters in the circles to label the photos with the captions that apply to them.

▷ Explore Online

a. Sparrows may have white or tan stripes on their heads. The white-striped sparrow is usually more aggressive. Because it can be seen more easily, it has to defend itself.

b. Tan-striped male sparrows help more with their offspring.

c. Both white-striped and tan-striped female sparrows prefer males with tan stripes. Male sparrows with tan stripes are less likely to be involved in fighting.

d. Both white-striped and tan-striped male sparrows prefer females with white stripes. The more aggressive white-striped female will defend her home and her young.

EVIDENCE NOTEBOOK Think about the sparrows. Why would a female prefer a tan-striped male? How would a tan-striped male instead of a white-striped male help the female and offspring survive? Write your answers in your Evidence Notebook.

5. Language SmArts You know that animals have different characteristics that help them survive in their environments. Which characteristics do you think would help an animal survive the most? Are there any characteristics that you would like to have?

_____

_____

_____

_____

_____

_____

Putting It Together

6. Complete the sentences. Write the words from the word banks that make the sentences correct.

> **shadowy places**   **light grasses**

a. Animals with darker colors, such as the black jaguar, are more

likely to hide in _____ while stalking prey.

> **stronger jaw**   **weaker jaw**

b. An animal with a _____ is more likely to break through bones for the nutrients inside or tear through a reptile's tough covering.

> **more likely**   **less likely**

c. When a trait is more desirable to females, the male will be

_____ to find a mate.

Battle of the Beans!

Explore Online

Objective

Collaborate to determine how an animal's body color might affect its ability to survive in its environment.

What question will you investigate during this activity?

_____

_____

_____

Materials
- 30 dry white beans
- 30 dry black beans
- 5 dry red beans
- large sheet of white paper
- large sheet of black paper
- cup
- clock with second hand or timer

Procedure

STEP 1 Working with a partner, place the white paper on the table. Randomly scatter the beans over the paper.

What do the beans and the paper model in this investigation?

_____

_____

STEP 2 One partner will keep time. The other will pick up as many beans as possible for 15 seconds and place them in the cup. Only one bean can be picked up at a time. The red beans are poisonous. Touching a red bean means your turn is over.

308

STEP 3 Record the number of black and white beans you picked up in a data table. Repeat the activity for two more trials.

Trial	White paper		Black paper	
	White beans	Black beans	White beans	Black beans
Partner A, Trial 1				
Partner A, Trial 2				
Partner A, Trial 3				
Partner B, Trial 1				
Partner B, Trial 2				
Partner B, Trial 3				

STEP 4 Now place the black paper on the table. Repeat the activity by placing all of the beans on the black paper. Do this three times, and record your data.

Why did you repeat the activity multiple times?

_____

_____

_____

STEP 5 Switch roles, and repeat Steps 1 through 4.

Analyze Your Results

STEP 6 How many red beans did you pick up or touch? How did this affect your data?

_____

_____

STEP 7 Explain the patterns you observed. Did the color of the paper make a difference in which color of bean was picked up the most?

_____

_____

Draw Conclusions

STEP 8 Compare your data with your partner's data and another group's data. How is the data shown in your data tables similar and different? Can you make any claims about how body color affects how animals are successful in their environments?

_____

_____

STEP 9 Based on your evidence, how do you think body color affects how animals are successful in their environments?

_____

_____

STEP 10 What other questions can you come up with about characteristics that help animals survive in their environments?

_____

_____

Better Together

Safety in Numbers!

Many animals live in groups, both on land and in water. Look at the photo to learn about an interesting animal that lives in the ocean.

The structures you see below are actually made up of groups of tiny animals called coral. Coral might look like ocean decorations, but they are living organisms. While people think they are rocks or ocean plants, coral are actually many tiny animals that live together in a group. As they grow together, they form coral reefs.

Coral is made up of tiny organisms.

7. What other animals live in groups? Make a list below. What benefits come with living with others?

_____

_____

_____

Living as part of a group can help animals survive. They can work together to hunt for food. Groups are well protected from predators. They also are better able to protect their young. And groups can work together to cope with changes in the environment.

Pods, Packs, and Protection

8. As you read the photo captions, underline the cause, and draw a circle around the effect of how the characteristics help the animals survive.

Zebras' running make it hard for other animals to single out a lone zebra when a herd starts to run. This makes the zebra harder to catch.

Hyenas work in packs to hunt for food. They can take down larger animals by working together.

To protect their offspring, sperm whales work together to raise their young. With better protection, more young reach adulthood.

Coping with the harsh cold of winter, male penguins huddle together. This behavior keeps their eggs warmer.

Ants have different jobs, such as weaving nests, hunting for food, and laying eggs. They meet their needs better in a group than they could by themselves.

The clownfish hides in the venomous tentacles of the anemone. Animals lured by the colorful clownfish are eaten by the anemone.

HANDS-ON Apply What You Know

Identify It!

9. Living things vary in color, size, and shape in ways that can make a big difference in whether or not they survive.

Your teacher will give each student in your group an item to draw. The specimens will be of the same type of plant or animal. Be sure to make your drawing as detailed as you can.

When everyone's drawings are complete, mix the items up into a random collection. Look at each student's drawing, and match it to the specimen he or she was assigned to draw.

EVIDENCE NOTEBOOK How does living in groups help the members of a group survive? How can being different from others in the group also be an advantage for individuals? Which do you think is more important? Write your ideas in your Evidence Notebook.

Teamwork

Living with groups of the same kind helps some animals survive.

Animal Groupings

10. Identify the reason these animal live in groups.

 Explore Online

| protection | hunting | reproduction | coping with change |

Notice how the fish are in a big group. How does this help them survive?

_____

Wolves travel in packs. How does this help them survive?

_____

Dolphins work together to raise young. How does this help them survive?

_____

Language SmArts
Taking Note

11. Why is it an advantage for animals to live in groups? Remember that the animals in a group have different characteristics. How might those different characteristics help the group survive if something were to happen?

_____

_____

_____

_____

Tip

The English Language Arts Handbook can provide help with understanding how to take effective notes.

Discover More

Check out the path . . . or go online to choose one of these other paths.

Careers in Science

- **People in Science**
- **Hidden Animals**

Wildlife Expert

Explore Online

Wildlife experts are scientists that study animals. Some of them focus on studying variations in the same type of animal. Different variations may help an animal be more successful in its environment.

Scientists need specialized cameras that magnify to study the tiny peacock spiders. These tools are used to find differences in the spiders.

The peacock spider is an example of an animal with variations. It can only grow up to 5 mm. There are peacock spiders in many different colors. Some males grow flaps that they use to attract mates. Others do not. Some males perform a special mating dance to attract females. In many cases, animals that have fancier characteristics are more likely to reproduce.

We know this because scientists have studied the peacock spider. Without wildlife experts, we would know a lot less about variation in animals.

Now you are going to be a scientist who researches an animal species with many different variations. Animals of the same species that have different traits or characteristics are said to have *polymorphic variations*. This means they have different versions of the same traits. Use this term in your research.

Have your teacher approve your research idea before you begin. Then gather information that explains the differences in the animal you chose. Find facts and details that explain how differences help the animal survive.

Use the information you find to make a presentation. For example, you can make a presentation with at least five slides, give an oral report, or draw a graphic design. You can sketch your plan in this space. Save your presentation, record your report, or turn in your picture. Submit your presentation to your teacher.

12. What animal will you be researching?

_____

_____

13. What differences will you try to learn more about?

_____

_____

14. What kind of presentation will you design?

_____

_____

Lesson Check

Name _____

Can You Explain it?

1. Now that you know how animals' characteristics help them survive, explain why one male bowerbird is more likely to find a mate. Be sure to do the following:

- Describe how the two nests are different.

- Explain which nest will be more likely to attract a female bowerbird.

- Explain how attracting a female will help the animals reproduce.

> **EVIDENCE NOTEBOOK** Use the information you've collected in your Evidence Notebook to help you cover each point above.

_____

_____

_____

_____

_____

Checkpoints

Answer each question about how plants and animals can be successful in their environments.

2. How might the spotted fur of a jaguar help it survive?

a. It helps a jaguars find a mate.

c. It helps the jaguar grow large.

b. It helps the jaguar blend into its environment to hide from prey.

d. It helps the jaguar cope with changes in the environment.

3. What advantages do these geese have by traveling in a large group?

    a. They are hidden from predators.

    b. They can fly slower.

    c. They can cope with a changing environment.

    d. They won't fall out of the sky.

4. Draw a line from the phrase that describes the effect to the animal's action that caused it.

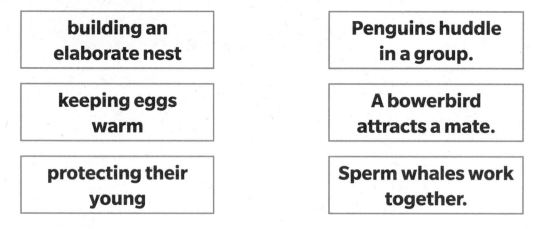

building an elaborate nest	**Penguins huddle in a group.**
keeping eggs warm	**A bowerbird attracts a mate.**
protecting their young	**Sperm whales work together.**

5. Check the column to show whether the animal's color provides protection or helps it attract mates and reproduce.

animal	protection	reproduction
clown fish		
white-striped sparrow		
black jaguar		
zebra		

6. Write the word that correctly completes the sentence.

Behaviors and physical _____ help animals succeed in their environments.

Lesson Roundup

A. Review what you have learned about how organisms are successful in their environments. Write the benefit of the trait shown in each image.

| reproduction | trapping food | hunting |

_____   _____   _____

B. Many animal groups help their members in different ways. Use the word bank to fill in the blanks below.

| care for young | cope with change |
| hunt | confuse predators |

a. Wolves that _____ in a pack are more successful than wolves that hunt alone.

b. The group of moving zebras helps _____.

c. When penguins huddle together during a snow storm, they are

showing how they _____.

d. Dolphins that travel together are better able to

_____.

What Happens When Environments Change?

Heavy rains may cause floods. A flood can cause extreme changes in an environment. Like people, animals may lose their homes or food source because of a flood. Animals have to adjust to the changes. If animals don't adjust or leave, they may die.

By the end of this lesson . . .
you'll be able to explain what happens to plants and animals when their sources of food, water, and shelter change.

Can You Explain It?

Explore Online

When rain or snow doesn't fall for a long time, the ground becomes very dry and plants may die. This change is harmful to animals that eat plants and use them for shelter. But when storms roll in, an even more extreme change can happen. Lightning can strike, causing fire. Wildfires can spread quickly and destroy many animals' homes.

1. This San Joaquin kit fox lost its home because of a wildfire. What do you think will happen to it now?

_____

_____

_____

_____

_____

_____

_____

Tip

Learn more about environments in How Can Organisms Be Successful In Their Environments?

EVIDENCE NOTEBOOK Look for this icon to help you gather evidence to answer the questions above.

Everything Changes

Here Today, Different Tomorrow

Some changes to environments happen quickly. For example, floods happen when there are heavy rains or snow melts off quickly.

Floods can change an environment by washing away land. Mudslides occur when land on water-soaked hills slide down the hills. All these changes affect living things in the environment.

Extra water from rain may cause rivers, lakes, or streams to overflow.

▷ Explore Online

When the land gives way in a mudslide, it takes trees and other plants with it.

 2. Language SmArts What other kinds of changes can you think of that might happen quickly in an environment?

_____

_____

_____

EVIDENCE NOTEBOOK Think about floods. What happens to plants and animals? Imagine a mudslide. How would a mudslide affect plants and animals? Add your ideas to your Evidence Notebook.

When an environment changes, it affects the plants and animals that live there. A fast change such as a flood or mudslide affects an environment. Plants may all die. Animals lose their homes and sources of food. Animals may also die if they can't make changes.

How Do Changes Affect Environments?

3. Circle at least one thing in each picture that was affected by the change in the environment.

 Explore Online

A volcano can cover land with lava and ash. Lava is melted rock from inside a volcano. It can change land. It may kill plants. The ash can cloud the sky so that the temperature of the land cools.

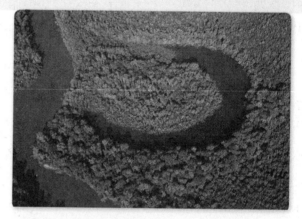

A river might change its course over many years and form an oxbow lake. When water changes, animals that live near rivers may move away or change. New organisms may take their place.

Drought, or lack of water, may cause plants to die. Less water also means less food for animals. Animals may need to search for food and water elsewhere or they may die out.

Humans cut down trees and clear land. This kills plants and destroys food sources of animals that live there. Animals may move into areas where they would not normally be found.

Types of Environmental Changes

4. Match the example of the environmental change to all the types of changes that the images show.

land change

human changes

water change

HANDS-ON Apply What You Know

Environmental Changes and You

5. How do you think a flood, mudslide, earthquake, or volcano might affect you? Make a list of ways these events could change your environment.

For each of those four events, describe what people can do to protect themselves against a big change to their environments. Make a poster with your findings, and share it with your class.

Putting It Together

6. Think of one or two kinds of environmental changes. What might happen to the animals that live in those environments as a result of those changes?

_____

_____

© Houghton Mifflin Harcourt • Image Credits: (tl) ©Koch Valérie/istock / getty Images Plus/Getty Images; (tr) ©Jeffrey Lepore/Science Source; (bl) ©Jedrzej Kami/EyeEm/Getty Images; (br) ©BackyardProduction/iStock/Getty Images Plus/Getty Images

Staying Alive

Fire!

Wildfires may start for many reasons. They often start when the forest is very dry and lightning strikes without any rainfall. The lightning creates a spark that can set dry bushes, grasses, and trees on fire. A wildfire can wipe out much of a forest environment.

A **population** is made up of all the members of a certain kind of plant or animal in a specific area in an environment.

7. Language SmArts What do you think might happen to the populations of plants and animals in a forest that has been destroyed by fire?

_____

_____

_____

© Houghton Mifflin Harcourt • Image Credits: ©Tony Bee/Getty Images

Reacting to Change

Different Reactions

8. Circle the animal or plant in each picture that is reacting to a change in the environment.

▶ Explore Online

During a wildfire, plants will die. But some plants reproduce. Some pine trees have cones that open and release seeds in a fire. The seeds settle on the forest floor and grow into new plants.

The Amargosa vole only lives in certain parts of California. It depends on certain plants for food. During a drought, plants die, so the voles move to new areas to find food.

This pika lives in the mountains of the northwest because it must stay cool to survive. If an area becomes too warm, the pika must move farther north where temperatures are cooler.

A sudden change in temperature that is not seasonal could upset the natural system in an environment. This plant died because of a freeze that happened out of season.

Dear Deer

9. Work as a class. Divide into two groups to play this game. Review the directions here, and then follow your teacher's instructions.

One group will all be deer. Record how many deer start the game. The other group make up the environmental factors: food, shelter, water. Each group lines up across from each other. The two lines face away from each other.

The deer will decide which environmental factor they need. Students in the second group should decide which factor they each want to be. There should be an equal number of each factor.

- If you want to be or need water, pretend you are ready to drink from a glass.

- If you want to be or need shelter, raise your hands.

- If you want to be or need food, put your hands on your stomach.

Students hold their poses but turn to face each other. If there are more deer than environmental factors, the extra deer must leave the group. After each round, record how many are in the deer line. Write below what happens to the population when there are not enough environmental factors for each deer. Follow your teacher's directions for other environmental changes that occur.

_____

_____

_____

10. Choose the words or phrases that best complete the sentences.

Plants and animals react when an environment changes.

> **survive and reproduce**
> **move to a new location**
> **rapid**
> **lose their habitat**

When a fire destroys a forest, pine trees are able to _____ by releasing seeds.

When a beaver builds a dam, it changes the flow of water. Other animals in the area may _____.

When the temperature of an environment gets too warm, animals that need cold temperatures to survive _____.

When _____ temperature changes happen to an environment, plants and animals may die because they cannot get away from the temperature change quickly enough or at all.

EVIDENCE NOTEBOOK How did the ability to get water, shelter, and food affect the population of deer in the game? How did the environmental changes affect the population? Write your answers in your Evidence Notebook.

Putting It Together

11. What do you think might happen to other plants and animals that live in a forest that has caught fire? What evidence supports your explanations?

_____

_____

_____

_____

Moving On Upstream

Going Against the Flow

Salmon are born in freshwater rivers. Then they swim downstream to the ocean, where they spend their adult lives. When they are fully grown, they return to the rivers to lay their eggs.

Swimming Upstream

12. Look at these photos and read their captions. Then answer the question that follows.

Salmon must swim upstream to lay their eggs. The eggs hatch, starting the salmon life cycle all over again.

This is a dam that has been built by humans. It is between the ocean and the salmons' nesting place.

Humans built this dam in the river. But the dam prevents the salmon from swimming upstream. What problem does this present for the salmon?

_____

_____

EVIDENCE NOTEBOOK Describe one way humans cause environmental changes that affect plants and animals. Write your answer in your Evidence Notebook.

What Humans Can Do

You have seen a few ways that humans can cause changes in the environment. Read the captions with these pictures to learn more about how humans can change the environment.

Humans Change Environments

13. Circle an area in each picture that shows a change humans made.

▷ Explore Online

Humans clear land to make way for roads, highways, and walls. Animal and plant habitats are destroyed.

Dams change habitats of animals that live around them. Dams also interfere with the habitats of the fish and other aquatic animals in the water.

When human homes are built, builders may clear the land for construction. Animals may lose their homes and sources of food.

Humans may grow plants that are harmful by mistake. These plants are not native to an area and take over the habitat of other plants, killing them and upsetting the balance of nature.

14. Circle what is most likely to happen to the population of each organism if its environment changes.

a. Some of this animal's habitat is now part of an airport runway. The animal's population will _____.
- ☐ grow
- ☐ move to a new habitat
- ☐ not be affected

b. This black bear's habitat has been reduced by construction. The bear no longer has enough food in its habitat to survive. The bear will _____.
- ☐ learn to live in houses
- ☐ destroy the new construction
- ☐ get by on food that is available

Language SmArts
Cause and Effect

15. Salmon need to get past the river dam to lay their eggs. How might they do it? Write your solution below. Then describe how your solution might affect the environment around the river.

_____

_____

_____

_____

_____

© Houghton Mifflin Harcourt • Image Credits: (tl) ©Design Pics Inc./Alamy; (tr) ©Eugene Sergeev/Alamy; (bl) ©BeyondMyLens/Getty Images; (br) ©Heiko Kiera/Shutterstock

Tip

The English Language Arts Handbook can provide help with understanding how to recognize cause and effect.

How Can It Cross the Road?

Objective

Collaborate with a group to design and model a solution to help caribou migrate. A highway blocks the path they once used. Now they need help in finding a new route around the human-made change to their environment.

What question will you investigate to meet this objective?

Materials
- craft sticks
- tape
- cardboard
- glue
- chenille sticks
- wood
- clay
- other materials you choose

_____

_____

Procedure

STEP 1 Migrating caribou have to cross a highway that blocks their migratory path. Think about the problems, and then write them down clearly.

_____

_____

STEP 2 Work with a group. Together, brainstorm solutions to the problem of the migrating caribou. How might you design a solution to help the caribou cross the highway? Or will you redesign the highway?

_____

_____

STEP 3 Work with your group to design a solution. Draw or build your design with materials of your choice.

STEP 4 Label the parts of your design or model. Write what those parts are and how the parts solve the problem below.

_____

_____

_____

_____

Analyze Your Results

STEP 5 Compare your design solutions to two other groups in the class. How are the designs similar? How are they different?

_____

_____

_____

_____

STEP 6 Which group do you think has the design solution that will work the best? Explain why you think so.

_____

_____

_____

STEP 7 What problems does each model create?

_____

_____

Draw Conclusions

STEP 8 Make a claim about the problems or issues your design may have, if any.

_____

_____

STEP 9 How might you improve your design? Explain.

_____

_____

_____

STEP 10 How can humans affect animal migration patterns? Cite evidence.

_____

_____

_____

_____

STEP 11 What other questions do you still have about animal migration:

_____

_____

_____

Discover More

Check out this path . . . or go online to choose one of these other paths.

| Engineer It | • Invasion
• Conservation Biologist |

Solving a Salmon Problem

Think back to the problem that dams cause for salmon. Salmon need to swim around the dams to get back to the stream where they hatched. These are the only places where salmon can lay their eggs. Engineers have invented solutions to help the salmon get to where they need to go.

Explore Online

river dam

This is a fish ladder. Salmon naturally leap out of the water. The salmon ladder uses this natural behavior to help them over the dam. When the salmon leap, they move up one step of the ladder. One step at a time, they get over the dam.

fish ladder

fish elevator

Engineers also designed a fish elevator. Multiple fish swim into the elevator at the base of the dam. Once they get in, they can't get out until the elevator is raised and the fish swim out at the top the dam.

A vertical-slot fish passage is another solution to the salmon problem. The fish swim through a slot at one side of the dam. The slot leads the fish up gentle ramps filled with water and pebbles. Eventually the fish find another slot to swim through. At the end, the salmon are safely at the top of the dam.

vertical-slot fish passage

16. How are the solutions for the fish passages alike and different? What are the benefits? What problems might these solutions cause? Write your answers below.

_____

_____

_____

_____

_____

_____

_____

Lesson Check

Name _____

Can You Explain It?

1. You have learned how environmental changes can destroy plant and animal habitats. Remember that the San Joaquin kit fox lost its home to a wildfire.

Explore Online

- What do you think will happen to the kit fox now?

- Where do you think it will live and catch its food?

EVIDENCE NOTEBOOK Use the information you've collected in your Evidence Notebook to help you cover each point above.

_____

_____

_____

_____

_____

Checkpoints

2. Circle the phrase that best completes the sentence. Construction

of homes and buildings leads to _____

a. fewer humans in an area.

b. habitat destruction.

c. more food sources.

3. How does the dam affect its surrounding environment? Circle the best answer.

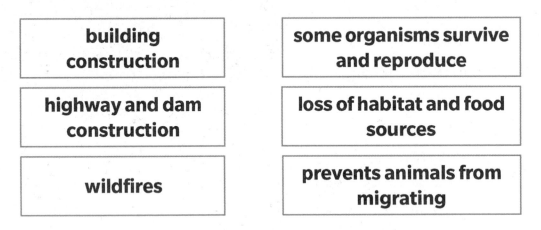

    a. It helps fish safely migrate.

    b. It floods the surrounding land.

    c. It improves the flow of river water.

    d. It decreases the amount of water.

4. Match the cause to the effect it has on the environment.

building construction	**some organisms survive and reproduce**
highway and dam construction	**loss of habitat and food sources**
wildfires	**prevents animals from migrating**

5. What are some ways that an environment can change because of natural causes? Circle all that apply.

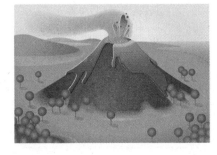

    a. volcanic eruptions

    b. beavers building dams

    c. roads and bridge construction

    d. dams that change the flow of water

6. Sort each change in the environment by whether it is natural or caused by humans.

oxbow lake	**construction**	**farming**
seasonal temperature changes		**volcanic ash**

Natural   Human

_____   _____

_____   _____

Lesson Roundup

A. Match the image to the type of environmental change it shows.

> **a.** Land change   **b.** Water distribution change   **c.** Habitat destruction

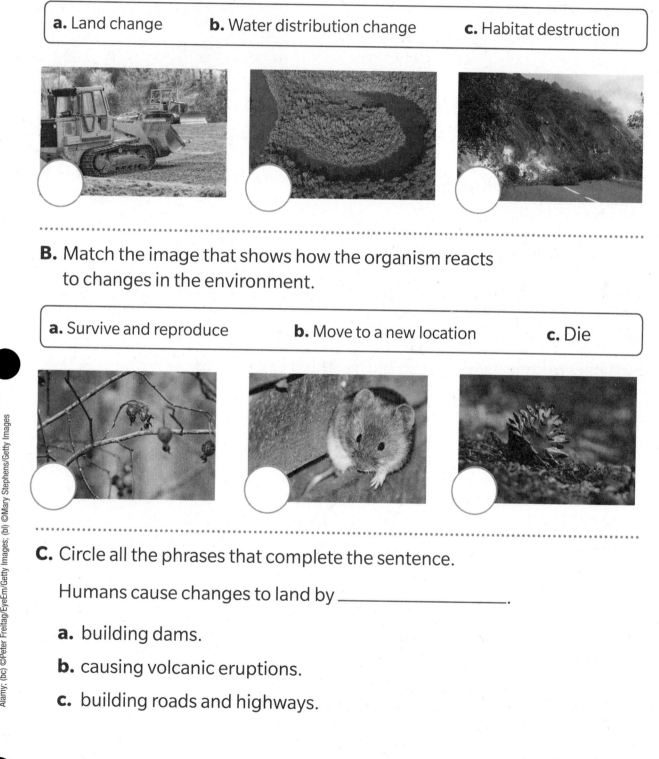

B. Match the image that shows how the organism reacts to changes in the environment.

> **a.** Survive and reproduce   **b.** Move to a new location   **c.** Die

C. Circle all the phrases that complete the sentence.

Humans cause changes to land by _____.

a. building dams.

b. causing volcanic eruptions.

c. building roads and highways.

ENGINEER IT!
Change It Up

What happens when the environment a plant is in changes? Using your plants from Lesson 1, design an experiment by making a change in the plants' environment. Gather evidence and explain how this change affects the plants.

How will being closer to sunlight affect the growth of this plant?

INQUIRY: What changes could you make to your plants' environment?

_____

_____

APPLY: Look back at what you've learned about the plants. Take notes about which information you will use to design your experiment.

_____

_____

BRAINSTORM: Brainstorm with your team about how you will design your experiment and collect evidence. Keep in mind the criteria and constraints.

Criteria	**Constraints**
☐ You may only make one change to the environment	☐ You will only have two weeks to collect data
☐ You must collect data each day during the experiment	☐ Your evidence must be measurable
☐ Your data collection must be recorded and used to create a graph to be used as evidence	☐ Your evidence must be presented using a type of graph (bar graph, pictograph, pie graph, etc.)

MAKE A PLAN: Consider the questions below. Answer the questions and make a list of needed materials and why you need them.

1. What change will you make to the plants' environment?

2. How will you collect data?

3. How will you interpret your data?

_____

_____

TEST: Design your experiment and make the change to the plants' environment. Record data each day.

_____

_____

EVALUATE AND REDESIGN: Did you meet the criteria and constraints? What changes could improve your experiment?

_____

_____

_____

COMMUNICATE: Present your data to your class using a graph.

☑ Checklist

Review your project and check off each completed item.

_____ Includes only one change to the environment.

_____ Includes data collected each day during the experiment.

_____ Includes evidence that is measurable.

_____ Includes evidence presented using a type of graph .

Unit Review

1. Which is an inherited trait in plants?

    a. the color of their flowers

    b. the amount of sunlight the plants receive

    c. the amount of water the plants receive

    d. the kind of animal that eats its leaves

2. Which inherited traits do animals have? Select all that apply.

    a. the colors of their fur

    b. the numbers of limbs they have

    c. the amounts of food they eat

    d. the habitats they live in

3. Select all that apply. A plant that gets too much of a need met might

    a. grow leaves too large.

    b. die from receiving too much sun.

    c. develop roots that grow too deep.

    d. have trouble growing due to too much water

4. You want to test how the amount of water given to a plant will affect it's traits. Describe an experiment that would have a control plant and three other plants that you could do to test the effect of water on a plant.

_____

_____

_____

_____

5. Match each physical adaptation to the description of the turtle's adaptations

    a. hard shell

    b. strong jaws

    c. period of inactivity

Fill in the blank with the letter that matches the adaptation.

____ saves energy when food is not available

____ uses to eat tough grasses

____ prevents predators from eating it

6. Select the correct answer.

| adaptations | traits | habits | families |

Organisms have _____ that allow them to survive

in their habitat. They also have _____ that make

them very successful living in their environment.

7. Look at the plant below. Select all of the characteristics that may protect it from being eaten by animals.

    a. spines

    b. flowers

    c. waxy skin

    d. green color

8. Match the physical adaptation to the animal that uses it to survive.

hard shell   eagle

mimicry   turtle

camouflage   viceroy butterfly

sharp claws   leopard seal

9. How might living in a group help animals survive? Select all that apply.

a. coping with change

b. fighting each other for food

c. hunting

d. protection

10. Look at the photo. Select all the ways this natural event changed the environment.

a. pollution

b. food loss

c. human change

d. migration blockage

Fossils

Explore Online

Unit Project: A Window to the Past

How can you use a diorama to model an ancient environment? You will build one to demonstrate. Ask your teacher for details.

Fossils at the natural history museum are set up to show the way the dinosaur lived and moved. How do you think some of these dinosaurs moved?

At a Glance

LESSON 1

What Is a Fossil? 348

LESSON 2

What Do Fossils Tell Us about the Past? 370

Unit Review 394

Vocabulary Game: **Bingo**

Materials

- 1 set of word cards
- 1 bingo board for each player
- counters, paper clips, or coins for game markers

fossil

extinct

Set Up

- Choose one student to be the caller. The caller will call out the words but not play.
- To make bingo boards, players write words from the unit in the squares to fill the board. Students can use words more than once.

How to Play

1. The caller chooses a word card, reads the word, and then puts the word card in a second pile.

2. Players put a marker on the word each time they find it on their bingo boards.

3. Repeat steps 1 and 2 until a player marks five boxes in a line going down, across, or on a slant and calls "bingo." Check the answers.

4. Have the caller check the word cards in the second pile against the bingo board.

Unit Vocabulary

 **aquatic:** Something that exists in or on water.

 **extinct:** Describes a kind of thing that is no longer found on Earth.

 **fossil:** The remains or traces of an organism that lived long ago.

 **terrestrial:** Something that exists in or on land.

What Is a Fossil?

Much of what we know today about life in oceans from long ago comes from fossils.

By the end of this lesson . . .
you'll be able to identify different types of fossils and explain what they can tell you about organisms from the past.

Can You Explain It?

▶ Explore Online

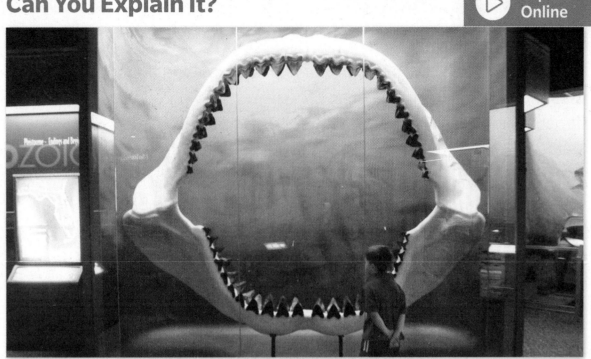

The fossil of this organism's jaw and teeth helps us see just how big the creature must have been!

1. Based on your observations of the image on this page, what can you infer about the animal? What kind of animal was it? How big do you think the animal was? What do you think it ate? Explain your reasoning.

_____

_____

_____

_____

_____

 EVIDENCE NOTEBOOK Look for this icon to help you gather evidence to answer the questions above.

What Are Fossils?

Fossil or Not?

The remains or traces of an organism that lived long ago is a **fossil.** Fossils can be made of an organism's hard parts or its soft parts. Hard parts include teeth, bones, and shells. Often, an organism's soft parts—tissues such as skin and organs—are not usually preserved because they break down over time.

Most fossils are preserved in rock. For example, when a fish dies and settles to the bottom of the ocean, its soft parts decay or are eaten by other animals. Over time, its bones and other hard parts are buried in the mud. When the mud hardens, the hard parts become preserved as fossils.

Fossil—Yes or No?

2. Look at the images on these two pages and read the descriptions. Then decide if the picture shows a fossil.

 Explore Online

a. This shell was pressed into the soft mud on the sea floor. Over time, pressure changed the mud to rock. The shell dissolved and left a hollow space in the rock. Over time, more mud filled the space to form an imprint of the shell.

Is this a fossil? _____

b. These shells belonged to animals that died on the beach not long ago. They are pressed into the sand.

Are they fossils? _____

c. These footprints were left behind as the organism walked in the sand.

Are they fossils? _____

d. These footprints were made long ago in soft mud. Over time, the mud changed to rock, preserving the footprints.

Are they fossils? _____

e. A strong storm knocked this tree over. The wood is starting to decay.

Is this a fossil? _____

f. This tree lived long ago. Its wood has been replaced by other materials called minerals. This tree is said to be petrified.

Is this a fossil? _____

Clues to the Past

Fossils tell us much about the past. They tell us about organisms that once lived on Earth. They tell us about the environments in which the organisms lived. Fossils can even tell us how some organisms have changed over time.

3. Choose an organism that lives on Earth today. Describe how it might become a future fossil. How long do you think the process will take?

_____

_____

_____

_____

_____

Evidence Provided by Fossils

4. Look at the images. Identify the object that was fossilized.

_____   _____

5. Look at the fossils on the previous page. What evidence does each fossil provide for the type of organism that left it and its environment?

_____

_____

_____

_____

Patterns in nature repeat over time. Some patterns repeat quickly. Others take a long time. The same processes that formed the fossils we find today are changing more organism remains into future fossils!

6. Language SmArts Research a fossil in a book or online. Make inferences about where the organism likely lived, what it ate, and how its fossil may have formed. Support your claim with evidence from the fossil.

_____

_____

_____

_____

Tip

Details and Evidence
The English Language Arts Handbook can provide help with understanding details and evidence.

 EVIDENCE NOTEBOOK How are all of the fossils you've seen so far the same? Make a list of the similarities in your Evidence Notebook.

So Many Types of Fossils!

Some fossils, like bones and teeth, are the remains of organisms. Others are simply the shapes of ancient organisms that were preserved in rocks. Some fossils are pieces of once-living things. Others are whole organisms! Read about some different types of fossils and how they formed.

The shell impressions in this rock are one type of fossil. Another type of fossil formed when the impressions were slowly filled with minerals.

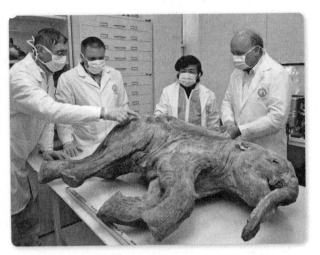

Some fossils, like this mammoth, form when an organism becomes trapped in water that freezes and becomes ice. This fossil is more than 40,000 years old!

This is petrified wood. This fossil formed when the wood of the plant was replaced by very hard minerals over time. *Petro-* means "rock."

This fossil formed when all the moisture of the leaf was pressed out, leaving only a thin coating of carbon behind.

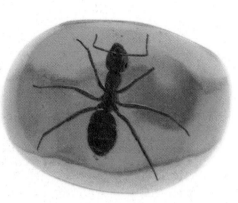

Organisms can get trapped in sticky tree sap and die. As the sap hardens, the organisms become fossilized in the sap, which is called amber.

These footprints formed when the soft mud around them turned to rock. Footprints are trace fossils that record the activities of once-living organisms.

7. Fossils are often the hard parts of once-living things. But an organism's soft parts can also be preserved. Which materials can preserve soft parts? Select all that apply.

sand   amber

ice   rock

8. Why do you think fossilized insects are often found preserved in amber?

_____

_____

_____

_____

Alive Today?

Some fossils look like organisms that live on Earth today. Others reveal **extinct** organisms — those no longer found on Earth.

Yes or No?

9. Read the descriptions for each of the items below. Research online to decide whether each type of organism is alive today. Write **yes** or **no** on the lines. Go online to do research.

Explore Online

a. This fossil is a dinosaur's head. The picture shows what the animal might have looked like.

Alive today? _____

b. This fossil shell is evidence of an organism that once lived on Earth. The picture shows what the animal might have looked like.

Alive today? _____

c. This fossil is part of an ocean creature called a blastoid. It lived long ago and was anchored to the sea floor by a stem-like column. The picture shows what it might have looked like.

Alive today? _____

Modeling Fossils

10. On a piece of paper, trace the outline of the sole of your shoe. Think about ways that your simple drawing is like a fossil. What can you determine about your shoe by examining just its outline?

Make a two-column chart. In one column, list the details you can determine about the shoe by looking only at the drawing. Then examine the actual shoe. In the other column, list the details you can determine by looking at the real thing. Repeat these steps, using your hand.

Turn your drawings and charts in to your teacher.

What can you tell about a person or organism that left footprints behind?

_____

_____

EVIDENCE NOTEBOOK Suppose you found two fossils of different body parts of the same organism. How can you use what you learned from the shoe and hand tracings to make inferences about the once-living organism? How does the fossil jaw you saw at the beginning of the lesson, help you identify features of the organism that left it?

Putting it Together

11. Describe some types of fossils, and explain what fossils can tell you about once-living things.

_____

_____

Walk This Way!

Objective

Collaborate with a partner to make a model and observe how trace fossils can provide evidence about a once-living organism.

What question will you investigate to meet this objective?

Procedure

STEP 1 Work with a partner. Connect two chopsticks near the top so that they open and close.

What do you think the chopsticks will represent in this activity?

STEP 2 Roll out three pieces of clay to model soft mud.

Predict how the length of the chopsticks will relate to the length of the *stride,* or distance between steps.

STEP 3 With one chopstick in each hand, "walk" the chopsticks across a piece of clay. Use the ruler to measure the stride. Record the length of the stride in the data table on the next page.

STEP 4 Record your measurements and observations for each trial in this data table.

Chopstick holder placement	Stride measurement (cm)
Top	
Middle	
Bottom	

STEP 5 Now move the chopstick holder down so that it is in the middle of the sticks. Repeat Step 3 with another piece of clay. Record the stride in your data table.

STEP 6 Now move the chopstick holder down so that it is near the bottom of the two chopsticks. Repeat Step 3 with the third piece of clay. Record your results in your data table. Compare your results with others. Were they the same?

Analyze Your Results

STEP 7 How are the model trace fossils in each trial the same?

_____

STEP 8 How are the model trace fossils in each trial different? What is the difference, in centimeters, between the longest and shortest stride?

_____

Draw Conclusions

STEP 9 Make a claim about how changing the position of the chopstick holder affects the model legs and footprint pattern?

_____

STEP 10 What kinds of evidence do fossil footprints tell scientists about the animal that made them?

_____

Clues from Fossils

How Big Was It?

Sometimes, it is hard to tell how large an organism was just by looking at fossil pieces of it. It is also sometimes hard to tell a fossil's size from a simple picture of it. Look at the pictures of some fossils on this page and how the organisms compared in size.

Giant ground sloth fossil   Cycad cone fossil   Trilobite fossil

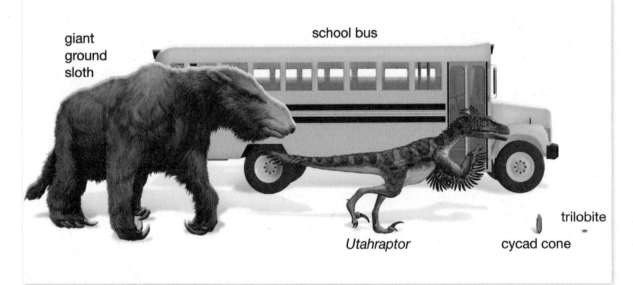

Compare them to the size of a school bus.

12. Based on the drawing at the bottom of the previous page, think of some common objects that can be used to show the size of each of the fossils listed below. Then complete the table.

Fossil	Object	How fossil compares in size to object
Trilobite		
Cycad cone		
Utahraptor		
Giant ground sloth		

Do the Math
Scale

13. Looking at the organisms next to the schoolbus helped you see how big those organisms were. A scientist will often take a picture as part of collecting data about a fossil. To show the size of the fossil, the scientist will place an object with a known length next to the fossil. The object becomes a visual reference similar to the bus.

Suppose a scientist uses a 4-centimeter paper clip as a visual reference. How large are the fossils described below?

Fossil A is half as long as the paper clip.

_____

Fossil B is 3 times as long as the paper clip.

_____

Fossil C is $4\frac{1}{2}$ times the length of the paper clip.

_____

Pieces and Parts!

Fossils of entire organisms are rare. Scientists usually only find pieces and parts of once-living things. Complete fossils such as those below give scientists greater insight into what some organisms used to look like. Can you figure out what's what?

Some of These, Some of Those

14. Look at the photos below. Compare the details in the fossils. Describe what you can tell about each fossil from the details you can see.

▷ Explore Online

Details: _____

_____

_____

_____

Details: _____

_____

_____

_____

_____

15. Language SmArts Using the evidence from the details you could see, which modern day animal do they resemble? Which features provide evidence for your conclusion?

_____

_____

Now look at the pictures below. An artist used the fossils to draw what the original organisms may have looked like. Compare the images below. Use the fossil to determine if you agree with the artist.

List any parts of the art that you think match the fossil.

_____

_____

_____

_____

List any parts of the art that you think do not match the fossil.

_____

_____

_____

_____

16. How does a more detailed fossil help scientists better understand what the organism was like?

_____

_____

_____

 EVIDENCE NOTEBOOK Recall the fossil teeth you saw at the beginning of the lesson. What have you learned here that can provide evidence about the organism that left the teeth behind? List any organisms you may know of that have similar teeth.

What Was That?

Some fossils closely resemble organisms alive today. Others, however, look *nothing* like organisms that live on Earth today. In fact, some fossilized organisms are so strange that it can be hard to imagine what the organisms looked like when they were alive! But no matter how strange or common fossils might look, they still provide scientists with much evidence about life in the past.

Match 'Em Up!

17. Draw a line from the picture of each organism to the fossil it may have left behind.

▶ Explore Online

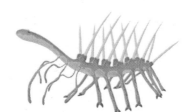 

Language SmArts
Constructing Explanations

18. How do scientists know that some organisms not alive today once lived on Earth?

_____

_____

_____

Tip

Constructing Explanations
The English Language Arts Handbook can provide help with understanding how to construct explanations.

Discover More

Check out this path . . . or go online to choose one of these other paths.

Careers in Science & Engineering

- **Dinosaur Parts**
- **Build a Fossil Museum**

Careers in Science & Engineering

What Is a Paleontologist?

Do you ever wonder what Earth was like millions of years ago? So do paleontologists! *Paleontologists* are scientists who study fossils to find out what ancient environments were like and what kinds of things lived in these environments.

Paleontologists don't just study dinosaurs. They study all the life forms that have flourished on Earth at different times and in different places. A paleontologist is like a detective, piecing together clues to learn more about the long and rich history of life on Earth.

Explore Online

Paleontologists at work in the South Dakota Badlands

Fossils displayed in the Zigong Dinosaur Museum, China

Paleontologists have to know a lot about biology and geology. Other science and math classes are also important. Some paleontologists work in labs. Some work outdoors. Others work in museums and offices.

19. What kinds of things do paleontologists study? What are some questions a paleontologist might try to answer?

_____

_____

20. One dinosaur studied by paleontologists is the *titanosaur*. This dinosaur is very large. Go online to research the largest titanosaur fossil found. How long was it? How tall? How much did it weigh? Record your research on the lines below.

_____

_____

_____

Now collaborate to make a life-sized drawing or model of a titanosaur. Describe the size of the model in relationship to parts of the school. For example, how many classrooms long was your model? Record your comparisons on the lines below.

_____

_____

Titanosaur replica

Lesson Check

Can You Explain It?

1. Now that you've learned more about fossils, explain what the fossil from the beginning of the lesson tells you about the past. Be sure to do the following:

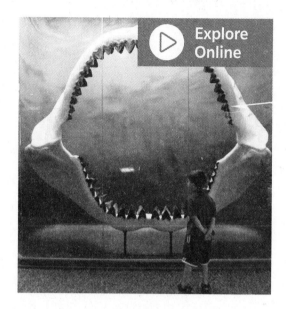

Explore Online

- Explain how the teeth give clues about the animal it came from.

- Describe how the teeth became a fossil.

EVIDENCE NOTEBOOK Use the information you've collected in your Evidence Notebook to help you cover each point above.

_____

_____

_____

_____

_____

Checkpoints

2. In what type of fossil has once-living material been replaced by minerals?

   a. petrified wood   **c.** amber

   b. a carbon film   **d.** a trace fossil

3. Circle the answer that best explains why the object in this image is a fossil.

a. It has no soft parts.

b. It was dug up by a paleontologist.

c. It took a very long time to form from a once-living organism.

d. There are similar shells on Earth today.

4. Circle all of the phrases that describe a fossil.

a. woolly mammoth frozen in ice

b. pinecone from a city park

c. impression of a leaf in a rock

d. an empty seashell on a beach

Decide whether the following statements are true or false. Circle the correct answer. Then, support your choice by writing how you know each statement is true or false.

5. The skeleton of a fish that died and became buried in the ocean floor a month ago is a fossil.

a. True

b. False

_____

6. All of the organisms that lived millions of years ago are extinct.

a. True

b. False

_____

Lesson Roundup

A. Mark all of the phrases that describe a fossil.

   a. muddy paw prints across a tile floor

   b. empty crab shells on a rocky beach

   c. a butterfly enclosed in amber

   d. imprints of leaves on a concrete sidewalk

   e. dinosaur footprints and petrified eggs

   f. a fish skeleton floating in a lake

B. Choose the word or phrase that best completes the sentences below. Words or phrases may be used more than once.

extinct	**very young**	**very old**
plants only	**animals only**	**living organisms**

Fossils come in all shapes and sizes. But no matter the shape or size, they all came from _____.

Fossils provide evidence of _____ organisms that no longer live on Earth.

C. Which of these would give a scientist the best evidence about the size of the once-living organism? Circle all that apply.

   a. fossilized footprints

   b. a petrified tree stump

   c. a frog trapped in amber

   d. a fish bone

What Do Fossils Tell Us about the Past?

You may have seen fossils at school or at a museum or found one in the ground. Scientists can learn a lot about Earth's past by studying fossils.

By the end of this lesson . . .
you'll be able to use fossils as evidence to explain what an organism's environment was like.

Can You Explain It?

 Explore Online

As you look at the image, consider what you know about fossils. This interaction between two animals was preserved in this fossil. Think about what can be learned from observing this fossil.

1. What can this fossil tell you about the environment where these two organisms lived? What clues from the fossil did you use to decide on your answer?

> **Tip**
>
> Learn more about fossils in *What Is a Fossil?*

_____

_____

_____

_____

_____

_____

 EVIDENCE NOTEBOOK Look for this icon to help you gather evidence to answer the questions above.

Wet or Dry?

Ancient Aquatic Ecosystem

Think about the fossil you just looked at. It is the evidence of two prehistoric organisms. It shows us more than just two organisms. We know that both organisms lived in the same ecosystem at the same time.

Exploring an Ancient Ocean

2. Look at the **aquatic,** or underwater, ecosystem below. It existed about 400 million years ago. Read on the next page about these organisms and how they may have lived. Write the letters from those descriptions to label the picture.

▷ Explore Online

a. The head of this fish was covered with armor plates, and the rest of its body was covered with thick scales.

b. These looked like present-day clams. Thick shells protected their soft bodies. Remains of their shells can be found as fossils today.

c. Feather stars were related to present-day sea stars. They lived attached to the sea floor.

d. These organisms lived inside a long shell. They were related to present-day squids and octopuses.

3. Make a claim about how each of these organisms ate by drawing a line from each image to the caption that describes the organism.

These organisms had feathery arms that caught food particles as they floated within reach.

These organisms had tentacles that they used to catch their food, such as fish.

These organisms used their powerful jaws to catch and eat sharks and other fish.

Language SmArts
Making Inferences

4. What evidence supports your claims in question 3 above? Provide evidence for each organism.

_____

_____

_____

_____

© Houghton Mifflin Harcourt

Tip

Making Inferences
The English Language Arts Handbook can provide help with understanding making inferences.

Ancient Terrestrial Ecosystem

Take a look at this **terrestrial,** or land, ecosystem from 50,000 to 11,000 years ago. Learn more about these organisms and how they may have interacted with each other.

Exploring a Land Ecosystem

5. Use the descriptions below to label the organisms.

▷ Explore Online

a. This ancient bird was over 1 meter in height. Its wings were almost 3 meters in length. Its legs, neck, and bill were all long.

c. By studying plant fossils, scientists have learned that plants from 50,000 to 11,000 years ago may have looked different from modern plants, but functioned in much the same way.

b. A saber-toothed cat is best known for its long, sharp front teeth, called sabers, which could be 30 centimeters in length.

d. The dire wolf was about the same length as a present-day gray wolf, but it weighed more.

Fitting In

6. Use the images to answer the question below.

dire wolf

ancient fish

oak leaves

feather star

Compare these organisms from aquatic and terrestrial ecosystems. What characteristics helped the organisms live in their environment?

_____

_____

_____

 EVIDENCE NOTEBOOK Consider the organisms from the beginning of the lesson. Do their features indicate a particular environment?

Putting It Together

7. Could a dire wolf live in an aquatic environment? Explain your reasoning.

_____

_____

_____

Yesterday and Today

We Can Learn from the Past

Think about the fossils you've seen. Do they look like any animals or plants that are alive today? Scientists will often study a present-day animal that is similar to a fossil. This approach can help them learn how the fossilized organism may have lived.

Comparing Fossils to Organisms Living Today

8. As you read about each set of organisms, think about how they are similar and how they are different. Write these in the boxes below.

▷ Explore Online

Ginkgo trees can reach heights of about 35 meters and live up to 1,000 years.

Fossils show that ginkgo trees have not changed very much in the last 100 million years.

Alike:	Different:

The nautilus uses its tentacles to catch fish, crabs, and shrimp. Similar ancient animals had shells that protected their soft bodies.

Fossils of shells reveal that their shells were long.

Alike:	Different:

9. Language SmArts Research what turtles from the very distant past may have looked like. On the lines, tell how they are different from modern turtles. Then, in the box below, draw a picture of an ancient turtle.

_____

_____

Modern sea turtles live in warm ocean water. They have a shell that covers their body and flippers.

A Closer Look

Woolly mammoths lived from about 10,000 to 5 million years ago, during the last ice age. Modern-day elephants, found in Africa and Asia, are related to woolly mammoths.

Woolly Mammoth versus Elephant

10. Contrast the organisms below. Circle one feature from each column that you think shows the most evidence for the environment in which they lived.

▶ Explore Online

Woolly mammoth	Elephant

a. Woolly mammoths had curved tusks that were up to 5 meters long.

b. Woolly mammoths were large, having a mass of 8,000 kg and reaching heights of 4 meters.

c. Woolly mammoths were covered with thick fur to help protect them from the cold temperatures.

d. Woolly mammoths had smaller ears than elephants.

e. Elephants have tusks that are up to $3\frac{1}{2}$ meters long.

f. Elephants are the largest modern land animal. They have a mass of up to 6,000 kg and reach heights of 4 meters.

g. Elephants have gray, wrinkled skin that is sensitive to touch.

h. Elephants have very large ears that help keep them cool.

Do the Math
Greater or Less Than

11. Choose the answers that correctly complete the sentences. Some answers may be used more than once.

>	<	less	shorter	longer	the same as
on land	in water	hot	warm	cold	more

a. 5 m _____ $3\frac{1}{2}$ m, so the woolly mammoth tusks were

_____ than the tusks of elephants.

b. 8,000 kg _____ 6,000 kg, so you can conclude that

woolly mammoths weighed _____ than elephants.

c. Both the elephant and woolly mammoth have legs. This is evidence that the woolly mammoth probably lived

_____ .

d. The woolly mammoth was covered in fur. This is evidence

that the woolly mammoth probably lived in a _____ environment.

EVIDENCE NOTEBOOK Look again at the picture at the beginning of the lesson. List some of the organism's features.

Putting It Together

12. Scientists assume that extinct animals and animals living today used similar body structures in the same way. What can you infer about extinct animals by comparing them to animals that are alive today?

_____

_____

What Can You Learn from Studying a Fossil?

Objective

Collaborate with your team to make observations about fossils. Based on your observations, you will describe the type of environment your fossilized organisms most likely lived in.

> **Materials**
> - fossil kit
> - hand lens
> - drawing paper
> - crayons or colored pencils

What question will you investigate to meet this objective?

_____

_____

Procedure

STEP 1 Use the hand lens and your senses of sight and touch to observe the fossils your teacher gave you.

STEP 2 Determine which of the fossils represent plants. Record the fossil number and observations, such as leaf shape and size, in the chart. Share your results with others. Did you all classify your fossils in the same way?

Plant Fossils	
Fossil number	Observations

STEP 3 Determine which fossils represent animals. In the chart below, record the fossil's number and observations about each fossil. Include the shape and size of limbs, body, teeth, and head, as well as other notable features.

Animal Fossils	
Fossil number	Observations

STEP 4 Select one of the fossils. Research which environment this organism most likely lived in. Which fossil did you select?

_____

STEP 5 Draw and color a picture of the environment your fossilized organism lived in.

Analyze Your Results

STEP 6 How did you know whether a fossil was from a plant or an animal?

_____

_____

STEP 7 Which observations that you made helped you decide what type of environment the organism lived in?

_____

_____

_____

STEP 8 What else did you learn about your fossil organism?

_____

_____

_____

Draw Conclusions

STEP 9 What do you think scientists learn about organisms from the past when they study fossils?

_____

_____

STEP 10 Choose one of the fossil animals in the kit. Make a claim about the type of food it may have eaten. Then give evidence from the fossil for your claim.

_____

_____

_____

STEP 11 Think of another question you have about fossils. Write it below, and then investigate to find an answer.

_____

_____

_____

How'd That Get There?

Common Features

What do scientists do when there are no similar animals alive today that are like the fossil organism. They look for living animals that have features or structures similar to the fossil. They compare the living organism and the fossil to see what they have in common.

Similar Parts

13. For each of the fossils below, identify an animal living today that is similar in structure. List your animal, and tell what physical features your animal has in common with the fossils below.

▶ Explore Online

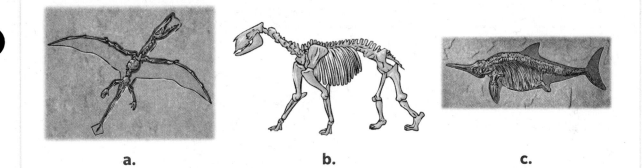

a. b. c.

a. _____

_____

b. _____

_____

c. _____

_____

Home Sweet Home

When scientists compare fossils from extinct organisms to organisms that are alive today, they can learn many things. One thing they can learn is what type of environment the extinct organism lived in. Can you use the features found in a fossil to figure out where it lived?

Where Did It Live?

14. a. Circle the features on the images below that are similar to the animals you compared them to on the previous page.

 Explore Online

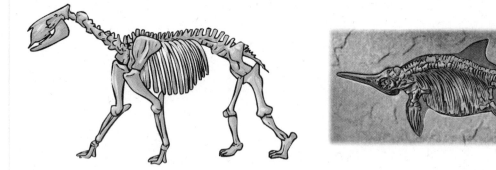

b. Tell whether each organism lived in an aquatic or terrestrial environment.

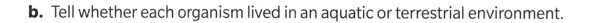

_____   _____

_____   _____

c. What structures in these fossils provide evidence that supports your answer above?

_____   _____

_____   _____

Look-Alikes

15. Go online, and find pictures of the animal called
Utahceratops and of a rhinoceros. The *Utahceratops* was a
dinosaur that lived millions of years ago. The rhinoceros is
found roaming tropical grasslands today.

Make a drawing showing the two animals.

16. Compare the rhinoceros to the *Utahceratops*.
What evidence from these images shows what the
environment of the *Utahceratops* might have been like?
Explain your reasoning.

_____

_____

_____

_____

_____

You Found It Where?

Scientists often find fossils of organisms that lived in oceans in areas of dry land today. Or they find a fossil of a plant that lived in a tropical climate in an area where the climate is cold today. How does this happen? How could a fossil of an organism that lived in a specific environment be found in an environment that is totally different today?

Same Place, Different Time

17. In the box below, draw what you think the environment looked like when this plant was alive.

This plant lived about 300 to 200 million years ago. It lost its leaves in the cooler season, and they grew back during warmer seasons. The plant grew all over the large landmass that existed during that time period.

What environment did this organism live in? How does this differ from where it was found?

_____

_____

_____

_____

18. This turtle lived in warm, tropical water 95 million years ago. Its fossil was found on an island where temperatures today are about −20 °C. Why couldn't the turtle live there now?

19. This tropical fish lived in a warm shallow sea. The fossil was found in the mountains. How could it have gotten into the mountains?

_____

_____

20. What is the evidence that these environments changed over time?

_____

_____

 EVIDENCE NOTEBOOK Think about the organism that left the fossil shown at the beginning of this lesson. What evidence would you need to describe the environment it lived in?

Engineer It
Tools of the Trade

You might be surprised that studying fossils requires engineering to solve some problems. Fossils form in places where they have to be excavated, or dug out, before they can be studied. It takes a certain set of tools to solve this problem. Not all engineering solutions use complicated technology. Many tools scientists use for digging up and studying fossils are simple. Read below to learn about these tools.

a.

b.

c.

d.

a. A paleontologist uses a geological hammer or mallet to break fossils out of the rock that surrounds them.

b. Brushes are used to dust away loose material from the fragile surfaces of fossils.

c. Many fossils are tiny or have very small details. A hand lens allows the paleontologist to look closely.

d. Paleontologists take pictures to document the whole process of excavation.

Language SmArts
Making Inferences

21. Suppose you discovered a new animal fossil. Tell how you would determine the type of environment that it lived in. Identify specific parts of the fossil that might be evidence for your claim.

_____

_____

_____

_____

_____

> **Tip**
>
> **Making Inferences**
> The English Language Arts Handbook can provide help with understanding how to make inferences.

Discover More

Check out this path . . . or go online to choose one of these other paths.

People in Science & Engineering

- **That's a Long Time Ago**
- **How a Fossil Forms**

People in Science & Engineering

Fossil Seekers

Explore Online

Karen Chin is a scientist who studies the fossilized remains of dinosaurs. However, unlike a lot of scientists who study fossils, she does not study bones or skulls. She studies the fossilized material that dinosaurs excreted.

These types of fossils are called coprolites. Scientists can learn a lot about an animal's diet by studying coprolites. For example, Dr. Chin has learned that certain plant-eating dinosaurs also ate wood.

Karen Chin

Mary Anning was an English fossil collector in the 1800s. She made several famous fossil discoveries. She also helped lead to the discovery that coprolites were fossilized feces.

Mary Gordon Calder also studied unusual fossils. In the 1930s, she worked with formations called coal balls. Coal balls are "blobs" of material that are almost coal, but are not fully formed. Coal balls preserve fragile plants from hundreds of millions of years ago.

Mary Anning

389

Coprolite Evidence

▷ Explore Online

22. Look at these coprolite fossils. Suppose each fossil contained various foods. Research types of animals that may have left them. Then, draw an organism for each fossil that may have left it.

1. Contained: seeds

2. Contained: bones

3. Contained: bones and seeds

23. If you could interview a scientist who studies coprolites, such as Karen Chin, what three questions would you ask?

_____

_____

_____

Lesson Check

Name _____

Can You Explain It?

1. What can this fossil tell you? Be sure to do the following:

Explore Online

   • Include evidence about the environment in which the animals lived.

   • Compare the animals with similar organisms alive today.

> **EVIDENCE NOTEBOOK** Use the information you've collected in your Evidence Notebook to help answer these questions.

_____

_____

_____

_____

_____

Checkpoints

Answer the questions below to show what you have learned about how fossils teach us about life in the past.

2. A fossil of a fish is found near the top of a mountain. What does this tell us about the environment? Circle all that apply.

   a. The environment has not changed over time.

   b. The environment changed from aquatic to terrestrial.

   c. The land was covered by water before the mountain formed.

   d. The land was dry before the mountain formed.

3. Write *terrestrial* or *aquatic* to identify the type of environment in which each organism lived.

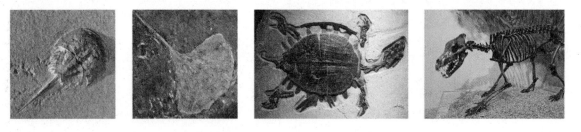

_____   _____   _____   _____

4. Look at the photo. Use the word bank to complete the sentences.

in water	legs	walking
on land	flippers	flying
in the air	wings	swimming

This organism lived _____. Scientists believe this

because it has _____ for _____.

5. Which is the most likely reason that woolly mammoths had fur covering their bodies but modern elephants do not? Circle the best answer.

a. The woolly mammoths lived on land, as do modern elephants.

b. The woolly mammoths lived in water, and elephants live on land.

c. The woolly mammoths lived in a warmer climate than elephants.

d. The woolly mammoths lived in a colder climate than elephants.

6. What can scientists learn from studying fossils? Circle all that apply.

a. about conditions of past environments

b. how organisms moved, what they ate, and how they interacted

c. how fossil organisms may be related to modern organisms

d. what noises animals made in the past

Lesson Roundup

A. Write the name of each feature under the environment for which it provides evidence.

tentacles	fins	leaves
wings	flippers	feet

Terrestrial   **Aquatic**

_____   _____

_____   _____

_____   _____

B. Match the fossil to the modern animal it is most like.

woolly mammoth	coyote

saber-toothed cat	elephant

dire wolf	tiger

C. The ginkgo tree is often called a "living fossil." Why do you think that is?

a. The leaf from the modern tree looks very different from the fossil leaf.

b. The leaf from the modern tree looks very similar to the fossil leaf.

c. The modern tree grows to the same height as the extinct tree.

d. The modern tree grows much taller than the extinct tree.

Past or Present?

Many plants and animals that lived long ago are still around, but some plants and animals are extinct. Look at the image and discuss it as a class.

This is a picture of a Stenopterygius fossil.

Your teacher will assign you a fossil to research. Use evidence from the unit and your research to analyze your organism. Determine if the organism is alive today, the type of environment in which the organism lived, and what other organisms lived during that time period.

BRAINSTORM: How will you determine if the plant or animal is alive today?

_____

_____

_____

RESEARCH: Look back at what you've learned about fossils. Research your organism on the Internet. Take notes about which information you will use in your explanation.

_____

_____

_____

MAKE A CLAIM AND CITE EVIDENCE: Use the information you gathered to make a claim about whether your organism is alive today or extinct.

_____

_____

_____

MAKE A PLAN: You will create a presentation. List the things you will include in your presentation.

_____

_____

_____

Communicate: Present your argument to your class.

☑ Checklist

Review your project and check off each completed item.

_____ Project includes a description of the environment in which the organism lived or lives.

_____ Project includes descriptions of at least two other organisms from the same time period.

_____ Project includes evidence from the unit.

_____ Project includes factual information used as evidence.

_____ Project includes an argument presented using multimedia.

Unit Review

1. Look at the images. Draw a circle around the fossil that was from an aquatic organism. Draw a square around the fossil that was from a terrestrial organism.

2. What should you do to learn about changes in a habitat over time?

  a. Make a map of the habitat.

  b. Ask people who moved there.

  c. Make a list of plants and animals that live there.

  d. Compare fossils to the animals that live there now.

3. Select the correct answer to finish the sentence.

The remains or traces of something that lived long

ago are _____.

> minerals
> rocks
> fossils

4. Most fossils are often the hard parts of once-living things that are preserved in rock. But an organism's soft parts can also be preserved. Which materials can preserve the soft parts of organisms? Select all that apply.

  a. sand

  b. amber

  c. rock

  d. ice

5. Select all the statements that correctly tell how scientists use tools to dig up fossils. Remember what a paleontologist goes through when they discover a fossil.

_____ Brushes are used to dust away loose material from the fragile surfaces of fossils.

_____ A paleontologist uses a geological hammer or mallet to break fossils into smaller pieces.

_____ Paleontologists take pictures to document the whole process of excavation.

_____ Many fossils are tiny or have very small details. A magnifier allows the paleontologist to look closely.

6. In which type of environment did the organism that left this fossil live?

a. aquatic

b. rock-like

c. terrestrial

d. forest-like

7. Select the correct answer to finish the sentence.

usually	rarely	typical	rare

Fossils of entire organisms are _____.

Scientists _____ only find pieces and parts of once-living things.

8. Which type of environment did this fossil live in?

  a. aquatic

  b. desert

  c. rock-like

  d. terrestrial

9. Number the steps into the correct order most fossils are preserved in rock.

_____ The animal's soft parts decay or get eaten by other animals.

_____ Over time, the animal's bones and other hard parts are

  buried in the mud.

_____ An animal dies and settles to the bottom of the ocean.

_____ The mud hardens and the hard parts become preserved.

10. Which statements are true about this animal?

  a. It is extinct.

  b. It is endangered

  c. It is similar to the elephant.

  d. It is hunted by people.

Weather and Patterns

▷ Explore Online

Unit Project: Safety Plan

How can you prepare for severe weather in your area? Your team will research and make a plan. Ask your teacher for details.

Lightning strikes from clouds to the ground in the continental United States an average of twenty million times a year!

At a Glance

LESSON 1

How Is Weather Measured? 402

LESSON 2

How Can We Predict the Weather? . 422

LESSON 3

What Are Some Severe Weather Impacts? 444

LESSON 4

What Are Some Types of Climates? 466

Unit Review 488

Vocabulary Game: Concentration

Materials • 1 set of word cards

Setup

• Mix up the cards face-down in even rows. Cards should not touch.

Directions

1. Take turns to play. Choose two cards. Turn them face up. If the cards match, keep the pair and take another turn. If the cards do not match, turn them back over.

2. The game is over when all cards have been matched. The player with the most pairs wins.

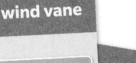

wind vane

wind vane

A tool that measures the direction of the wind.

Unit Vocabulary

atmosphere: The mixture of gases that surround a planet.

climate: The pattern of weather an area experiences over a long period of time.

hazard: Something that can cause damage to a person or property.

precipitation: Water that falls from the sky. Rain, snow, sleet, and hail are kinds of precipitation.

rain gauge: A tool for collecting and measuring precipitation.

thermometer: A tool used to measure temperature.

weather: What is happening in the atmosphere at a certain place and time.

wind vane: A tool that measures the direction of the wind.

How Is Weather Measured?

Some types of weather can bring bright flashes of lightning!

By the end of this lesson . . .
you'll be able to identify types of weather and some of the tools used to measure weather conditions.

Can You Explain It?

▷ Explore Online

Angela is excited. She's going camping for the next three days. But she's not sure what clothes to pack. She wonders what the weather will be like. How can she find out?

1. Think about the kind of clothes Angela will need for the weather that's coming. What should she pack?

_____

_____

_____

_____

_____

_____

 EVIDENCE NOTEBOOK Look for this icon to help you gather evidence to answer the question above.

What's It Like Out?

Observing Weather

Imagine going outside on a sunny morning. The sky is blue. A few fluffy, white clouds are visible. Suddenly, dark clouds appear, and rain pours down. **Weather** is what the air is like outside. Sunshine, wind, and clouds are parts of weather. Rain and snow are weather, too.

Different Weather

2. Use the words *rainy, sunny, snowy, foggy, hot,* or *cold* to describe the weather in each picture.

▷ Explore Online

EVIDENCE NOTEBOOK Record the different weather conditions you saw in the images. In which types of weather would you wear a coat?

Weather occurs in the **atmosphere,** or air around Earth. Weather can be hot or cold, wet or dry, cloudy or clear, windy or still. A strong wind can blow down a tree. A fallen tree is the result of windy weather, but the fallen tree is not a type of weather.

Weather or Not?

3. Circle each word that describes a type of weather. Draw a line through words that describe something caused by weather.

 Ice-covered trees

 Thunderstorm

 Puddle

 Tornado

 Blizzard

 Dry riverbed

Language SmArts
Describing

4. Recall a type of weather that you've been in. Tell what type of weather it was and what it was like. Then tell which parts were weather and which parts were caused by the weather.

_____

_____

_____

Weather Gadgets

Measuring Weather

▷ Explore Online

You know you can observe weather, but did you know that you can measure weather, too? You can measure the amount of **precipitation**—the liquid or solid water that falls from the clouds. You can also measure the direction of the wind and air temperature. If you measure weather over time and compare the data, you can see weather patterns.

This **rain gauge** measures the amount of rain that fell in an area.

This **wind vane** points in the direction from which the wind is blowing.

This **thermometer** measures the air temperature.

5. Write the weather tool next to the measurement that could come from one of the tools listed above.

<u>rain gauge</u> 1 inch

<u>thermometer</u> 75 °F

<u>windvane</u> 88 °F

<u>windwane</u> from the east

<u>thermomet</u> 2 inches

<u>windvr</u> from the south

Wind Pictures

6. The Beaufort wind scale uses numbers and words such as *light breeze* to describe the wind's force. Pictures in the scale show how objects are affected by wind blowing at different speeds.

Research the Beaufort wind scale to find out how many levels of wind it describes. Then draw your own pictures to show four different wind speeds, and answer the question below.

This picture shows no wind.

Circle the highest level on the Beaufort wind scale.

2

8

(12)

16

7. Record the measurement from each tool on the lines below.

_____ inches   from the _____   _____ °F

© Houghton Mifflin Harcourt • Image Credits: (bc) ©Icon Digital Featurepix/Alamy Images; (br) Comstock/Getty Images

EVIDENCE NOTEBOOK In your evidence notebook, list the weather tools shown above. Tell how each tool gives you more information about the weather than when you just step outside to observe it.

How's the Weather?

Observe the weather conditions shown below. Each row shows the weather for a different day.

 Explore Online

Weather Watching

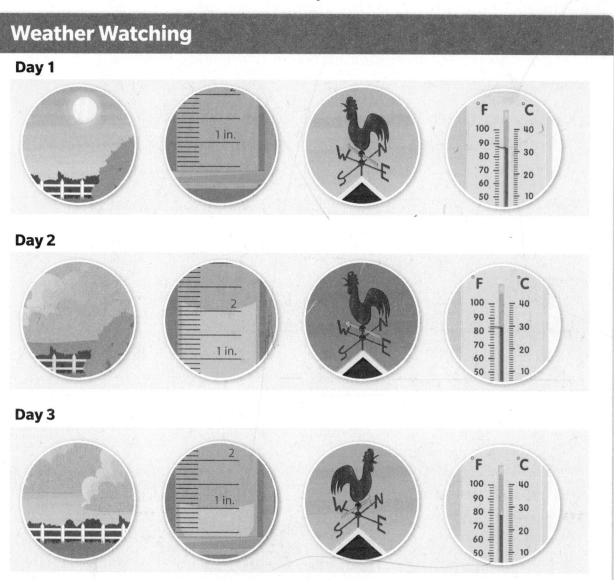

Day 1

Day 2

Day 3

8. Record the data for each day in the table below.

Weather Observations and Measurements				
Day	**Description of sky**	**Amount of rainfall**	**Wind direction**	**Temperature**
Day 1	Sunny	_0_ inches	from the _west_	_88_ °F
Day 2	cloudy	_2_ inches	from the _west_	_82_ °F
Day 3	Windy	_1_ inches	from the _north_	_19_ °F

Do the Math
Analyzing Data

9. Use the data on the opposite page. Answer the questions below. Look at the amount of rainfall for each day. What is the difference between the most and the fewest inches of rainfall?

the difrecence is 2 inches

Look at the wind direction for each day. What wind direction is most common?

west

Look at the temperature for each day. What is the difference between the highest and lowest temperatures?

8 degrees

Language SmArts
Details and Evidence

10. A barometer is also a tool that measures weather. Research what a barometer measures and what that measurement can tell you about the weather. Record your findings on the line below.

_____

_____

_____

Analyzing Weather Data

Objective

Collaborate with your team to observe, measure, and analyze weather data to predict future weather.

What question will you investigate to meet this objective?

_____

_____

Procedure

STEP 1 With your teacher, find a time and place to collect weather data. Be sure to put your weather tools in the same place each day for 5 days.

On what dates will you observe the weather and collect data?

_____

_____

STEP 2 Put your rain gauge where rain can fall into the tube. Leave it outside all day. At the end of each day, read the amount of rainfall. Be sure to record the results at the same time each day. Record the data on your data table. Then empty the gauge to collect rain for the next day.

Where will you put your rain gauge to collect the most accurate data?

_____

STEP 3 Put your wind vane where the wind can blow directly onto the tool. In your data table, record the direction from which the wind is blowing.

How will you record data when the arrow points between two directions?

_____

_____

STEP 4 Put the thermometer in the same place each day at the same time. Wait 10 minutes. Then read the air temperature, and record it in your data table.

STEP 5 In addition to making measurements, you will also observe the weather conditions using your senses. Look at the sky, feel the air, and observe the rain and wind. Record your observations in the data table.

Weather Observations and Measurements				
Date	Observations	Amount of rainfall	Wind direction	Temperature

Analyze Your Results

STEP 6 What weather patterns did you observe over the 5 days?

_____

_____

STEP 7 Compare your data with another student's data. Are your data the same? If not, how can you explain the differences?

_____

_____

Draw Conclusions

STEP 8 You can represent some of your recorded data on a bar graph. Draw a bar graph to show the temperature for each day.

STEP 9 Make a claim about what you expect the temperature to be like for the next five days.

_____

_____

Cite evidence to support your claim.

_____

_____

STEP 10 What other question would you like to ask about weather patterns?

_____

_____

Weather Everywhere

Weather Maps

These maps use color to show weather features. The warmest temperature is shaded orange. The heaviest precipitation is purple.

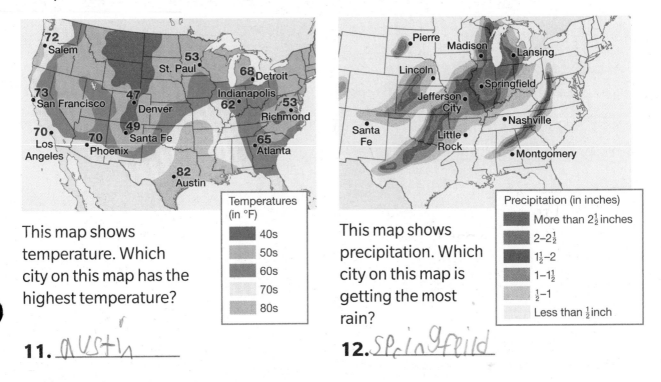

This map shows temperature. Which city on this map has the highest temperature?

Temperatures (in °F)
- 40s
- 50s
- 60s
- 70s
- 80s

11. _Austin_

This map shows precipitation. Which city on this map is getting the most rain?

Precipitation (in inches)
- More than $2\frac{1}{2}$ inches
- 2–$2\frac{1}{2}$
- $1\frac{1}{2}$–2
- 1–$1\frac{1}{2}$
- $\frac{1}{2}$–1
- Less than $\frac{1}{2}$ inch

12. _Springfield_

Engineer It!
Other Weather Tools

Scientists use satellites to help them study and predict weather.

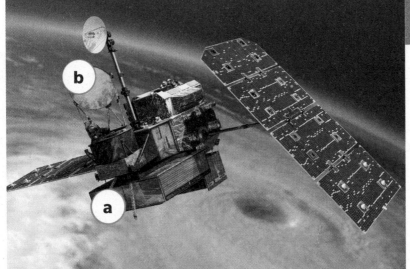

Explore Online

a. This part of the satellite scans, or searches, for precipitation.

b. This part is a precipitation radar. It takes measurements of the rain or snow falling at certain places and times.

Where's the Weather?

The map below shows temperatures across the United States. The key shows the temperature range for each color.

Reading Temperature Maps

13. Fill in the data table below with the temperatures on the map.

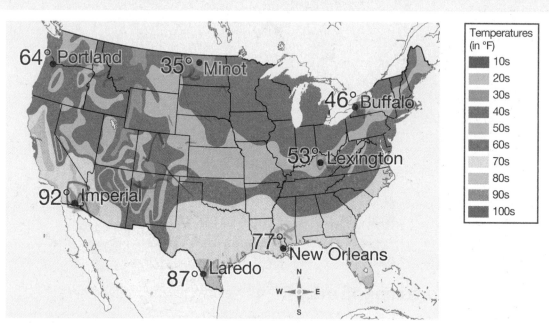

Weather across the United States			
City	New Orleans, LA	Portland, OR	Buffalo, NY
Temperature	77	64	46
Precipitation			

Do the Math
Temperature Changes

14. What is the difference in temperature between the hottest city and coldest city above?

Compare the map for precipitation below to the map on the previous page. Fill in the data chart on the prior page.

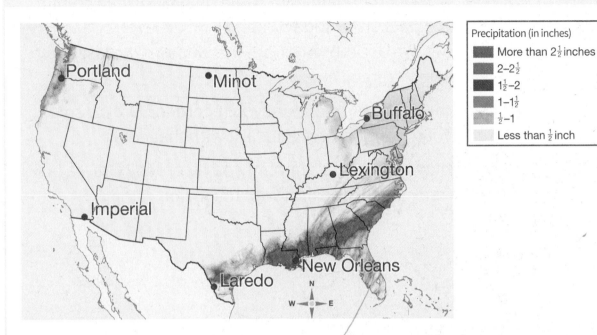

15. What conclusions can you draw from the two maps? Choose all that apply.

   a. A weather map can show the weather for more than one place at a time.

   b. If you know the weather in one city, you know the weather in any other city.

   c. Weather can be different in different locations at the same time.

   d. If two cities have the same kind of precipitation, they always have the same temperature.

EVIDENCE NOTEBOOK Choose one of the cities from the maps on the previous page. Record the weather data for that city in your notebook. Then pretend that Angela, from the beginning of this lesson, is going to that city. Use evidence to describe what she should pack.

Color Your Location

16. Fold a blank piece of paper in half. On one half of the paper, draw a thermometer. On the other half, draw a rain gauge. Research your current weather details so far today. Then fill in the level for each tool to show those details. Use the keys from the maps on the last two pages to complete the steps below.

a. What color shows the temperature you recorded? Draw a small box next to your thermometer, and fill it with that color.

b. What color shows the rainfall amount you recorded? Draw a box next to your rain gauge, and fill it with that color.

Putting It Together

17. Use the bar graphs to answer each question below.

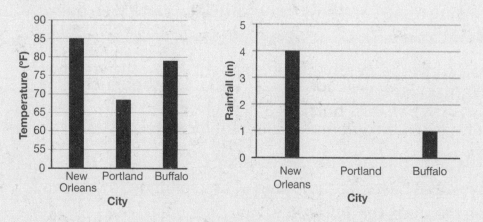

a. Circle the number that shows how much warmer it was in New Orleans than in Buffalo.

5 °F   6 °F   9 °F

b. Circle the number that shows how much more rain fell in New Orleans than in Portland.

2 inches   3 inches   4 inches

Discover More

Check out this path . . . or go online to choose one of these other paths.

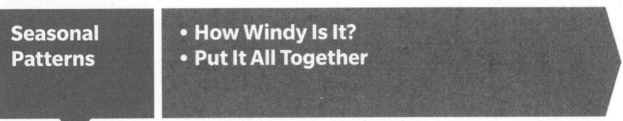

Seasonal Patterns

- How Windy Is It?
- Put It All Together

A Normal Season

Spring is often warm and rainy.

Summer can be very hot.

Fall can be cool and windy.

Winter can be very cold.

Think about different conditions and kinds of weather, such as snow, rain, sunshine, clouds, hurricanes, or tornadoes. The number of times these weather conditions occur is affected by the season and month of year it is. How many times do these types of weather happen each month of the year in your state?

Work with a partner or on your own. Select and research one of these kinds of weather: snowfall, rainfall, sunny days, cloudy days, hurricanes, or tornadoes. Find out how often that weather happened each month during the last year in the state where you live. Enter the numbers in the data table on the next page.

20. Which weather type did you select? _____ Now record your weather data research in the table below.

Month	Number of times this weather type occurred
January	
February	
March	
April	
May	
June	
July	
August	
September	
October	
November	
December	

List the resources you used for your research: _____

_____

21. Collaborate with classmates who researched other types of weather. Use the data to answer these questions.

a. Which season had the most rain? _____

b. Which season was the driest? _____

c. Which season had the most dangerous weather? _____

d. Which month was the sunniest? _____

e. Which month had the most snowfall? _____

f. Which month had the greatest number of cloudy days? _____

LESSON 1
Lesson Check

Name <u>Javion Miles</u>

Can You Explain It?

1. Now that you've learned more about weather, explain how you can use weather information to decide what Angela should pack for her trip. Be sure to do the following:

- Identify types of weather data.

- Describe what different types of weather data tell you.

- Tell how that information helped you decide what Angela should pack.

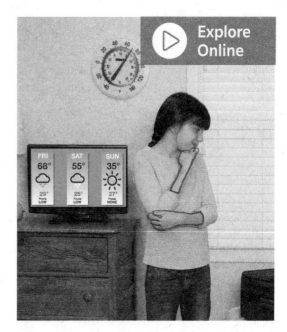

EVIDENCE NOTEBOOK Use the information you've collected in your Evidence Notebook to help you cover each point above.

_____

_____

_____

_____

Checkpoints

2. Label each picture with the name of the tool used to measure the weather condition. If the condition can't be measured with a tool, write *observation* on the line.

<u>rain gage</u>   <u>thermometer</u>   <u>thermometer</u>   <u>windvane</u>

419

3. Record the measurements shown on the lines below each tool.

__thermometer__   __rain gauge__   __Wind vane__

Use the bar graphs to answer questions 4 through 6. Select all correct answers that apply.

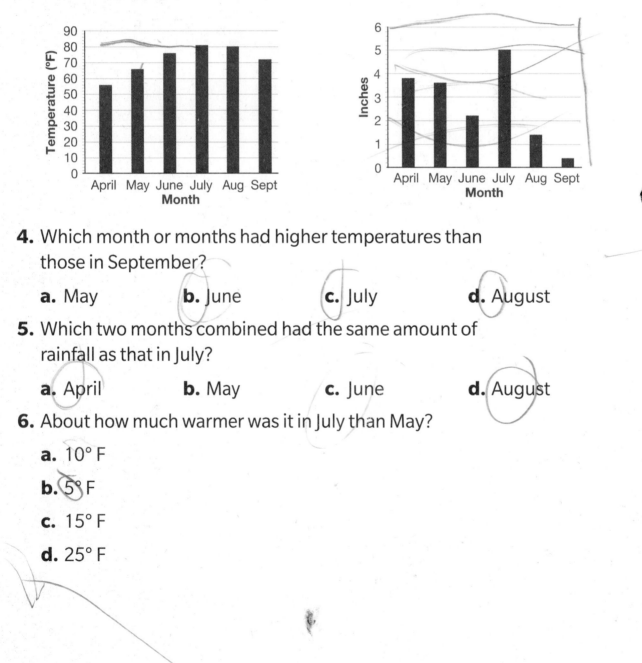

4. Which month or months had higher temperatures than those in September?

a. May   **b.** June   **c.** July   **d.** August

5. Which two months combined had the same amount of rainfall as that in July?

a. April   **b.** May   **c.** June   **d.** August

6. About how much warmer was it in July than May?

a. 10° F

b. 5° F

c. 15° F

d. 25° F

Lesson Roundup

say'inmi'es

A. Circle all the words below that describe types of weather.

a. puddle **b.** fog **c.** rain **d.** tornado

e. cloudy **f.** hail **g.** icicle **h.** fallen tree

B. Read the information from the weather instruments, and record them on the lines.

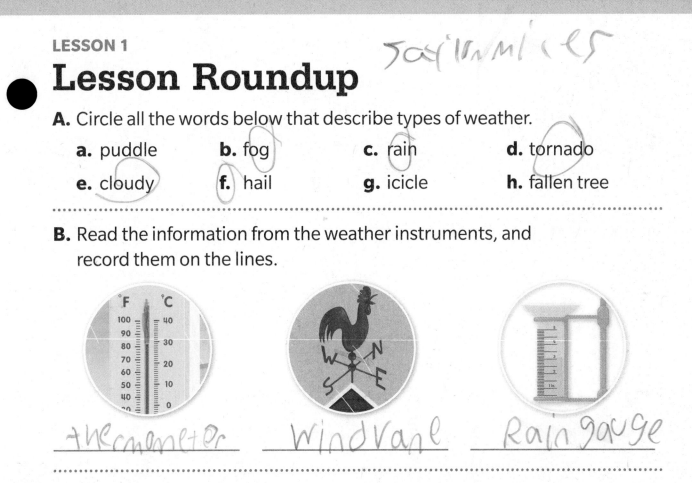

thermometer   windvane   Rain gauge

C. Circle the bar graph that correctly shows the temperature data in the table.

Average High Temperatures	
Month 1	78 °F
Month 2	84 °F
Month 3	90 °F

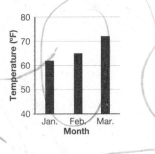

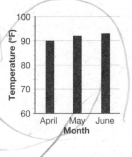

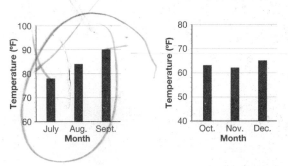

How Can We Predict the Weather?

What clues from this image can tell you what the weather is like there? What do you think the weather will be like in two months?

By the end of this lesson . . .
you'll see how patterns can be used to predict weather.

Can You Explain It?

▶ Explore Online

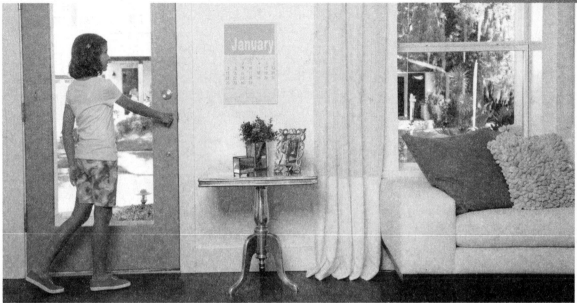

It's January, and Maritza can't wait to go outside to play with her friends. But first, she had to decide what to wear. Did she make a good choice?

1. It is January in the picture, but Maritza is going outside in shorts and a T-shirt. Why did she make this choice? Write your answer on the lines below.

Tip

Learn more about weather in How Is Weather Measured?

_____

_____

_____

_____

_____

_____

 EVIDENCE NOTEBOOK Look for this icon to help you gather evidence to answer the questions above.

Time and Temperature

Things Change

Observe the weather today. Was it the same yesterday or the day before? What about a month ago? Probably not. Weather changes from day to day, week to week, and month to month. Think about how the weather can change.

Look at each month below. The data show the average temperature and precipitation for each month in Chicago.

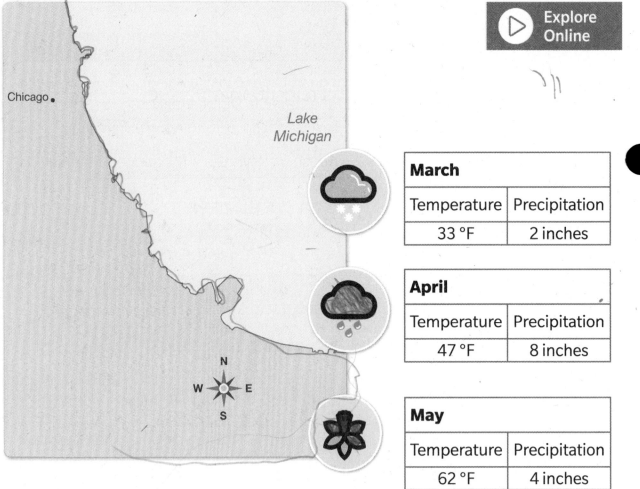

Explore Online

March	
Temperature	Precipitation
33 °F	2 inches

April	
Temperature	Precipitation
47 °F	8 inches

May	
Temperature	Precipitation
62 °F	4 inches

EVIDENCE NOTEBOOK Record the temperature data of Chicago in your Evidence Notebook. Now examine the temperature for each month. What patterns do you notice? Predict what the average temperature will be in Chicago in June.

© Houghton Mifflin Harcourt

2. Language SmArts Look at the data on the previous page. Describe two weather conditions that change over time. Give an example of how these conditions might change over several months.

_____

_____

_____

_____

Do the Math

Using a Map for Math

3. Read each statement about the data from the map on the opposite page. Circle all the statements that are true.

   a. The average temperature in March is 29 °F more than in May.

   b. The total precipitation in March and May is 2 inches less than in the month of April.

   c. The average temperature in May is 15 °F less than in April.

   d. Temperature and precipitation both show the pattern of increasing each month.

   e. The average temperature in April is 14 °F more than in March.

   f. The total precipitation in April is 4 inches more than in May.

4. Use the data from the map to fill in the average precipitation. Then solve each problem.

Month	Average precipitation	Greater than > or less than <	Precipitation this past year
March	2 in.	>	1 in.
April	8 in.	<	9 in.
May	4 inches	<	5 in.

425

Weather Conditions

5. Record the average temperature and precipitation in Chicago during March, April, and May in the table below.

▷ Explore Online

Chicago			
	March	April	May
Average temperature	33°F	47°F	62°F
Average precipitation	2 in.	8 in.	4 in.

Chicago in springtime

6. Use the data in the table to make two bar graphs. One bar graph will show the average temperature data for March, April, and May in Chicago. The other will show precipitation data.

Cities all over the world record weather data every day so that forecasters can look for patterns and use them to make predictions.

HANDS-ON Apply What You Know

Averages in Your Town

7. Research the average temperature and total precipitation for your city during the months of March, April, and May. Make a data table with the information.

Then, make two bar graphs to compare the average temperature and total precipitation within the months.

Putting It Together

8. Look at the bar graph you made for temperature in Chicago. Do you see a pattern? If so, what is it?

_____

_____

_____

Predict the average temperature for Chicago in June. What evidence do you have that supports this prediction?

_____

_____

Do you see any patterns in the precipitation bar graph? Describe what the graph shows.

_____

_____

A Year of Change

Give It a Year

If weather can change over three months, think about how it might change over a whole year. These images show how the weather in Chicago can change within a year. Observe how the weather changes from month to month and season to season.

Chicago's Four Seasons

9. Review the images of weather in Chicago.

▷ Explore Online

January is winter in Chicago. The weather is cold, and snowstorms are common.

March is spring. The weather gets warmer, and strong winds can blow. Warmer weather melts snow and ice.

Thunderstorms roll through the city on hot summer afternoons in July.

Fall begins in September. Some days are cloudy and gray, and temperatures are cool.

10. Circle all of the statements that describe weather throughout the year in Chicago.

a. March can be windy.

b. Snowstorms are common in September.

c. January can be stormy with lots of snow.

d. Hot weather in July can bring afternoon thunderstorms.

11. Wind direction is one weather condition that changes over time. This table shows the most common wind direction in Chicago each month.

Month	Average wind direction
January	West
February	West
March	West
April	South
May	Southwest
June	Southwest
July	Southwest
August	Southwest
September	South
October	South
November	Southwest
December	West

a. Look at the data in the data table. Do you see any patterns?

_____

_____

_____

_____

b. Do the patterns occur during particular seasons?

_____

c. If so, what is the pattern, and in which season did it occur?

_____

_____

_____

_____

Seasonal Changes

Weather conditions such as temperature and precipitation are always changing. Meteorologists measure these conditions every day. They find the average of their measurements and record them in tables like this. Average measurements help us see patterns in the weather. They help us understand how weather changes over time.

Average Temperatures

Use the average temperatures in the data table to answer the questions below.

	Spring	Summer	Autumn	Winter
Year 1	44 °F	71 °F	51 °F	22 °F
Year 2	49 °F	71 °F	55 °F	28 °F
Year 3	51 °F	69 °F	55 °F	29 °F
Year 4	47 °F	72 °F	50 °F	19 °F

12. Which season's data would be the easiest to predict for Year 5? _____

13. What would be a good prediction for this season? _Summer_

14. Which season is most likely to average 60 °F? _____.

15. Which two years were the coolest? _____.

16. Analyze the temperature data in the table. Use it to determine which of these statements is correct. Circle all that apply.

   a. The winter of year 4 was the coldest.

   b. The autumn of year 1 was the warmest.

   c. Year 4 had the warmest summer.

   d. Year 4 had the coolest spring.

17. Pick two years from the table to compare, and draw a bar graph for each.

 EVIDENCE NOTEBOOK Record in your Evidence Notebook the data for the current season. Now research the data for your area in the same season. Compare and contrast the weather data for the two different locations during the same season. Record your observations.

Language SmArts
Compare and Contrast

18. Which weather conditions showed some type of pattern over the seasons? Can those patterns help you predict future weather? If so, how?

_____

_____

_____

_____

Tip

Compare and Contrast
The English Language Arts Handbook can provide help with understanding how to compare and contrast.

HANDS-ON ACTIVITY
Weather Here and There

Objective

Collaborate to research and analyze weather data for a particular location.

What question will you ask about temperature and precipitation change over one season?

_____

_____

Materials

- class map of the United States with specific cities marked
- group map of the United States with specific cities marked
- newspapers or Internet
- graph paper
- colored pencils
- self-stick notes in a variety of colors

Procedure

STEP 1 Your teacher will assign a specific city on the map to your group. Locate the city on the map. What state is your city located in? Is the city close to any major water?

_____

_____

STEP 2 With your group, research the average precipitation and temperature in degrees Fahrenheit for your city during the last 24 months. How did you divide the research within your group?

_____

_____

STEP 3 Record your research in a data table.

STEP 4 Now use your temperature and precipitation data table, graph paper, and colored pencils to build four bar graphs. Make two bar graphs for precipitation, one for each year. Then make two bar graphs for temperature, one for each year.

City: _____

Year 1 Precipitation

Year 2 Precipitation

Year 1 Temperature

Year 2 Temperature

STEP 5 Share your data and
bar graphs with the class. As
other groups are presenting their
data, notice any similarities and
differences between their cities and
your city. List any similarities and
differences between your city and
the other groups' cities.

_____

_____

_____

STEP 6 After all groups have presented their data and graphs,
mark your group map with self-stick notes to show the cities
that have the highest and lowest temperatures over the last
24 months. Then mark the cities that have the most and least
amounts of precipitation. Use the following color code.

- Yellow—least precipitation
- Green—most precipitation
- Pink—highest temperatures
- Blue—lowest temperatures

Look at the cities with the self-stick notes. List observations
or patterns you notice about these cities below.

_____

_____

_____

_____

_____

_____

Analyze Your Results

STEP 7 Use your temperature bar graph, and find another city researched in the class that has similar data. What similarities in locations of the two cities do you notice?

_____

_____

_____

STEP 8 Examine the temperature data for your city. Which season had the warmest weather? Which season had the coolest temperature?

_____

_____

_____

Draw Conclusions

STEP 9 Choose one month out of the year. Look at all the precipitation data for that month for your city. State a claim about what the precipitation will be next year for the month you chose.

_____

_____

_____

STEP 10 Choose one month out of the year. Look at all the temperature data for that month for your city. What would you expect the temperature to be next year for the month you chose? Cite evidence for your claim.

_____

_____

_____

Predicting Weather

Finding Patterns

Consider the patterns in weather data you collected for cities around the country. Some cities may get a lot of rain in the fall. Other cities might get most of their precipitation in the spring. You can use these patterns to make predictions about the weather.

Temperature Patterns

19. Look at the table. Some data are missing. Use the patterns you observe in the given data to determine the missing data. Select from the choices in the box.

▶ **Explore Online**

| 79 °F | 63 °F | 56 °F | 80 °F | 60 °F | 30 °F | 44 °F | 14 °F |

Monthly Average Temperature (°F)				
	Riverside, CA		**Anchorage, AK**	
	Year 1	Year 2	Year 1	Year2
January	53	53	13	14
February	55		17	
March	60	60	30	22
April	63		33	35
May	65	69		46

Anchorage, AK

📋 **EVIDENCE NOTEBOOK** Examine the data from the table showing temperatures in Riverside, California, and Anchorage, Alaska. Observe how the temperature changes for each month and year. What other pattern do you notice between the two years? Write your observation in your Evidence Notebook.

20. The table below shows monthly precipitation totals for two cities across two years . Look for patterns in this table. Then use your observations to answer the questions below.

Total Monthly Precipitation (inches)				
	Fargo, ND		Portland, ME	
	Year 1	Year 2	Year 1	Year2
January	1	0	3	2
February	1	1	8	3
March	1	5	6	3
April	2	1	4	5
May	2	2	1	5

Portland, ME

21. Which city receives more precipitation for these months? Does temperature or precipitation show a more predictable pattern?

_____

_____

22. Language SmArts Why is it important to collect data about the weather? How do we use these data in our everyday lives?

_____

_____

_____

East and West Coast Weather

Look at the bar graphs below. One graph represents average temperatures in Philadelphia, Pennsylvania, on the east coast of the United States. The other bar graph shows precipitation in Honolulu, Hawaii, in the Pacific Ocean.

Philadelphia, Pennsylvania

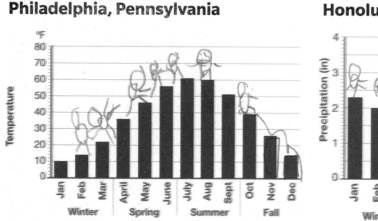

Honolulu, Hawaii

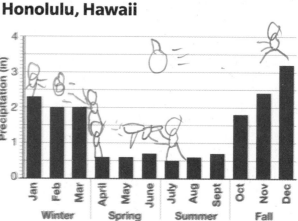

Putting It Together

23. Use information from the bar graphs to circle the best prediction for temperature and precipitation from the statements.

Temperature

a. The high temperature in February will be higher than the temperature in November.

b. The high temperature in July will be about 20 °F less than the high temperature in August.

c. The high temperature in November will be higher than the temperature in December.

Precipitation

d. January will have more precipitation than October.

e. The average precipitation in May will be about 5 inches more than in June.

f. February will have less precipitation than June.

Discover More

Check out this path . . . or go online to choose one of these other paths.

People in Science & Engineering

• **Weather Outside of the United States**
• **National Weather Patterns**

People in Science and Engineering

Pam Heinselman, Meteorologist

Pam Heinselman is a meteorologist. Her research deals with using a special type of radar to predict weather changes and the need for weather warnings. Understanding and knowing sooner when hazardous weather may occur helps people prepare earlier for disastrous weather.

Pam Heinselman

24. What else would you like to know about how technology helps with weather warnings? List your questions below.

_____

_____

_____

In 2010, Lidia Cucurull won an award for her contributions to predicting weather more precisely. Meteorologists, like Lidia, have used satellites for years to help predict and inform people what the weather will be in the near future. However, through years of research and observations, Lidia developed a system that uses radio signals from Global Positioning System (GPS) satellites. This system helps to predict the weather with more accuracy and for a longer time period.

Lidia Cucurull

25. Compare and contrast the contributions between Pam Heinselman and Lidia Cucurull below.

_____

_____

_____

_____

_____

_____

_____

_____

Lesson Check

Name _____

Can You Explain It?

1. Think back to the beginning of this lesson. What can you say about Maritza's choice of clothing for the season and weather? Be sure to do the following:

Explore Online

- Consider what you know about weather in different locations.

- Consider how patterns of data can help you make predictions.

EVIDENCE NOTEBOOK Use the information you've collected in your Evidence Notebook to help you cover each point above.

_____

_____

_____

_____

_____

Checkpoints

Circle the best answer to the question.

2. Which of these would help you to predict average weather conditions in a certain place?

   a. Knowing what the weather was like on that day 100 years ago.

   b. Observing how weather patterns repeat year after year.

   c. Finding the highest and lowest temperature in each month.

Use the data tables to answer the questions below.

3. Predict which months are most likely to have snow next year. It must be 32°F or below for snow to occur. Circle all that apply.

a. February

b. December

c. April

d. September

e. January

4. Predict which months will have the hottest temperatures next year.

a. August, September, October

b. May, June, July

c. June, July, August

d. November, December, January

5. Predict which months will have the least precipitation next year.

a. September, October, November

b. March, April, May

c. June, July, August

d. December, January, February

6. The data show that the rainiest part of the year begins in the month of

_____ and ends in the month

of _____. _____ and

_____ are the months most likely to have about 8 inches of rain next year.

Denver, Colorado

Month	Average temperature
January	31 °F
February	32 °F
March	48 °F
April	50 °F
May	57 °F
June	67 °F
July	74 °F
August	72 °F
September	62 °F
October	50 °F
November	39 °F
December	30 °F

Miami, Florida

Month	Total precipitation
January	2 inches
February	2 inches
March	3 inches
April	3 inches
May	5 inches
June	10 inches
July	7 inches
August	9 inches
September	10 inches
October	6 inches
November	3 inches
December	2 inches

Lesson Roundup

A. You look at the data for average Chicago temperature each month. You see average temperatures of 47 °F, 59 °F, and 70 °F. Which three months are you most likely looking at?

a. March, April, May

b. July, August, September

c. August, September, October

d. September, October, November

| prove | explain | changes | compare |

B. Bar graphs can help you _explain_ data. Reviewing data in the bar graphs can help you _compare_ patterns. Looking

at those patterns can show you how the data _changes_

over a year. These patterns can be used as evidence to help you

prove your claims about what will happen next.

C. Which shows a pattern in weather data? Circle the best answer.

a. total precipitation of 4 inches in June

b. average temperature of 50 °F in June, 65 °F in July, and 60 °F in August

c. average temperature of 60 °F in July and 39 °F in November

d. record-high precipitation of 10 inches in August

What Are Some Severe Weather Impacts?

Severe weather such as this ice storm is common in winter.

By the end of this lesson . . .
you'll be able to identify hazardous weather and critically examine solutions to problems caused by that weather.

Can You Explain It?

▷ Explore Online

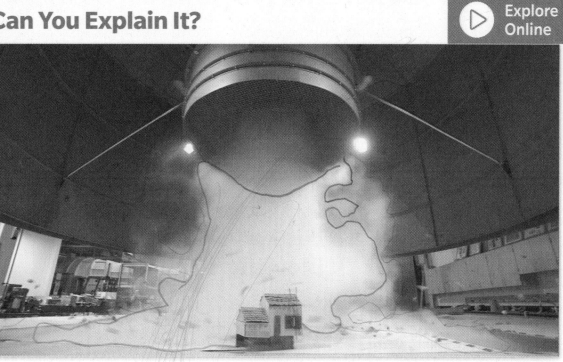

This machine makes air swirl over the roof of this model house.

1. What do you think the machine in this picture is for? Why is it swirling air over the top of the model house? Write your answers below.

Tip

Learn more about weather in How Is Weather Measured? and How Can We Predict the Weather?

_____

_____

_____

_____

_____

_____

EVIDENCE NOTEBOOK Look for this icon to help you gather evidence to answer the questions above.

© Houghton Mifflin Harcourt

445

Cause and Effect Weather

Severe Weather Threats

Some effects of weather are hard to see. Other effects of weather are seen every day. And even more effects are quite easy to see. Try this mini-activity and think about what type of weather effect you are modeling.

HANDS-ON Apply What You Know

The Answer Is Blowing in the Wind

2. Place a sheet of paper on your desk. Blow gently on the paper. Record your observations. Now blow with more strength. What did you observe this time? How did the force you used to blow on the paper affect what happened to the paper? How might the strength of the wind during a storm affect objects in the environment? Repeat the activity with a textbook. Record your observations and explain any differences.

Severe weather is any type of weather that can harm people or property. See the photos below and on the next page to learn about some types of severe weather.

A tornado is a swirling column of fast-moving air. Tornadoes form when cold and warm air meet, causing the air to rotate. They can damage property and hurt people. Some tornadoes are much stronger, faster, and more violent than others. They are most common in spring and fall.

Hurricanes are huge storms with heavy rain and winds of 74 mph or more that form over oceans. When they move over land, the winds and rising waters can cause flooding and major damage. Hurricanes are most common in summer and fall.

Lightning is the biggest danger in thunderstorms. Some lightning strikes cause injuries and even deaths. Lightning often hits objects and causes fires. A direct hit from lightning can split trees.

A blizzard is a big winter snowstorm with strong winds and blowing snow. Winds in a blizzard reach 35 mph or more. Blowing snow can make it hard to see. Ice can make roads slippery. Many car and truck accidents result from icy roads and blowing snow.

3. Language SmArts Think about the severe weather you just saw in the photos. Which types of severe weather do you have where you live?

Weather Makes It Happen

Severe weather can bring all kinds of risks. Different areas have different types of severe weather. Most tornadoes occur in the United States. In fact, the central part of the United States is called Tornado Alley. In the United States, hurricanes threaten the Gulf coast and east coast in summer and early fall. Hurricanes can damage wide areas. People who live where severe weather occurs need to be prepared.

 EVIDENCE NOTEBOOK Look at the images on the previous pages again and group types of severe weather that cause similar types of damage. Can you tell which type of severe weather has occurred based on the evidence from the effects of that weather?

Sort It Out

4. Look at the pictures of the damage severe weather can cause. On the lines below, write the type of weather that may have caused the damage. Some types of damage belong with more than one type of weather.

Hurricane   Blizzard

Blizzerd

thundecstorm

thundecstorm

thundecstorm

Putting It Together

5. Circle the correct answer.

a. Which type of severe weather can create damage over the largest area?

thunderstorm   tornado

hurricane   ice storm

b. Which types of severe weather have strong winds? Circle all that apply.

hurricane   tornado

blizzard   ice storm

Using the Data

How Scientists Do It

Scientists who study the weather are called meteorologists. They collect data about weather that has already happened to help them predict future weather events.

Meteorologists want to predict severe weather accurately. Most severe weather also brings weather hazards. A **hazard** is something that can cause damage to a person or property.

Weather radar and satellites help meteorologists see weather that is currently happening. They can also see which direction the weather is headed. This helps them see where severe weather is going to strike.

 EVIDENCE NOTEBOOK What types of weather are more likely to occur in your area? Make a list of the weather types. You'll use this list later in the lesson, so leave room for notes.

Name that Weather

Think about what you already know about severe weather. Read the city profiles for three cities on this page and the next pages. Then answer the questions based on the information given.

Weather in St. Louis

- Because it is in the middle of the United States, St. Louis has had many tornadoes. The worst one was in 1896.
- On January 30–31 in 1982, St. Louis suffered through a blizzard that dropped 13 inches of snow. Drifts piled 6–7 feet high.
- On average St. Louis has thunderstorms 48 days every year.

It's hot for a fall day in St. Louis—80 °F and sunny. In late afternoon, the white puffy clouds grow taller and darker. The sun disappears and gusty winds start to blow. Heavy rain falls and thunder follows flashes of lightning. Within an hour, the rain has stopped and the sun is shining again.

6. What is one reason St. Louis has many tornadoes?

_____

7. What kind of severe weather was described in the paragraph?

_____ Blizzerd tornad thunderstorm

8. What possible weather hazards did the people of St. Louis have to deal with in the storm? Circle all that apply.

    a. lightning   **c.** flooding

    b. icy roads   **d.** strong winds

9. List one way you may stay safe during this type of weather.

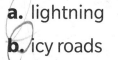

caror house

Weather in Jacksonville

- In the summer months, it rains almost half the days in Jacksonville.
- On average in Jacksonville, it drops below freezing temperature only 15 days a year.
- In January 2010, there was a very light snow in Jacksonville.

In Jacksonville, the day begins with a sky covered by low, gray clouds. It's 70 °F outside, and there is light rain as winds begin to gust. As the warm day continues, clouds thicken, winds increase, and rain pours down. By mid-afternoon, winds are howling outside at almost 80 mph and floodwaters come ashore from the Atlantic Ocean.

10. What is the most likely season in the paragraph and why?

Summer

11. What kind of severe weather did Jacksonville just experience?

Bthunderstorm

12. What possible hazards did the people of Jacksonville have to deal with? Circle all that apply.

a. (flooding)   **c.** (strong winds)

b. icy roads   **d.** freezing temperatures

13. Think about ways you may stay safe during this type of weather. List one way.

house or shelter

Weather in Denver

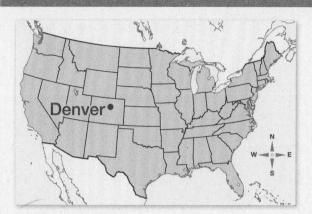

- In Denver, the temperature falls below freezing on average 156 days per year.
- On average in Denver, there are 33 days with snow.
- On average, there are five tornadoes in the Denver area every year.

It's a cold day in Denver that begins with snow flurries. The snow falls harder and faster throughout the morning. Winds pick up and are soon blowing at 48 mph. The wind blows the snow so hard that the air appears white. Streets become slippery. Soon, snow piles up on roads and against houses.

14. On average, how many below freezing days do not have snow?

_____

15. What kind of weather did the people of Denver just experience?

_____

16. Which hazard do the people of Denver face most often?

    a. flooding   **c.** tornadoes

    b. blizzards   **d.** temperatures below freezing

Putting It Together

17. Research another city, and identify severe weather that happens there. Write the name of the city below. What is the best way to stay safe during severe weather there? Explain your reasoning.

_____

_____

HANDS-ON ACTIVITY
Smashing Floods

Objective

Collaborate with a partner to engineer flood protection. Flooding is a big hazard of severe weather. Imagine you must find a way to protect your community from flooding.

What question will you investigate to meet this objective?

_____

_____

Materials

- water table or 9 x 12 pan
- sand
- water
- containers for pouring water
- model house
- small stones
- plastic straws
- strips of fabric

Procedure

STEP 1 With a partner, determine your project's plan or goal.

What problem do you want your design to solve?

_____

_____

STEP 2 List the criteria. How will you know it works? Then describe any constraints, or limits, of your plan.

_____

_____

_____

STEP 3   Sketch at least two design plans. Share your designs with a classmate. Then choose the one you think is best.

Which design did you choose and why ?

_____

_____

STEP 4   Build your design. Describe in writing how you can test your design. Then test it.

_____

_____

STEP 5   Use the results of your test to identify ways to improve your design. Exchange your improved design ideas with a classmate. Review your classmate's improved design. Identify other ways the design might be improved. How will you improve your design?

_____

_____

STEP 6   Change your design to include any of your classmate's suggestions that you think will make it better. Test your design again to see whether it works better than before. Take pictures to show the test and its results. How does your design compare to the designs of other students.

_____

_____

Analyze your Results

Enter your answers on the lines below each question.

STEP 7 What part of your design worked best when tested?

_____

_____

STEP 8 What part of your design didn't work when tested?

_____

_____

STEP 9 What is one part you would change before retesting your flood protection?

_____

_____

Draw Conclusions

STEP 10 Make a claim about the most effective part of your design.

_____

_____

_____

STEP 11 Cite evidence to support your claim.

_____

_____

_____

Reducing Risk

Engineering for Weather

We can't stop severe weather. But people can design solutions that protect people and property from severe weather. You know that a hazard is a danger. People can find different ways to minimize weather hazards. Engineers work to design structures to reduce the amount of damage caused by severe weather. For example, to stop water from coming into a building in a hurricane, walls on the first level can be made of brick or stone that will hold up to floodwaters.

When the conditions are just right, precipitation falls as ice instead of rain or snow. Heavy ice covers trees, power lines, streets, sidewalks, and bridges.

Icy weather is very hazardous, especially for driving.

© Houghton Mifflin Harcourt • Image Credits: (b) ©CristiNistor/iStock/Getty Images Plus/Getty Images; (t) ©Alissa Sanderson/Getty Images

Severe Weather Solutions

So how do engineers solve the issue of icy roads during ice storms? Here's one way some engineers want to handle it.

Solar roadways and sidewalks are designed with solar panels that you can drive, walk, and park on. Engineers hope that the panels will be able to store energy from the sun that can melt ice and snow. They are still testing to make sure that the roads can stand up to heavy traffic and that all of the features of the roadway work correctly.

 18. Language SmArts Imagine your school is in an area where blizzards are common. Identify two structures in your neighborhood that might take damage from the ice and snow. Then tell how you would redesign the structures to handle ice and snow.

_____

_____

_____

19. Look at the solutions for some severe weather hazards below. Try to identify the cause and effect that these objects solve.

A lightning rod is a metal rod attached to a tall building or structure. It is designed to attract lightning during a thunderstorm and direct the energy safely to the ground.

Cause: _____

Effect: _____

A snowplow is designed to drive through snow while pushing the snow to one side of the road. Some snowplows also spread salt on roads to help melt ice and snow.

Cause: _____

Effect: _____

EVIDENCE NOTEBOOK Look back at the severe types of weather in your area. What sort of engineered features are used to keep the people and property in your area safe? How do those features work?

Select the Best

The solutions on the previous pages help protect people and property from the hazards of severe weather. Each has benefits. Yet there are also drawbacks. For example, a snowplow removes mounds of snow from streets. But it dumps the snow in piles that can block sidewalks or trap parked cars on the sides of roads.

20. Think about the solar roadway you saw earlier. Research more about it. Decide whether you think it's a good solution or a bad solution. Write your answer below, and explain your reasoning.

_____

_____

_____

Language SmArts
Research

21. Which solution do you think is best at protecting people from the hazards of severe storms? Explain your choice. Discuss the benefits and drawbacks of the solution and its design.

_____

_____

_____

22. Research another tool that solves the same problem and compare them. Which works better and why?

_____

_____

© Houghton Mifflin Harcourt • Image Credits: ©Wiskerke/Alamy

Tip

Research
The English Language Arts Handbook can provide help with understanding how to research.

Discover More

Check out this path . . . or go online to choose one of these other paths.

Careers in Science & Engineering

- **Reporting Severe Weather**
- **Historical Weather Patterns**

Careers in Science and Engineering

Explore Online

Hurricane Hunters

Why would anyone fly into a hurricane? Hurricane hunters do exactly that to collect data from inside the storm. The data goes into computers that predict the strength of hurricanes and where they will go.

Hurricane hunting started in 1943 during the height of World War II. A hurricane struck Houston, Texas near an airfield where British and American pilots were learning how to fly. Some of the pilots decided to see whether the planes would hold up to the powerful winds. American pilot Colonel Joseph Duckworth and his navigator, Lieutenant Ralph O'Hair, flew into the center of the hurricane and back out in an AT-6 Texan airplane.

By 1946, the Air Force had started a hurricane hunter program. Because their planes can fly above the eye of the hurricane, they can observe and measure the size of the storm. Because the planes were made to fly very long distances, they can take off and land far from the dangerous area created by the hurricane. And because the early planes were large and made to carry a few people and a lot of cargo, they could have all sorts of instruments to measure the hurricane weather.

When a dropsonde is dropped from an airplane, it slowly measures and tracks weather conditions as it falls to Earth.

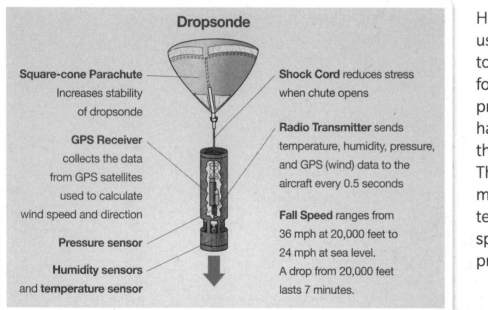

Dropsonde

Square-cone Parachute
Increases stability of dropsonde

GPS Receiver
collects the data from GPS satellites used to calculate wind speed and direction

Pressure sensor

Humidity sensors and **temperature sensor**

Shock Cord reduces stress when chute opens

Radio Transmitter sends temperature, humidity, pressure, and GPS (wind) data to the aircraft every 0.5 seconds

Fall Speed ranges from 36 mph at 20,000 feet to 24 mph at sea level. A drop from 20,000 feet lasts 7 minutes.

Hurricane hunters use a dropsonde to collect data so forecasters can predict what will happen during the hurricane. The dropsonde measures altitude, temperature, wind speed, and air pressure.

22. Suppose you could meet a hurricane hunter. List three questions you would ask. Research and record answers to your questions.

i would ask them how do they survive a hurricane. what doo you need to survive a hurricane.

Lesson Check

Name _____ 76%C

Can You Explain It?

1. Now that you know more about severe weather, explain what was happening to the building at the beginning of the lesson. Be sure to do the following:

   • Identify the type of weather.

   • Identify the feature being tested.

   • Tell how this testing helps keep people safe from severe weather.

EVIDENCE NOTEBOOK Use the information you've collected in your Evidence Notebook to help you answer these questions.

_____

_____

_____

_____

_____

Checkpoints

2. Which types of damage would be caused by a hurricane? Circle all that apply.

   a. slippery, icy roads

   b. trees knocked down by strong winds

   c. snow piled high on streets

   d. flooded streets

3. Choose the correct word from the word bank to complete the sentences.

We can record patterns of weather to make

Predictions about what kind of weather might

happen next. Meteorologists issue warnings about

nice weather to help people protect

themselves and their _Property_ from harm.

criteria

data

predictions

good

severe

nice

property

designs

4. Which types of damage could be the effect of a tornado? Circle all that apply.

a. rivers overflowing their banks

b. roads washed away by flooding

c. trees torn out of the ground

d. buildings with crumbled walls

5. Which of these could reduce the impact of severe weather? Circle all that apply.

a. sandbags piled up along a flooding river

b. plows working the streets after a blizzard

c. cutting grass before a thunderstorm

d. lightning rods

6. Your friend designs a jacket for staying dry during heavy rain. It is made out of yellow cloth and has a collar but no hood. Which changes to the design would make the jacket work better in heavy rain? Circle all that apply.

a. add a hood to keep your head dry

b. add stripes that reflect light so people can see you

c. make the jacket out of black cloth

d. add a way to make the cuffs on the wrist fit tighter

e. make the jacket out of waterproof material

LESSON 3
Lesson Roundup

A. Choose the correct word from the word bank to complete each sentence.

| winds |
| blizzards |
| slippery |
| flooding |

Hurricanes bring long periods of heavy rain that can cause ~~winds~~. Damage from tornadoes comes mostly from strong ~~flooding~~. Ice storms cause car accidents because of _slippery_ roads. Heavy snow blocks roads during _blizzerd_.

B. Which of these tools would a meteorologist use to predict severe weather? Circle the best answers. There may be more than one.

1. radar
2. rain gauge
3. satellite
4. data from previous years
5. researching when the sun sets

C. Label each image with the severe weather type the tool helps with.

_____ _____ _____ _____

What Are Some Types of Climates?

The temperature and weather patterns where these blue penguins thrive would not be good for many other organisms.

By the end of this lesson . . .
you'll recognize weather patterns from different parts of the world.

Can You Explain It?

 Explore Online

The blue penguin lives on the coasts of Australia and New Zealand. The size of the blue penguin's habitat is being reduced in some areas. Building a preserve somewhere else could help.

1. Where would be a good location for scientists to start a preserve to relocate the blue penguins?

_____

_____

_____

_____

_____

 EVIDENCE NOTEBOOK Look for this icon to help you gather evidence to answer the question above.

Out of Place

Different Birds, Different Homes

Different penguins live in different places around the world. The map shows where two species of penguin live. Notice how the emperor penguin and the blue penguin look the same. How do they look different? Also compare their habitats. How are the places where they live alike or different?

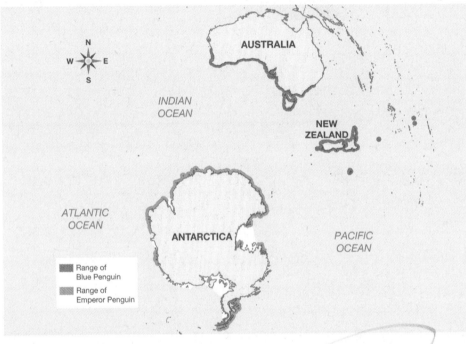

This map shows where the penguins live.

Emperor penguins are the largest penguin species, standing about 114 cm tall. Emperors live on the frozen coast of Antarctica. They fish for food in icy waters. Emperor penguins live on the open ice during the harsh winter. They huddle in large groups to keep warm. Antarctica also has cold summers.

The blue penguin is the smallest penguin species. They are also called fairy penguins or little penguins. Blue penguins stand only about 33 cm tall—about one-third the size of the emperor penguin. They live on the southern coast of Australia and on the coast of New Zealand. They make nests in burrows on coastal sand dunes or in openings between rocks on the shore. Like other penguins, blue penguins eat fish that they catch in coastal waters.

EVIDENCE NOTEBOOK Think about how these two types of penguins are different. How do their environments differ? List the ways each penguin is suited to its climate.

2. Language SmArts Recall that the habitat of some blue penguins is being reduced. One way people could help the penguins is to relocate them. Emperor penguins live in Antarctica. Could the blue penguins be relocated to Antarctica, too? Use evidence from the text to explain the reasoning for your answer.

_____

_____

_____

_____

_____

Feels Like Home

Climate is the normal weather in an area over a long period of time. When you say that it is warm outside today, you are describing weather. When you say that the weather is usually warm in summer, you are describing climate.

View the photos. They show various locations in New Zealand throughout the year. As you look at the photos, think about the climate where the blue penguin lives. What is it like?

The penguins live in a part of New Zealand with a mild climate. The normal high winter temperature is about 53 °F. Winter is the wettest season.

Normal daytime spring temperatures in northern New Zealand are about 60 °F. Coastal wildflowers in the penguin's nesting area start to bloom in spring.

The penguins on the northern coast of New Zealand have a different climate. Their summers are warm and have a lot of rain. Summers are warm and dry in southern Australia.

Days become cooler in fall on the northern coast of New Zealand. But temperatures stay mild, and clouds bring many days of rain.

3. Use the descriptions from the photos to describe the type of climate in which blue penguins need to live. Be sure to consider each season.

_____

_____

_____

You learned about climate areas where different penguins live. These small areas are part of much larger climate zones. Each of Earth's climate zones has different patterns of weather. You can see the different climate zones on this map.

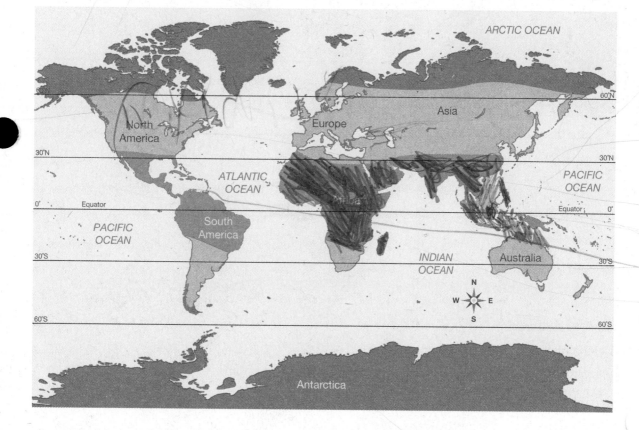

4. Observe the climate zones on the map. Describe any patterns you see.

_____

_____

Climate Is Everywhere

Observe Earth's climate zones again below. Each climate zone has certain overall features. However, areas within each zone can have different features than what is normal. Use the descriptions below to map the letters to the zones.

Zones

5. Use the map and the descriptions of each climate zone below to complete the activity at the top of the next page.

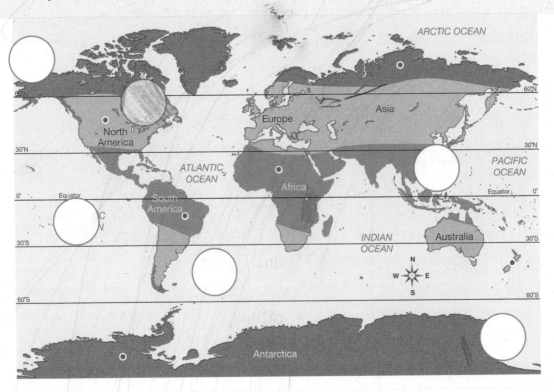

Tropical Zones

These zones are the hottest. It is hot or warm all year. The part of the zone near the equator has heavy rain throughout the year. Parts farther from the equator have a wet season and a dry season.

Temperate Zones

These zones have hot or warm summers and cool or cold winters. Precipitation falls as both rain and snow in some places in the zones. Other parts are dry.

Polar Zones

These climate zones are the coldest. They have cold winters and cool summers. Precipitation is usually light, and most of it is snow.

Write the name of the climate zone being described on the line beneath each description. Then use the letters to mark the zones on the map on the previous page.

a. This climate zone is so cold that most precipitation is frozen.

Poler

b. This climate zone is hot in summer, fall, and winter.

tempeate

c. Winters are cold and summers are hot here.

Tropical

d. People in this zone see both rain and snow during the year.

Temperate

e. Summers are cool or cold in this zone.

Poler

f. At the center of this zone, heavy rain is common.

Tropical

 EVIDENCE NOTEBOOK Examine the map of the climate zones for patterns. What do you notice about where each zone is on the map? How can you use this information about the climate pattern to help locate a new location for the penguins?

6. Circle the temperature and precipitation description that describes each climate zone. Go back and look at the climate zone descriptions if you need to.

Climate zone	Temperature	Precipitation
Polar	• Cold or cool all year • Cold only in winter	• Light rain in the winter • Precipitation is mostly snow.
Temperate	• Hot summers, warm winters • Hot or warm summers, cool or cold winters	• Wet summers, dry winters • Wet and dry areas; snow can fall in winter.
Tropical	• Hot or warm all year • Hot summers, cold winters	• Light or no precipitation • Heavy rain all year near the area between the zones

In the Zone

How can you figure out which climate zone a place is in? If you have a map, you can look at its location. You can also observe temperature and precipitation patterns.

Far and Away

7. Look at the temperature and precipitation data for each city below. Label the climate zone for each city.

 Explore Online

Nairobi is a city in Kenya, a country in eastern Africa. Nairobi is in the mountains, which makes the weather a little different from that in surrounding areas. Cities that are in the mountains are cooler than nearby cities. It usually gets most of its rain in the spring.

- High temperature: 83 °F in summer
- Low temperature: 53 °F in winter
- Highest amount of precipitation: 5.9 in. in November
- Lowest amount of precipitation: 0.6 in. in July

Climate zone: _____

Upernavik is a town in Greenland. It is on the coast of Baffin Bay. People might need coats in the middle of summer in Upernavik, but they rarely need umbrellas.

- High temperature: 46 °F in summer
- Low temperature: −10 °F in winter
- Highest amount of precipitation: 1.1 in. in July
- Lowest amount of precipitation: 0.3 in. in March

Climate zone: _____

Explain the Zones

8. Get a ball about the size of a globe. Make a model of Earth by marking the north pole, equator, and south pole. Touch all of the areas that you marked, and record whether each location was cool or warm.

Your teacher will use a hair dryer to direct hot air toward the equator on the model for one minute. Do not put the ball too close to the hair dryer. Predict how the temperature will change in each location.

After one minute, touch each location again. How did the temperature change in each zone? Was one area warmer than another? Consider your results and make a claim about what may cause different climate zones on Earth. Cite your evidence.

 Language SmArts
Details and Evidence

9. In which climate zones do you think the emperor penguin and the blue penguin live? Give evidence to support your reasoning.

_____

_____

_____

_____

Tip

The English Language Arts Handbook can provide help with understanding how to provide details and evidence.

Looking for a New Home

Objective

Collaborate with your team to determine a new location for blue penguins.

What question will you investigate to meet this objective?

_____

_____

Procedure

STEP 1 With a small group, choose a location from the map. Each group should select a different location. Which location will you research and why?

_____

_____

_____

STEP 2 Research the climate in your location. Also research the climate in Adelaide, Australia. Find monthly data for temperature and precipitation for one year. Record the data from both locations in a table. How will these data help you determine whether this is a good location?

_____

_____

STEP 3 Write the location and climate data on a self-stick note. Place the self-stick note on the map near your location. What type of climate zone is your location in?

_____

_____

_____

STEP 4 Look at your data for all locations on the map along with the climate data for Adelaide. Which location has the most similar temperature patterns? Which location has the most similar rain patterns?

_____

_____

Analyze Your Results

STEP 5 Discuss your comparisons with another group. Decide which locations would not work as a habitat for the blue penguins and eliminate those locations. Which locations did you eliminate?

_____

_____

STEP 6 Choose any locations with a climate closest to Adelaide. With your group, research five more years of data to determine the climate patterns of the place you chose. Which location did you choose? Would the climate in the area support a penguin colony?

_____

_____

STEP 7 Reread the description for the climate zone of your location. Notice any differences in your city's data and the description. Also look at the other self-stick notes on the map. Are there climate differences within the zones? If so, what do you think causes the differences?

_____

_____

STEP 8 Which climate zone type is Adelaide in?

_____

STEP 9 Do any of the locations on the map match Adelaide's climate data? If so, which one and why?

_____

_____

Draw Conclusions

STEP 10 Make a claim about how patterns in data can help you interpret that data, using weather as an example.

_____

_____

_____

STEP 11 How did analyzing patterns in data help you find a good location to relocate the blue penguin? Cite evidence to support your answer.

_____

_____

Something Different

Survival

Like all living things, plants get what they need to survive from their environment. Different types of plants need different amounts of water. They also grow better at different temperatures.

Precipitation and temperature are two factors that vary depending on the type of climate. So it makes sense that different climates support different types of plants.

Engineer It!
Artificial Climate

Sometimes people want to grow plants where the climate does not naturally support them. For those places, engineers can design artificial climates. The artificial climate must supply the plants with the water, gases, and temperature, as well as the light, they need.

The International Space Station has an artificial climate that supports astronauts and allows them to experiment with growing plants.

The research about growing plants in space might lead to gardening in artificial habitats on Mars. Then people who travel to Mars could grow food.

10. What are some problems that the designer of an artificial climate for plants needs to solve?

_____

_____

Not Always the Same

Most of the time, the climate for a location stays similar from year to year. Sometimes the weather does not follow the normal pattern. Look at the images below. They show three ways this can happen.

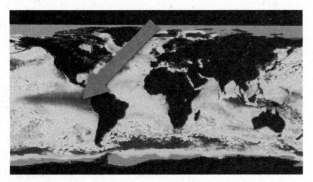

El Niño occurs when waters in the Pacific Ocean are warmer than normal. As a result, climate patterns change.

During the 1982–1983 El Niño, heavy rains caused severe flooding in Peru while Australia had a harmful drought.

Mount Pinatubo is a volcano that erupted in 1991. This sent a huge cloud of ash and sulfur dioxide gas 22 miles into the air.

The cloud of ash circled Earth. It blocked the sun's energy, causing temperatures to drop around the world for two years.

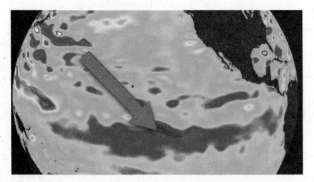

During a La Niña, waters in the Pacific Ocean are cooler than normal. La Niña also affects global climate patterns.

During a La Niña in 2010–2011, the southern part of the United States had less rain than normal.

Do the Math

Display the Difference

11. Look at the temperature data for the years surrounding a volcanic eruption such as that of Mt. Pinatubo. Make a bar graph to show the temperatures for each year.

Year	Temperature
1	53 °F
2	50 °F
3	51 °F
4	52 °F
5	53 °F

During which year do the data indicate that the eruption likely occurred? _____ What is your evidence?

_____

 EVIDENCE NOTEBOOK Consider how a volcanic eruption might change the climate zones over two years. Which zones would get bigger? Which would become smaller?

Putting It Together

12. Choose the words that correctly complete the sentences.

floods	higher	lower	droughts	ash

The 1982–1983 El Niño brought heavy rain and _____ to Peru. A La Niña in 2010–2011 caused _____ in the southern United States. In 1991, Mt. Pinatubo erupted. It blasted hot gases and _____ into the air. This made the world's temperature _____ than normal for two years.

Discover More

Check out this path . . . or go online to choose one of these other paths.

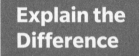

Explain the Difference

- **Migrating Monarchs**
- **Other Factors**

Not a Match

As you know, each climate zone has general features. Yet each zone has variations. For example, most of the tropical zone is hot. But there are places in the tropical zone that are cold enough to have snow. How can you explain this?

You learned that sometimes certain events cause a change to climate. Could this be what's going on? Look at the two maps on these pages to find evidence to explain why this happens.

United States Climate Zones

- Desert
- Mediterranean
- Semiarid Steppe
- Marine West Coast
- Highland
- Humid Continental Cool
- Humid Continental Warm
- Humid Subtropical
- Tropical

This map shows variations in climate for the United States.

You know that most of the United States is in the temperate climate zone, but the map on the last page shows differences in the climate. Examine that map to see which parts are cooler and which parts are warmer.

13. What patterns do you see between where the warmer and cooler temperatures are?

_____

14. Does this pattern fit with the global patterns you saw in the lesson?

_____

_____

15. Do you see any variations to this pattern?

_____

_____

The map below shows land features of the United States. Compare the two maps to find patterns that could help you explain the differences.

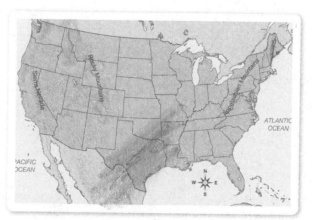

16. Is there anything shown on this map that might explain the change in pattern shown on the climate map?

_____

_____

Lesson Check

Name _____

Can You Explain It?

1. Now that you've learned about climate, explain where you would relocate the blue penguins and why. Be sure to:

- Describe features of the new habitat you selected for the blue penguins.

- Identify reasons that other locations would not work as a new habitat for the penguins.

▷ Explore Online

EVIDENCE NOTEBOOK Use the information you've collected in your Evidence Notebook to help you cover each point above.

_____

_____

_____

_____

Checkpoints

2. You are in a forest with cold winters, cool summers, and a lot of snow. What type of climate zone are you in?

   a. midway zone   **b.** polar zone

   c. tropical zone   **d.** temperate zone

3. Choose the correct words to complete the sentences.

There are similar patterns of temperature and _precipitation_ through most of a climate zone. Climate zones are usually warmer closer to the _equator_ and colder closer to the _Poles_.

> poles
> tropical
> temperature
> equator
> precipitation

4. In the spring, the weather is cool, and there is some rain. By summer, the temperatures are much higher, and there is little rain. When fall comes, the temperatures cool off, and there is some rain. In winter, it is very cold, and there is usually some snow on the ground. What climate zone does this describe?

a. forest zone   **c.** polar zone

b. tropical zone   **d.** temperate zone

5. How is a tropical zone different from a temperate zone? Circle all that apply.

a. Tropical zones are dry all year.

b. Tropical zones are hot all year.

c. Tropical zones receive rain most of the year.

d. Tropical zones are closer to the equator.

e. Tropical zones are only in jungles.

6. Choose the correct answer below.

An unusual warming of the tropical area of the Pacific Ocean can cause flooding in some areas and droughts in other areas. What is this event called?

a. La Niña   **c.** El Niño

b. volcanic eruption   **d.** Blackberry winter

Lesson Roundup

A. Look at the data in the table. Identify the climate type:

_____

Now use the data to predict the climate in 2020.

	2010		2011		2012		2020	
	Temp (°F)	Precip (in.)	Temp (°F)	Precip (in.)	Temp (°F)	Precip (in.)	Temp (°F)	Precip (in.)
Spring	37	2	36	2.5	38	2		
Summer	78	1	82	1.5	79	1		
Fall	38	1.5	37	2	39	1.5		
Winter	19	1	18	1.5	20	1		

B. Which of these describe climate? Circle all that apply.

a. weather experienced day to day

b. average yearly rainfall

c. daily rainfall

d. average yearly temperature

e. daily temperature

f. the monthly weather

C. Which of these can cause temporary differences in the climate in some areas? Circle all that apply.

a. Mountains elevate an area higher than the area around it.

b. Melting ice releases cool air in a region.

c. Volcanic eruptions blow out a lot of ash into the air.

d. La Niña lowers temperatures in the Pacific Ocean.

e. El Niño raises temperatures in the Pacific Ocean along Central and South America.

f. Shade caused by clouds cools off the area.

A New Job?

Your local TV station needs a new meteorologist, and you want the job. Everyone who applies is asked to forecast the daily average (mean) temperature and precipitation for two cities. Whoever gives the most accurate one-week forecasts will get the job.

A future meteorologist?

DEFINE YOUR GOAL: What is your goal for this project?

_____

_____

RESEARCH: Use print and online sources to learn more about how meteorologists forecast weather. Consider how past weather can help predict future weather. Note useful information. Cite your sources.

BRAINSTORM/DISCUSS: Your teacher will assign your team its two cities. Look at a calendar, and write down the one-week period your team's forecasts will cover. (Start with tomorrow.) Brainstorm and discuss what you know about forecasting and weather patterns.

MAKE YOUR FORECASTS: Use these questions to help you with your goal. Answer each one, then write your 2 one-week forecasts. Remember to break your forecasts down by date.

1. What cities are you doing forecasts for?

_____

_____

_____

2. What dates are you giving forecasts for?

_____

3. What two things about the weather are you forecasting?

There are many different weather websites available for research.

_____

4. Which season from past years would have the most useful weather data? Why?

_____

_____

5. Which dates did you look at to help you make your predictions?

_____

_____

TRACK YOUR FORECASTS: On each day of your one-week forecast period, track your accuracy on the Weather Underground website. Create a table that compares the day's weather to your prediction.

COMMUNICATE: Make and give a short presentation about your team's project. Compare your accuracy with other groups.

✅ Checklist

Review your project and check off each completed item.

_____ All questions on this page are answered.

_____ Brainstorming and research notes are completed.

_____ Forecast data is tracked in a table.

_____ Presents the goal, planning, data, and results orally to the class.

Unit Review

1. What is this person most likely doing? Circle the correct answer.

   a. describing a tornado

   b. telling about a meteor

   c. predicting the weather

   d. reading temperature graphs

2. Which of these are instruments for gathering data about the weather? Circle all that apply.

   a. a hazard

   b. a forecast

   c. a wind vane

   d. a rain gauge

   e. a thermometer

3. Complete the sentences using the words in the word bank.

arrays	meteorologists	satellites	climates

   Weather _____ orbit Earth to gather data

   about the atmosphere. _____ use this

   information to help predict weather.

4. The two types of dangerous weather most associated with winter

   are ice storms and _____.

   a. hurricanes

   b. blizzards

   c. tornadoes

5. You are completing a weather data chart for last summer and winter. What temperature or precipitation does each letter represent?

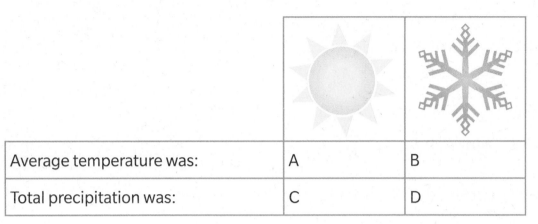

Average temperature was:	A	B
Total precipitation was:	C	D

Write the correct letter from the chart on the lines below.

5 ft. of snow _____

82 °F _____

34 °F _____

9 in. of rain _____

6. Which statement describes climate more than weather? Circle the correct choice.

a. The sky has been cloudy all week.

b. It will be dry today and then rain tomorrow.

c. The wind died down once the storm passed.

d. It is hot in the summer and mild in the winter.

7. _____ weather such as flooding and tornadoes can harm people and property.

a. Historical

b. Severe

c. Mild

8. Which statements apply to hurricanes? Circle all that apply.

   a. They carry hail.

   b. They form over oceans

   c. They often cause flooding.

   d. They contain blowing snow.

   e. They are usually small.

9. Complete the sentences using the words in the word bank.

polar	**temperate**

Emperor penguins are large and live in a _____ climate.

Blue penguins are small and live in a _____ climate.

10. Circle the choice that does not name a climate zone.

   a. polar

   b. tropical

   c. consistent

   d. temperate

Interactive Glossary

As you learn about each item, add notes, drawings, or sentences in the extra space. This will help you remember what the terms mean. Here are some examples:

fungi (FUHN•jee) A group of organisms that get nutrients by decomposing other organisms.

hongos Un grupo de organismos que obtienen sus nutrientes al descomponer otros organismos.

Mushrooms are a type of fungi.

Glossary Pronunciation Key

With every glossary term, there is also a phonetic respelling. A phonetic respelling writes the word the way it sounds, which can help you pronounce new or unfamiliar words. Use this key to help you understand the respellings.

Sound	As in	Phonetic respelling	Sound	As in	Phonetic respelling
a	bat	(BAT)	oh	over	(OH•ver)
ah	lock	(LAHK)	oo	pool	(POOL)
air	rare	(RAIR)	ow	out	(OWT)
ar	argue	(AR•gyoo)	oy	foil	(FOYL)
aw	law	(LAW)	s	cell	(SEL)
ay	face	(FAYS)		sit	(SIT)
ch	chapel	(CHAP•uhl)	sh	sheep	(SHEEP)
e	test	(TEST)	th	that	(THAT)
	metric	(MEH•trik)		thin	(THIN)
ee	eat	(EET)	u	pull	(PUL)
	feet	(FEET)	uh	medal	(MED•uhl)
	ski	(SKEE)		talent	(TAL•uhnt)
er	paper	(PAY•per)		pencil	(PEN•suhl)
	fern	(FERN)		onion	(UHN•yuhn)
eye	idea	(eye•DEE•uh)		playful	(PLAY•fuhl)
i	bit	(BIT)		dull	(DUHL)
ing	going	(GOH•ing)	y	yes	(YES)
k	card	(KARD)		ripe	(RYP)
	kite	(KYT)	z	bags	(BAGZ)
ngk	bank	(BANGK)	zh	treasure	(TREZH•er)

A

adaptation
(ad•uhp•TAY•shuhn) A trait or characteristic that helps an organism survive. p. 284

adaptación Rasgo o característica que ayuda a un organismo a sobrevivir.

aquatic (uh•KWAH•tik) Something that exists in or on water. p. 372

acuático Que existe en o sobre el agua.

atmosphere
(AT•muhs•feer) The mixture of gases that surround a planet. p. 405

atmósfera Mezcla de gases que rodea el planeta.

B

balanced forces (BAL•uhnst FAWRS•iz) Forces that cancel each other out because they are equal in size and opposite in direction. p. 91

fuerzas equilibradas Condición que ocurre cuando todas las fuerzas se cancelan por ser fuerzas iguales y opuestas.

C

camouflage (KAM•uh•flazh) An adaptation that allows an organism to blend in with its surroundings. p. 289

camuflaje Adaptación que le permite a un organismo mimetizarse con su entorno.

climate (KLY•muht) The pattern of weather an area experiences over a long period of time. p. 470

clima Patrón de tiempo que experimenta una región durante largos periodos.

C

constraint (KUHN•straint) A real-world limit on the resources of a solution such as available time, money, or materials. p. 16

restricción Algo que limita u obstaculiza.

criteria (kry•TEER•ee·uh) The desired features of a solution. p. 8

criterios Estándares para medir el éxito.

D

design (dih•ZYN) To conceive something and prepare the plans and drawings for it to be built.

diseñar Concebir algo; preparar el plano y los dibujos de ello para construirlo.

D

design process (dih•ᴢʏɴ ᴘʀᴀʜꜱ•es)
A process that engineers follow to develop
solutions that meet a want or need, for
example — Find a Problem, Research,
Brainstorm, Make a Plan, Build, Evaluate and
Redesign, and Communicate.

proceso de diseño Proceso que los
ingenieros siguen para desarrollar soluciones
que cumplan con un requisito o una
necesidad.

E

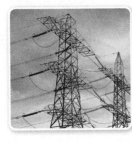

electricity
(ee•lek•ᴛʀɪꜱ•uh•tee) A form
of energy. p . 115

electricidad Una forma de
energía.

engineer (en•juh•ɴᴇᴇʀ) A person who
uses science and math to design structures,
machines, and systems to solve problems.
p. 6

ingeniero Persona que utiliza las
matemáticas y las ciencias para diseñar
tecnología que resuelva algún problema.

E

engineering (en•juh•NIR•ing) The use of scientific and mathematical principles to develop something practical.

ingeniería Uso de principios científicos y matemáticos para desarrollar algo práctico.

environment (en•VY•ruhn•muhnt) All the living and nonliving things that surround and affect an organism. p. 265

medio ambiente Todos los seres vivos y no vivos que rodean y afectan a un organismo.

extinct (ek•STINGKT) Describes a kind of thing that is no longer found on Earth. p. 356

extinto Describe organismos que ya no habitan en la Tierra.

force (FAWHRS) A push or a pull, which may cause a change in an object's motion. p. 70

fuerza Empujón o tirón que puede causar un cambio en el movimiento de un objeto.

fossil (FAHS•uhl) The remains or traces of an organism that lived long ago. p. 350

fósil Restos o rastros que deja un organismo que vivió hace mucho tiempo.

frame of reference (FRAYM UHF REF•uhr•ins) A background that remains the same, allowing you to determine if an object is changing position. p. 142

marco de referencia Contexto que se mantiene igual, permitiendo determinar si un objeto está cambiando de posición.

G

gravity (GRAV•ih•tee)
A force that pulls two objects toward each other, such as the force between Earth and objects on it. p. 96

gravedad Fuerza que atrae dos objetos el uno hacia el otro.

H

habitat (HAB•ih•tat)
The place where an organism lives and can find everything it needs to survive. p. 285

hábitat Lugar donde vive un organismo y donde puede encontrar todo lo que necesita para sobrevivir.

hazard (HAZ•urd)
Something that can cause damage to a person or property. p. 450

riesgo Algo que puede causar daño a una persona o un bien.

L

life cycle (LYF SY•kuhl) Changes that happen to an animal or a plant during its life. p. 186

ciclo de vida Etapas que experimenta un ser vivo en la medida que crece y se transforma.

M

magnet (MAG•nit) An object that attracts iron and a few other—but not all—metals. p. 110

imán Objeto que atrae el hierro y algunos otros metales (pero no todos).

metamorphosis (met•uh•MAWR•fuh•sis) A series of changes that some animals go through. p. 218

metamorfosis Fase del ciclo de vida de algunos animales en la que estos experimentan grandes cambios en la forma de sus cuerpos.

M

mimicry (MIHM•ih•kree)
An adaptation that allows an animal to protect itself by looking like another kind of animal or like a plant. p. 289

mimetismo Adaptación que le permite a un animal protegerse, al tomar el aspecto de otro tipo de animal o planta.

motion (MOH•shuhn)
A change of position of an object. p. 140

movimiento Cambio de posición de un objeto.

N

net force (NET FAWHRS) The combination of all of the forces acting on an object. p. 91

fuerza neta La combinación de todas las fuerzas que actúan sobre un objeto.

O

organism
(AWR•guh•niz•uhm) A living thing. p. 236
organismo Ser vivo.

P

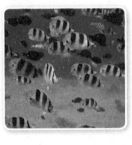

population
(pahp•yuh•LAY•shuhn) All of the members of a certain kind of plant or animal in an environment. p. 325

población Todos los miembros de un cierto tipo de planta o animal en un ambiente.

position (puh•ZISH•uhn) The location of an object in relation to a nearby object or place. p. 140

posición Ubicación de un objeto en relación a otro lugar u objeto cercano.

P

precipitation
(pri•sip•uh•TAY•shuhn)
Water that falls from the sky.
Rain, snow, sleet, and hail
are kinds of precipitation.
p. 406

precipitación Agua que cae
del cielo. La lluvia, la nieve,
el aguanieve y el granizo son
tipos de precipitación.

problem (PRAHB•lem) A question to be
considered, solved, or answered.

problema Cuestión para considerar, resolver
o responder.

pupa (PYOO•puh) The stage
of complete metamorphosis
in which an insect changes
from a larva to an adult.
p. 218

crisálida Fase de
metamorfosis completa en la
que un insecto se transforma
de larva en adulto.

R

rain gauge (RAYN GAYJ) A tool for collecting and measuring precipitation. p. 406

pluviómetro Instrumento que se usa para recoger y medir la precipitación.

S

solution (suh•LOO•shuhn) An answer to a problem.

solución Respuesta a un problema.

speed (SPEED) The measure of an object's change in position during a certain amount of time. p. 144

velocidad Medida que expresa el cambio de posición de un objeto durante un tiempo determinado.

S

static electricity (STAT•ik ee•lek•TRIS•uh•tee) The buildup of electric charges on an object. p. 118

electricidad estática Acumulación de cargas eléctricas en un objeto.

T

technology (tek•NAHL•uh•jee) Engineered products and processes that meet a want or need. p. 6

tecnología Diseño de productos y procesos que cumplen con una necesidad o un requisito.

terrestrial (TUH•rest•ree•uhl) Something that exists in or on land. p. 374

terrestre Que existe en o sobre la tierra.

T

thermometer
(ther•MAHM•uh•ter)
A tool used to measure
temperature. p. 406

termómetro Instrumento
que se usa para medir
temperatura.

trait (TRAYT) A physical
characteristic of a person,
animal, or plant. p. 237

rasgo Característica física
de una persona, animal o
planta.

U

unbalanced forces
(uhn•BAL•uhnst FAWRS•iz)
Forces that cause a change in
an object's motion because
they don't cancel each other
out. p. 91

fuerzas desequilibradas
Fuerzas que provocan un
cambio en el movimiento de
un objeto porque ellas no se
cancelan entre sí.

W

weather (WEH•ther)
What is happening in the atmosphere at a certain place and time. p. 404

tiempo Lo que ocurre en la atmósfera en un cierto lugar y momento.

wind vane (WIND VAYN)
A tool that measures the direction of the wind. p. 406

veleta Instrumento que mide la dirección en la que sopla el viento.

Index

A

adaptations
    behavioral, 287
    in bird beaks, 294–296
    camouflage, 283, 289, 305
    color, 308–310
    definition, 284
    to environments, 288, 291
    group living, 311–313
    to habitats, 285–286, 292–293
    mimicry, 289
    physical, 285–286, 288
    by plants, 284, 289, 291, 304
    robotic, 297–298
    for survival, 291–293, 304–307
adhesives, 99

aerospace engineers, 103
airplane design, 103–104
amber, 355
Anderson, Stuart and Cedar, 189
animals. *See also* **birds; fish; insects**
    adaptations by, 285–287, 288, 291, 292
    alligator, 214, 273
    alligator snapping turtle, 282
    amargosa vole, 326
    ammonite, 373
    amphibians, 217
    anemone, 313
    antelope, 242, 243
    behavior of, 273, 277–278, 287, 303, 315
    brachiopods, 373
    chalicotherium, 383, 384
    cheetah, 138
    coral, 311
    crinoid, 373

    dire wolf, 374–375
    dog, 210, 212, 273
    Dunkleosteus, 373
    elephant, 378
    elk, 242
    environment and, 272–278, 323
    frog, 287
    gecko, 99
    habitats, 285, 292–293
    horseshoe crab, 376

    hyena, 312
    ichthyosaur, 383, 384
    inherited traits in, 242–248
    jaguar, 305
    leopard seal, 288
    life cycles, 208–228
    living in groups, 311–314
    lizard, 226, 275, 286, 287
    moose, 242, 243
    naked mole rat, 287
    octopus, 283
    opossum, 289
    orca, 312
    peacock spider, 315
    pika, 326
    pterosaur, 383
    saber-toothed cat, 374–375
    sea turtle, 377
    spotted salamander, 217
    survival characteristics of, 291, 305
    trilobite, 360–361
    turtle, 227, 228, 282, 377
    utahceratops, 385
    utahraptor, 360–361
    woolly mammoth, 378
    zebra, 312
Anning, Mary, 389
artists, 166
atmosphere, weather and, 405

B

bar graphs, 415–416, 438, 481
barometer, 406
Beaufort Wind Scale, 407
Berenbaum, May, 277
bicycle electrical generator, 117
biomechanists, 171–172
birds
    birds of prey, 96–97
    bowerbird, 303
    ciconla maltha, 374–375
    egret, 215
    emu, 285
    flamingo, 272
    parrot, 285
    penguins, 211–213, 312, 466–471, 476–478
    sparrow, 243, 306
blastoid, 356
blizzard, 447
Bloodhound SSC (supersonic car), 139, 149
Butterfly Metamorphosis Relay, 220

C

Calder, Mary Gordon, 389
Careers in Science and Engineering
    aerospace engineer, 103
    artist, 166
    biomechanist, 171–172
    chemist, 55
    electrician, 125
    engineer, 6, 8, 18
    entomologist, 277
    hurricane hunter, 461–462
    meteorologist, 439–440, 450
    paleontologist, 365–366, 388

robotic engineer, 154, 297–298

wildlife expert, 315

zoologist, 229

chemists, 55

Chin, Karen, 389–390

claim, *in Hands-On Activity,* for example, 50, 79, 102, 124, 193

climate, 470–474, 479–484.
See also **weather**

coal balls, 389

color, 272–273, 304–306, 308–310

compass, 113

complete metamorphosis, 218–219

cones, tree, 196–197

constraints
in camping gear list, 11–15

in desalination, 55

in engineering plant species, 203–204

in *Hands-On Activity,* 11–13, 29–30, 47, 454, 456

in irrigation project, 23–26, 29, 47, 54

in space exploration, 16–17

coprolite, 389–390

coral reef, 311

criteria
in design process, 11–15, 47–48

in evaluating solutions, 54

in *Hands-On Activity,* 11–13, 47–48, 454, 456

in irrigation project, 23, 26, 32, 47–48

in plant engineering, 203–204

in problem definition, 8–10

in space exploration, 16–17

in testing, 26, 35, 48

in water treatment, 55

Cucurull, Lidia, 440

D

dams, 329, 330, 335

Darden, Christine, 103

death, in life cycle, 210, 213–214, 219, 227

desalination, 55–56

design. *See also* **constraints;**
criteria
analyzing results, 13, 31, 46, 49–50, 78–79

building a prototype, 29–30, 35

drawing conclusions, 13, 31, 50, 79

evaluating, 30, 54

peer review, 34, 53

problem definition, 8–10, 27–28

product packaging, 38

recording, 12, 30, 48, 49, 54

redesigning, 51–52

sketching, 29

testing, 32–35, 44–46, 47–50

direction of motion, 146–147

Do the Math
calculating speed, 144–145

display the difference, 481

egg-splosion!, 228

greater or less than, 379

hello up there!, 238

how many dogs?, 76

improving running speeds, 172

interpreting graphs, 415

looking for patterns, 409

strong pull, 93

use less water, 36–37

using a map for math, 425

dog sledding, 69, 72, 73, 76, 82

dropsonde, 462

drought, 323

Duckworth, Colonel Joseph, 461

E

eggs, 212–215, 217–219, 226

El Niño, 480

electrical field, 119

electrical meter, 116

electricians, 125

electricity
body-powered generators, 117

electromagnets, 120, 121–124

generation and transport of, 115–116

static, 118–119

electromagnet, 120, 121–124

energy, 115, 117

Engineer It!
adhesives, 99

art in motion, 166

artificial climate, 479

dog sled race, 73

flow hive, 189

foot energy, 117

lucky lizards, 275

plant species, 203–204

satellites in weather prediction, 413

severe weather solutions, 458

supersonic car track, 149

tools for studying fossils, 388

tracking devices on animals, 211

engineering
caribou migration, 332–334

flood protection, 454–456

flowering plants, 203–204

gardens, 267

greenhouses, 267

irrigation, 29–37

marble motion paths, 163

metal stresses, 35

nests, 216

© Houghton Mifflin Harcourt

protection against
environmental changes, 324
robotic adaptations, 297–298
zoos, 230

engineering design process.
See also **constraints;
criteria**
analyzing results, 13, 31, 46,
49–50, 78–79
building a prototype, 29–30,
35
drawing conclusions, 13, 31,
50, 79
evaluating, 30, 54
peer review, 34, 53
problem definition, 8–10,
27–28
product packaging, 38
recording, 12, 30, 48, 49, 54
redesigning, 51–52
sketching, 29
testing, 32–35, 44–46, 47–50

engineers, 6
aerospace, 103
interviewing, 18
learning from failure, 43–44,
51–52
robotic, 154, 297–298
testing by, 35

entomologists, 277

environment
animal adaptations to,
272–278, 288, 305–307
cold, 292, 312
dry, 292–293
engineering solutions to fish
passage, 335–336
extreme changes in, 320–326
forest fires, 321, 325–326
human changes in, 329–331
plant adaptations to, 264–
266, 292–293, 304

Everglades, 214

evidence
in *Evidence Notebook,* for
example, 5, 43, 99, 159, 221
in *Hands-On Activity,* for
example, 50, 77, 78, 101, 193
in *Hands-On, Apply What You
Know,* for example, 71, 220
in *Lesson Check,* for example,
19, 39, 57, 85, 105
in many lessons, for
example, 21, 33, 93

Evidence Notebook
Multiple assignments are
given in every lesson.
Example references are
shown below, 5, 43, 99, 159,
221, 266, 303, 337, 379, 424,
462, 485

explanation
in *Can You Explain It?,* for
example, 19, 23, 43, 69, 89,
109
in every lesson, for example,
32, 34, 44, 45, 72, 73
in *Hands-On Activity,* for
example, 12–13, 31, 78–79,
248
in *Lesson Check,* for example,
19, 39, 57, 85, 105

extinct organisms, 356

F

fish, 214, 362–363
clownfish, 313
salmon, 329, 335
vampire fish, 285

fish elevator, 336

fish ladder, 335

flipbook, 142, 190

floods, 320, 322, 454, 457

flowers, 186–187, 190,
195–197, 304

footprint fossil, 355, 358

forces, 68–87
balanced and unbalanced,
89, 91–92, 148
in birds of prey, 96–97
contact force, 90, 100–102
direction of, 80–81
at a distance, 114, 118
in dog sledding, 72, 73, 76, 82
friction, 94–95, 149
gravity, 25, 96–99
magnetic, 108–114
motion and, 77–79
net force, 98
observing, 71
as pushes and pulls, 70–71,
72, 90, 112–113, 118
in simple machines, 83–84
in stopping cars, 92, 93
strong and weak, 74–75, 76

forest fires, 321, 325–326

fossils, 348–392
comparing original and
present environments,
386–387
coprolites, 389–390
definition, 350–351
determining original
environment, 372–375,
383–385
estimating scale, 360–361
of extinct organisms, 356,
360–361
future fossils, 353
information from, 352–353,
371, 380–382, 383–387
living organisms compared
with, 376–379
modeling, 357
as parts of organisms,
362–363
picturing organisms from,
364
trace fossils, 355, 358–359
types of, 354–355

Foucault pendulum, 167
frame of reference, 142–143
friction, 94–95, 149
Fuller, Mark, 153

G

genealogy, 249
generating station, 115
generators, body-powered, 117
genetics specialists, 249
germination, 186, 198–199
Global Positioning System–
   Radio Occultation, 440
GPS (Global Positioning
   System) device, 73, 211
graphs, bar, 415–416, 438, 481
gravity, 25, 96–99

H

habitats
   adaptations to, 285–286,
   292–293
   climate and, 470–471
   penguin relocation project,
   476–478
   preservation of, 467, 469
Hands-On Activities
   backpacking trip supplies,
   11–15
   bird beaks, 294–296
   caribou migration solutions,
   332–334
   climate in a new location,
   476–478
   color and survival, 308–310
   contact forces, 100–102
   electromagnets, 121–124
   flood protection
   engineering, 454–456
   forces affecting motion,
   77–79
   fossil information, 380–382
   irrigation modeling, 29–31

mealworm metamorphosis,
222–224
model testing, 47–50
monster traits, 246–248
pendulums, 168–170
plant growth, 191–193
trace fossil footprints,
358–359
walking speed, 150–152
water needs of plants,
268–271
weather data analysis,
410–412, 432–435
Hands-On, Apply What You
Know
   Beaufort Wind Scale, 407
   butterfly metamorphosis
   relay, 220
   compass and magnet, 113
   drawing specimens, 313
   electrical meter reading, 116
   environmental needs of
   deer, 327
   flowering plan life cycle
   flipbook, 190
   fossil modeling, 357
   fossils compared with living
   animals, 385
   frame of reference flipbook,
   142
   friction from materials, 95
   garden planning, 267
   handedness survey, 245
   illustrated adaptations, 290
   marble motion path design,
   163
   matching game of animals
   and adaptations, 286
   needs met by products, 7
   nest design, 216
   playground pushes and
   pulls, 71
   protection against
   environmental changes, 324

scale of objects, 361
stressing metal until it
breaks, 35
temperature in Earth zones,
475
testing plan, 45
weather averages graphing,
427
weather map reading, 416
wind strength modeling, 446
height, as inherited trait,
238–239
Heinselman, Pam, 439
high-voltage lines, 115
honey production, 189
hurricane hunters, 461–462
hurricanes, 447, 448, 457,
461–462

I

ice storms, 444, 457, 458
Imager (weather satellite), 413
incomplete metamorphosis,
218–219
inheritance. *See also* **traits**
   in animals, 242–248
   family tree, 250
   parents and offspring, 235,
   236, 244
   in plants, 236–241
   siblings, 240
insects
   ant, 313
   bee, 188, 189, 200
   cicada, 218–219
   cockroach, 276, 277
   ladybug, 209, 218–219
   mealworm, 222–224
   monarch butterfly, 289
International Space Station,
479
interview questions, 18

irrigation systems
  building a prototype, 29–31
  conserving water, 36–37
  constraints and criteria, 23–26, 29, 47–48
  peer review, 34, 53
  testing, 32–35, 46, 47–50
  types of, 24–25
  water needs of plants, 23, 27–28, 268–271
Irwin, Steve, 229

J

Jansen, Theo, 166

K

Kittles, Rick, 249

L

La Niña, 480
laboratory safety, XVIII
laminar flow, 153
Language SmArts
  asking questions, 81
  cause and effect, 146, 163
  compare and contrast, 37, 82, 143, 195, 216, 431
  describing, 117, 245, 290, 331, 405, 425
  evidence, 475
  examples and details, 165
  gathering information, 287
  interviewing, 154, 172
  main idea and details, 199
  making inferences, 143, 267, 274, 373, 388
  note taking, 245, 314
  predicting, 292, 307, 322
  presentations, 73, 104, 126
  researching, 98, 104, 117, 126, 353, 362–363, 377, 406, 447, 453, 458
  thinking ahead, 46

  understanding diagrams, 187
  using data, 437
  using evidence, 469, 470–471
larval stage, 218–219
Leftwich, Megan, 154
Lesson Check, 19–20, 39–40, 57–58, 85–86, 105–106, 127–128, 155–156, 173–174, 205–206, 231–232, 251–252, 279–280, 299–300, 317–318, 337–338, 367–368, 391–392, 419–420, 441–442, 463–464, 485–486
Lesson Roundup, 21, 41, 59, 87, 107, 129, 157, 175, 207, 233, 253, 281, 301, 319, 339, 369, 393, 421, 443, 465, 487
lever, 84
life cycles of animals
  alligator, 214
  dog, 210, 212–213
  egret, 215
  fish, 214
  lizard, 226
  metamorphosis, 217–220, 222–224
  penguin, 212–213
  spotted salamander, 217
  white-tailed deer, 214
life cycles of plants
  flowering plants, 186–187
  interruptions of, 200–202
  nonflowering plants, 198–199
  observation of, 191–193
  pollen, 188, 197, 203–204
  seeds, 186, 188, 196–199
lightning, 118, 321, 447, 459
lightning rods, 459
Lum, Olivia, 55

M

magnet, 110–114, 120–124
magnetic field, 111–112
magnetic force, 112–113, 114
metamorphosis, 217–219, 220, 222–224
meteorologists, 439–440, 450
model, 29–31, 47–50, 190, 204, 220, 230, 294–296, 332–334, 357, 358–359, 475
molting, 218
motion
  art in, 166
  designing paths for, 163
  direction of, 146–147
  of the Earth, 167
  forces and, 77–79, 148
  frame of reference in, 142–143
  measuring, 150–152
  patterns of, 160–163
  of pendulums, 167, 168–170
  planning fastest route, 147
  position, 140–141
  predicting, 164–165
  speed, 144–145, 150–152
mudslides, 323

N

NASA, problem solving by, 16–17
nymph stage, 218–219

O

O'Hair, Lieutenant Ralph, 461
offspring, 235, 236, 242
oxbow lake, 323

P

paleontologists, 365–366, 388

parents, 236, 242

peer review, 34, 53

pendulum, 167, 168–170

People in Science and
    Engineering
    Anning, Mary, 389
    Berenbaum, May, 277
    Calder, Mary Gordon, 389
    Chin, Karen, 389–390
    Cucurull, Lidia, 440
    Darden, Christine, 103
    Fuller, Mark, 153
    Heinselman, Pam, 439
    Irwin, Steve, 229
    Jansen, Theo, 166
    Kittles, Rick, 249
    Leftwich, Megan, 154
    Lum, Olivia, 55
    Turner, Charles Henry, 277
    Wright brothers, 104

petrified wood, 354

phases array radar, 439

Pinatubo, Mount, 480–481

plants. *See also* **trees**
    adaptations by, 284,
    289–290, 291–293
    African violet, 27
    aloe, 27
    arctic poppy, 264
    bearberry, 293
    bee orchid, 289
    blackberry, 284
    Boston fern, 27
    cactus, 27, 196
    cycad, 360–361
    dandelion, 186
    environment and, 264–266,
    323
    flowering, 184–190,
    195–197
    forest fires and, 326
    Gerbera, 27
    inherited traits in, 236–241
    insect-eating, 304
    jade plant, 27
    life cycles of, 186–187,
    198–199
    light and, 264
    needs of, 264
    nonflowering, 194–199
    pitcher plant, 304
    purple tansy, 292
    survival characteristics of,
    291–292
    sweet pinesap, 289
    tomato, 196
    tumbleweed, 188
    umbrella plant, 27
    water needs, 23, 27–28,
    268–271
    yucca, 27

polar zones, 472–473, 484

pollination, 188, 196, 200, 304

pollution, plant life cycle and,
    200

polymorphic variations, 316

population, 227, 325

position, 140–141

precipitation (weather), 406,
    413–414, 437–438, 473

precipitation radar, 413

presentation preparation, 18,
    73, 104, 126, 202, 316

problem (for engineering)
    defining, 6, 8–10
    identifying constraints in,
    16–17, 26
    problems to solve, 11–13,
    74, 202, 203–204, 329,
    332–334, 335–336, 388,
    454–456, 479
    strategies for solving,
    24–25, 28, 34, 55

product packaging, 38

pulley, 83, 84

pupa stage, 218

Putting It Together
    in every lesson, for example,
    10, 17, 26, 46, 52, 54

Q

question (for science)
    in *Hands-On Activity,* 77, 100,
    121, 191, 222, 246, 268, 294,
    308, 380, 432
    in lessons, for example, 81,
    126, 366

R

rain gauge, 406, 407, 410

ramp, 84

reasoning, 375, 377, 385, 453,
    460, 469, 475, 484

reproduction
    animal, 212–213, 225, 303,
    315
    behavioral characteristics
    and, 303, 315
    plant, 186–187, 196–199

robotic engineers, 154,
    297–298

Rube Goldberg device, 44–45

S

safety in science, XVIII

satellites, weather, 413, 440,
    450

scale (relative size), 361

scale (weight), 100–101

scales (fish), 363

scar, 273

science, 18, 34

seeds, 186, 188, 196–199, 292

seesaw, 83

sequence, 10, 190

siblings, 240–241

simple machines, 83–84

snow plow, 459, 460

solar roadways and sidewalks, 458, 460

solutions (for engineering)
  evaluating, 54
  examples of, 6–7, 16–17, 55, 335–336
  in *Hands-On Activity*, for example, 13, 29–31, 47–50, 332–334
  researching, 24–25, 28
  reviewing, 34
  testing solutions, 8–10, 32–33, 35, 44–45

sonic boom, 103

space exploration, 16–17, 98, 103, 479

spark, 119

speed, 144–148, 150–152, 407

spring scale, 100–101

static electricity, 118–119

storms
  blizzards, 447
  hurricanes, 447, 448, 457, 461–462
  ice storms, 444, 457, 458
  lightning, 118, 321, 447, 459
  thunderstorms, 428, 459
  tornados, 446, 448

Strandbeests, 166

stride, 358

sunlight, 264, 273

supersonic cars, 149

survival
  adaptations for, 291–292, 304–307
  color and, 304–307, 308–310
  living in groups and, 311–314

systems
  ecosystems, 372, 374–375
  irrigation, 29–31, 46, 47–50
  natural, 326

technology as, 6
  for weather prediction, 440

T

Tacoma Narrows Bridge, 43, 51–52

technology
  airplane design, 103–104
  bicycle electrical generator, 117
  bridges, 43, 51–52
  compass, 113
  dams, 329, 330, 335
  definition, 6–7
  fish elevator, 336
  International Space Station, 479
  lightning rod, 459
  pendulum, 167, 168–170
  phases array radar, 439
  precipitation radar, 413
  Rube Goldberg device, 44–45
  simple machines, 83–84
  tracking device, 140, 211
  transformer, 115
  Van de Graaff machine, 119

teeth, 285

temperate zones, 472–473, 483–484

temperature
  in climate zones, 473
  predicting from patterns, 436–438
  reptile gender and, 273
  seasonal patterns, 430–431
  on weather maps, 413–414

thermometer, 406, 407, 411

Thrust SSC (supersonic car), 149

thunderstorm, 428, 459

timeline, 212, 223

tornado, 446, 448

Tornado Alley, 448

tracking device, 140, 211

traits
  characteristics for survival, 291–292, 304–307, 311–314
  definition, 235, 237
  in different animals, 243
  environment and, 265–266, 272–274, 277–278
  handedness as, 245
  height as, 238–239
  in parents and offspring, 235, 236, 244
  polymorphic variations, 316
  in siblings, 240–241

transformer, 115

trees
  apple, 195
  cedar, 197
  ginkgo, 377
  mangrove, 291
  maple, 196
  palm, 197
  pine, 195
  redwood, 196
  sand live oak, 291

tropical zones, 472–473, 484

Turner, Charles Henry, 277

U

unbalanced forces, 89, 91–92, 148

V

Van de Graaff machines, 119

vertical-slot fish passage, 336

volcano, 323, 480

W

water conservation, 36–37

water flow, 153

water treatment, 55–56

weather. *See also* **climate**

    averages, 424–427, 430–431, 436

    climate and, 470

    data analysis, 410–412, 425–427

    definition, 404

    engineering protection from, 457–460

    hurricane hunters, 461–462

    meteorologists, 439–440, 450

    modeling effects of, 445, 446

    monthly changes, 417–418, 424–427, 436

    observation and measurement, 408–409, 410–411

    prediction, 436–438

    seasonal changes, 428–431

    severe weather profiles, 451–453

    severe weather threats, 446–450

    tools for studying, 406–407, 413, 439–440, 450, 462

    types of, 404

    weather maps, 413–414

    wind speed, 407

weight, 98

wheel and axle, 84

wildfires, 321, 325–326

wildlife experts, 315

wind, 407, 429, 445, 446

wind vane, 406, 407, 411

Wright brothers, 104

X

xeriscaped landscapes, 36–37

Z

zero net force, 91

zoo, 230

zoologists, 229